The Google Generation

CHANDOS
INFORMATION PROFESSIONAL SERIES

Series Editor: Ruth Rikowski
(email: Rikowskigr@aol.com)

Chandos' new series of books are aimed at the busy information professional. They have been specially commissioned to provide the reader with an authoritative view of current thinking. They are designed to provide easy-to-read and (most importantly) practical coverage of topics that are of interest to librarians and other information professionals. If you would like a full listing of current and forthcoming titles, please visit our website www.chandospublishing.com or email info@chandospublishing.com or telephone +44 (0) 1223 891358.

New authors: we are always pleased to receive ideas for new titles; if you would like to write a book for Chandos, please contact Dr Glyn Jones on email gjones@chandospublishing.com or telephone number +44 (0) 1993 848726.

Bulk orders: some organisations buy a number of copies of our books. If you are interested in doing this, we would be pleased to discuss a discount. Please email info@chandospublishing.com or telephone +44(0) 1223 891358.

The Google Generation

Are ICT innovations changing information-seeking behaviour?

BARRIE GUNTER,
IAN ROWLANDS
AND
DAVID NICHOLAS

Chandos Publishing
Oxford • Cambridge • New Delhi

Chandos Publishing
TBAC Business Centre
Avenue 4
Station Lane
Witney
Oxford OX28 4BN
UK
Tel: +44 (0) 1993 848726
Email: info@chandospublishing.com
www.chandospublishing.com

Chandos Publishing is an imprint of Woodhead Publishing Limited

Woodhead Publishing Limited
Abington Hall
Granta Park
Great Abington
Cambridge CB21 6AH
UK
www.woodheadpublishing.com

First published in 2009

ISBN:
978 1 84334 557 2

© B. Gunter, I. Rowlands and D. Nicholas, 2009

British Library Cataloguing-in-Publication Data.
A catalogue record for this book is available from the British Library.

Typeset by Domex e-Data Pvt. Ltd.
Printed in the UK and USA.

Contents

Acknowledgements   ix

About the authors   xi

1   Introduction   1

    Search for the Google Generation   3

    Understanding the diffusion of new technologies   3

    Finding a new generation of information seekers   6

    Before the Internet   7

    The Internet era   8

    The broadband effect   10

    A distinctive 'Google Generation'?   11

    The Internet as information source   12

    Web 2.0   13

    The Internet, learning and higher education   14

    What does the future hold?   15

2   The rise of the information society   19

    What does history teach us?   21

    How to configure information and communication change   23

    How important is information access?   27

    Media landscape: pre-Google Generation era   28

    Media landscape: Google Generation era   30

    Use of different media by young people   33

    Summary   38

3	**The Internet era**	**41**
	Media profiles	43
	Internet use by age	44
	The broadband effect	49
	Generations and Internet use	52
	Online information searching	59
	Concluding remarks	63
4	**'Google Generation': What is the evidence?**	**65**
	Web 2.0	67
	User literacy	71
	Cognitive skills and interactive technologies	74
	A generational perspective	80
	Google Generation and learning scenarios	82
	Concluding remarks	90
5	**Emergence of new forms of knowledge production, search and acquisition**	**93**
	Changing contexts for scholarly output production and use	94
	The digital transition	96
	Subject domains and information use	106
	Changing user behaviour	109
	Supporting Google Generation users	118
	Concluding remarks	120
	Notes	122
6	**The emergence of digital scholarship**	**123**
	Overview of studies reviewed	125
	Methods used	126
	The academic research evidence	127
	Use of information technology	127
	Searching expertise	129

Evaluating electronic resources 131

Use of library and information services 133

Opinion, assumption and anecdotal evidence 134

The claims 134

Concluding remarks 145

Notes 146

7 **What next?** 147

Convergence of technology, application and consumption 148

The social web 149

Finding the tipping point 151

Google Generation: e-learning and higher education 153

Formality of learning 163

Uptake of digital media and higher education 164

References 173

Index 203

Acknowledgements

The book is largely based on the work of the British Library/JISC funded research project The Behaviour of the Researcher of the Future (The Google Generation). For further details of the project and associated reports please see *http://www.ucl.ac.uk/infostudies/research/ciber/ downloads/*. Special thanks are due to Maggie Fieldhouse, Carol Tenopir and Peter Williams who made important contributions to a number of the original reports produced for this project and from which parts of this text were drawn.

About the authors

Barrie Gunter MSc, PhD is currently Professor of Mass Communication and Head of the Department of Media and Communication at the University of Leicester, having previously held the post of Professor of Journalism Studies in the Department of Journalism Studies at the University of Sheffield. Professor Gunter's research interests include the study of digital media developments and their impact upon consumer, social and political behaviour and upon the use of 'old' media.

David Nicholas MPhil, PhD is Director of the Department of Information Studies at University College London. He is also the Director of the UCL Centre for Publishing and the CIBER research group. Previously, he was Head of Department in the Department of Information Science at the City University. Professor Nicholas's research interests largely concern mapping behaviour in virtual spaces, the virtual scholar and the health information consumer.

Ian Rowland PhD is a Reader in Information Studies in the Department of Information Studies at University College London. He is also Research Director in the Centre for Publishing at UCL. Dr Rowland's research includes the study of scholarly communications, bibliometrics and the use of e-books and e-journals in higher education.

The authors may be contacted via the publishers.

Introduction

Information and communication technologies have evolved at an unprecedented pace in the past two decades changing the way people live their lives. While traditional sources of information such as word of mouth and early mediated forms of communication such as print, radio, television and telephone retain some importance, they are rapidly being superseded by networked electronic and computerised communications systems, most notably the Internet. Developments in information and communications technologies have transformed people's lives by opening up new channels through which they can communicate with each other, engage in business, consumer-related and personal financial transactions, and learn about the world. This book is concerned principally with the significance of these developments for learning, with special reference to the way this occurs in higher education. Is the printed word on paper being increasingly supplanted by the electronic word displayed on a screen? If so, what are the implications of this phenomenon for the way education institutions supply information to and teach their students and for the way tutors can most effectively engage with their students in future? Will there need to be a rethink of formats and techniques of course delivery? Will the role played by libraries, as information repositories, also have to change? Or have these changes been overinflated in their reach and their impact? These are issues that will be considered and examined in this book.

Since the mid-1990s, as computerised communications networks have spread beyond specialist user communities such as the academy and military, their applications have also become increasingly diversified. Initially used for relatively simple word processing and data analysis tasks, computers have evolved into multipurpose work stations that can handle huge quantities of multimedia content and communications devices that can provide links to others all round the world via different modalities and enable users to engage in a multitude of diverse transactions that can substitute for offline mail, telephone calls and face-to-face meetings.

Technology mergers have created a communications environment in which distinctive media such as print, broadcasting and telecommunications now operate businesses in direct competition with each other in the same markets. Television pictures are no longer only available through television sets. They can also be obtained via desktop and portable computers and mobile telephones. Similarly radio broadcasts are accessible via these same alternative technologies (as well as via television sets). Meanwhile, telecommunications is no longer a simple voice communications medium. Mobile telephones can communicate via text and pictures.

Perhaps the most significant development in communications in the past 20 years is the Internet. This medium provides users with access to massive quantities of information on virtually every subject anyone can think of. It is also an interpersonal communications system through which users can maintain contacts with people they know as well as search for and find new contacts. It comprises the biggest library in the world and provides easy access to a huge community of users who can become friends, advisors, counsellors, teachers, suppliers or customers. Although an increasingly important source of entertainment for many of its users, the Internet has always had close links to the educational world and is emerging as one of the most valued and trusted sources of information and learning for rapidly growing numbers of people. As this book will discuss, online media technologies have been readily embraced in the world of education (New Media Consortium, 2007). We should not be too surprised about this given that the Internet was well established as a form of communication within higher education, especially in the United States, long before it was adopted by mass consumers. The enthusiasm for adoption of online tools in educational contexts has been driven in part by the acknowledgement that their widespread use – especially by younger generations – across a diverse array of non-educational contexts might indicate a sea change in the way people learn. Yet, as we will see in this book, this observation is not always borne out by empirical evidence concerning how young people search for information for educational purposes.

With the expansion of the amount of information that is available to people and the growing ease with which it can be accessed, we shall be asking whether significant changes have occurred in the way individuals confront and use information. We need to know whether old information sources are being usurped by new ones. We also need to know, in the case of new information search technologies, whether they do cater effectively to convenience of information access and in a form with which users are comfortable. Has the Internet conditioned distinctive information search behaviours or habits?

Search for the Google Generation

Given that a generation of people exists today that has never known the world without the Internet, does that generation exhibit distinctive qualities in relation to the way it seeks and uses information and display idiosyncratic preferences concerning the way they like information to be packaged that sets it apart from pre-Internet generations? In particular, is there any evidence that the younger generation of today that is accustomed to the ubiquitous availability of a range of communications technologies searches for and uses information in qualitatively distinctive ways from their elders? If this is the case, to what extent might this generational distinctiveness in orientation towards information have important implications for the future of learning and, more especially, for the role that libraries – those traditional information repositories – might play in educational contexts? If there is an emergent community of young information seekers whose information-related behaviours are firmly tied to search engines and online repositories, are we witnessing the emergence of a new generation – a Google Generation? Such questions represent a primary theme of enquiry for this book.

Understanding the diffusion of new technologies

In examining the evidence for the emergence of a distinctive new generation of information users – a new community of information users who might be called a 'Google Generation' – are we witnessing a new social phenomenon that could have important implications for information providers? In this book, we will consider what evidence exists for the concept of a distinctive generation of information seekers and users. We will consider changes that have been witnessed to the way people seek out and use information sources online. We need to determine whether the patterns of behaviour we can observe in relation to the use of online information search tools represent radically different approaches to people's information search strategies. It does not automatically follow that because the information technology is new the mental search strategies used by information seekers have also changed in fundamental ways.

The study of information and communication technology innovation, adoption and diffusion is not a new field triggered by the emergence of the Internet. Attempts to map out and understand innovation diffusion pre-date the modern Internet era by several decades. The 'diffusion model', for instance, has been used to study how different technology innovations have penetrated the user populations for which they were intended (Rogers, 1986; Rogers and Shoemaker, 1971). A constant S-shaped curve has consistently been found to describe the path followed by most innovations from their point of introduction to a stage where they became widely used.

Innovations tend initially to be used by small numbers of people – amounting to perhaps 5 per cent of the population – often called 'innovators' who like to try out new products and services. Having been trialled in this way, innovations then spread to a slightly larger group of 'early adopters' (between 10 and 25 per cent of the population) and then if these like the innovation, it gradually spreads to larger and larger groups of people until the innovation may eventually end up being used by most people (Rogers, 1995).

Historical tracking has indicated that not all innovations that are eventually adopted by most people penetrate society at the same pace. One important factor in this context is whether an 'innovation' is completely new or whether it represents a new version of an existing technology. A key concept in understanding the spread of new information and communication technologies is the 'tipping point', which refers to a critical mass of adopters who can then trigger dramatically accelerated penetration of an innovation. Diffusion researchers have reported previously that new technologies must first achieve a critical mass before they spread to become adopted by the majority. This 'critical mass' tends to comprise between one in ten and one in four of potential users of an innovation within a specific population. Once this level of adoption has been reached dramatic growth can then occur (Rogers, 1995). This concept is explored further in later chapters in this book and can be used to judge whether some new online tools and technologies still in minority use have yet reached their 'tipping point' beyond which one might predict rapid and widespread adoption.

Another feature of innovation adoption is that the penetration of innovations is not always evenly distributed throughout any specific population. Some people may adopt a technology while others never do. Hence a 'digital divide' may develop whereby some people adopt innovations and others do not. A range of political, economic, social and cultural factors have been found to predict the occurrence and nature of digital divides. For instance, some countries have experienced more rapid and more widespread adoption than others of specific information technologies, including the Internet, and this has been found to be influenced by the strength of the national market economy and the political system in place (Norris, 2001). If there is a 'Google Generation' the pace at which it emerges could therefore vary in different parts of the world as a function of the opportunities provided for technology innovation and adoption by different economic, political and social systems.

One general observation that can be made about technology innovation and adoption, particularly in the developed world, is that the pace at which innovation tipping points are reached seems to be speeding up. While radio took 38 years to become widely available, television took 13 years, personal computers took 16 years and the World Wide Web took just four years. For specific applications of the Internet, such as social networking, this pace of development has accelerated even further. As noted earlier, the pace of innovation adoption can be increased where new technologies represent new versions of old technologies. With each successive wave of technology developments, however, the number and range of technologies that could spawn new versions of themselves increase. This in turn expands opportunities for innovation and facilitates greater pace of technology growth. Moreover, the expansion of technologies has increased competition for users' or consumers' attention and loyalty among a greater range of technology applications. This phenomenon has created a stronger need to be 'first to market' with a new development. Such market imperatives have also driven the pace of information and communication technology innovation.

The spread of information and communication technology innovations is influenced significantly by the readiness of potential users to recognise their relevance. Although there may be some early adopters who will try out innovations because of their exploratory nature, wider adoption depends upon whether there is a significant market for the applications underpinned by a technology innovation. Innovations are therefore sensitive to social factors such as whether an information technology satisfies specific needs that people have. Adoption of new communications media and their displacement of older media, for instance, can depend upon whether the 'new' satisfies specific user needs and does so better than the 'old' (Ferguson and Perse, 2000).

Finding a new generation of information seekers

The principal question addressed by this book is whether there is evidence that developments in information and communication technologies, manifest especially in the Internet and its associated information repositories and search and communications tools, have driven fundamental changes in the way people search for information. If such change has occurred, what are the implications for the way information is sought and used in education settings? Then, in turn, what are the implications of these developments for higher education and the role played by libraries?

Evidence will be drawn from a wide range of sources in the following chapters. A large amount of this evidence was already in the public domain and derives from both academic and non-academic research. In addition, we report new evidence that derives from the authors' own research into the information-related behaviour of young people. In organising all this evidence into a systematic analysis of information behaviour, we distinguished in our own research between three generations in society, defined in terms of their age in 2007. These groups are:

- Google Generation, born 1994 and later;
- Generation Y, born between 1978 and 1993;
- Generation X, born before 1978.

These groups will be referred to again at different points in this book in connection with evidence on information and communication technology adoption and use in different contexts. From 1994, the Internet started to surface as an information source and communications medium for the general population, whereas previously it had been used predominantly by the academic and military worlds. In the years that followed, not only did the Internet itself evolve rapidly in terms of its information carrying capacity and range of applications, so too did other technologies such as television (which became increasingly interactive) and telephony (which embraced a wide range of information and communication applications in addition to voice-only communications). A critical question is whether these developments have conditioned radically different styles of information behaviour among their regular users compared with others who have not adopted these new technologies. The 'Google Generation' label is therefore applied hypothetically to people who have enthusiastically adopted the new information and communication technologies, but it is regarded as being especially relevant to those individuals who have never known a world without the Internet. Whether or not this group does represent a new learning generation with different information-seeking habits, demands and expectations from preceding generations is open to question. The purpose of this book is to examine relevant evidence in order to establish whether there is a distinctive new generation of information seekers whose information behaviours are not the same as those of older, pre-Internet information users and to consider – if this is so – the implications this social change has for those whose business is information and learning.

Before the Internet

In the pre-Internet era, the dominant information and communication technology equipment included television and radio, and video recorders, with only minorities of people possessing personal computers (PCs). PCs were a new technology at this time and were most rapidly taken up by households with children.

From the mid-1980s to the mid-1990s, there was clear evidence that consumption of television and radio was notably lighter among younger generations The age group equivalent to the generation of today to which we refer as the Google Generation, exhibited the least amount of TV viewing and radio listening. Across this ten-year span, however, all age groups exhibited increased average weekly amounts of viewing and listening. As evidence presented in Chapter 2 will show, children doubled their radio listening during this period and also had the biggest proportionate increase of any age group in terms of TV viewing.

During this period, around two-thirds of the population in the UK read books, but among teenagers aged 16–19, girls were much more likely to read than were boys. This gender divide persisted among young adults in their 20s. In the Internet era, the media consumption habits of people in developed countries have changed in response to the growth of new information and communication technologies with media markets becoming increasingly fragmented. These developments have serious implications for some media businesses. One illustration of this phenomenon has been shifting patterns of news consumption since the mid-1990s. Research in the United Kingdom has indicated that online news had become firmly established in the second half of the first decade of the twenty-first century. At the same time, longer established news media such as newspapers and television saw their markets decline, with young people in particular seemingly becoming disengaged from these news providers (Currah, 2009).

Up until the mid-1990s, the media environment of the average household had not changed greatly since the early 1980s. But within two or three years of this point, the position changed as growing numbers of people acquired home computers, computer games and other entertainment-related technology. Such changes were most prevalent in households with children. By 2000, more and more personal computers with modems had been acquired facilitating access to the Internet. It is not only fixed-location communication technologies that have evolved in their applications. Mobile technologies likewise have become increasingly significant in their prevalence and prominence in people's lives. Mobile telephones are no longer simple voice communication devices. The more advanced models can be used to search for information on and download content from the Internet and to receive television and radio transmissions.

The Internet era

In 1997, about half of pre-teenage and teenage children in Britain and Europe had a PC. But very few (under one in ten) had a PC with a modem, which indicated that the Internet had not yet been widely adopted. By the end of the 1990s, however, evidence from across Europe indicated that by their mid-teens, four in ten young people used the Internet at all, two-thirds used PCs for purposes other than to play games, and seven in ten played electronic games (Livingstone and Bovill, 2001b).

Even so, more than seven out of ten mid-teens still read books and over eight in ten said they read newspapers. So the traditional information media continued to hold on to large user groups. In fact, while many young people did display a keen interest in the new technologies and media such as computers, electronic games and the Internet, some still preferred to stay mainly with older established media (Johnsson-Smaragdi, 2001). In terms of adoption therefore the early Internet community has a distinctly youthful complexion, but the new technology did not capture the imaginations or interest of all young people.

The early impact of newer media on older media became more apparent in the new millennium. Across large media markets in Europe and North America, use of the Internet grew rapidly and consumption of television, radio and some print media – notably books – declined, especially among young people. Displacement of old media by newer media occurs partly because users must adjust their finite time budgets as the choice of media to consume grows. Thus, if an individual has a limited amount of time to spend on media consumption and a new medium emerges, he or she may have to reduce the time allocated to older media to make way for the new one (Kayany and Yelsma, 2000). However, there is a set of more complex psychological processes that come into play to determine which medium – new versus old – achieves the ascendancy. This observation is especially true when a new medium effectively plays to the same needs and interests as an older medium. The media consumer will then choose the medium that satisfies their needs the best (Ferguson and Perse, 2000; James et al., 1995).

Across the 2000–7 period, dramatic changes occurred in the adoption of many new information technology innovations. Initially, this phenomenon was manifest in the rapid spread of the Internet. This development was age-related. Younger people – though not just the Google generation – adopted the Internet more quickly than others. This pattern was observed in Europe, North America and other parts of the world. The most significant divide during the early part of this period was between the under- and over-50s (rather than the under- and over-30s).

Indeed, there was a trait that was distinctive from age that seemed to be a powerful indicator of innovation adoption, especially where new information media were concerned. Adopters of one new medium tended also to be people who had adopted other new media earlier in their lives. While such experimentation might be correlated to some degree with age and other demographics such as education and income level (Atkin and LaRose, 1994; Dutton et al., 1987), these factors have not invariably emerged as primary defining attributes. People who are swift to adopt new information technologies tend to be those who have adopted other similar innovations (Jeffres and Atkin, 1996; Lin, 1994). Computer adoption and Internet adoption have been found to be especially closely related – not surprisingly perhaps given the dependence of one on the other – but both have also been linked to adoption rates for a range of other telecommunications technologies (Lin, 1998).

As the first decade of the new millennium wore on, not only was there a marked expansion in the size of the Internet user population, but also in the range of devices used to gain access to online information. By 2006 in the UK, for example, although PC-based access was still dominant, the use of mobile phones, handheld computers and even digital television was also emerging. The Internet laggards were those people aged over 65, but even among this age group clear growth in online behaviour could be observed.

The broadband effect

One of the significant drivers of the expansion of Internet access from 2002 was the penetration of broadband. This type of connection meant that significant increases occurred in the volume of information that could be readily communicated over the Internet and the speed with which information could flow. Broadband technology represents a higher-speed communications medium that has the capacity to convey larger quantities of content electronically via wired and wireless transmission systems. In the context of the Internet, this meant that image and video content could be more effectively transmitted to end-users in real time without any downgrade in the quality of reception. The earlier generation of narrowband technology was effective enough for transmission of simple text-based documents but was much less effective for video transmission. In a narrowband environment, users might have to wait for hours to download a television programme or movie. With a broadband network, this downloading time could be reduced perhaps to a few minutes.

The adoption of broadband was not just associated with more people going online, but also with an increased diversity of information transaction applications. This technology was needed to cater to the ever-expanding demands of users in the online world. It also had significant economic implications because it also increased the range of business opportunities that could be developed via telecommunications systems. Broadband meant that more users could be accommodated by a communication network. It also meant that large amounts of information content in many different formats could be effectively transmitted. The evolution of the Internet from a fairly limited text-based communications system to a versatile system able to handle multi-modal forms of communication depended on broadband.

As Chapter 3 shows, broadband has been associated with increasingly complex online applications. It is also associated in turn with increasingly sophisticated use of the Internet by those who go online.

As with Internet adoption in general, it has tended to be younger people who have taken the lead, but older generations have quickly followed. The capacity afforded by broadband connections, however, has enabled Internet users to send and download much larger online cargoes and to engage in interactive and transactional activities where long lag times for responses to messages sent are not tolerated.

A distinctive 'Google Generation'?

Earlier we introduced the premise that the Internet and its associated information search tools may have conditioned a new information-seeking generation that differs from older (pre-Internet) generations in the way they try to find information and the way they use it. The hypothesis that a young, Internet-savvy generation – a 'Google Generation' – exists that has distinctive information-seeking needs and styles and that perhaps also possesses more advanced technology literacy than older generations is not conclusively proven by Internet penetration statistics alone, although evidence linked to the adoption of different online applications has revealed age-related differences (Brynin et al., 2004; Cole et al., 2004). As we will see in Chapters 3 and 4, despite the early lead taken by the younger generation first in initial Internet adoption and second in adoption of specific online applications, the older generations have been catching up (Dutton and Helsper, 2007; Madden, 2005).

Younger Internet users have tended to display greater diversity in their online behaviour patterns than older Internet users. For example, while many age groups up to 65 years used the Internet for basic functions such as e-mail, more advanced activities such as file-sharing, personal transactions and online content creation were much more prevalent among people aged under 30 that among older Internet users (Madden, 2005; Madden and Fox, 2006). It is significant to note, however, that most Internet users up to the age of 60 were already displaying an increasingly diverse range of information-related uses of the Web by 2005 (Lenhart, 2007; Madden and Fox, 2006). What was apparent from these studies of Internet users was that among the younger generations (what we have called the 'Google Generation' and Generation Y) was that the Internet had emerged as an important tool through which to obtain education-related information (Rainie and Tancer, 2007).

The Internet as information source

The Internet is now widely acknowledged by its users as an important source of information across a range of information domains. Indeed, for many users, it has become an 'essential' source for a diverse array of information including news, health, science, travel, leisure and education. As we shall see in Chapter 4, although many Internet users also rely on other older media for information, especially television, there is evidence from among those aged under 50, and more so among those aged under 30, that the Internet is fast emerging as their premier information source (Currah, 2009; Madden and Fox, 2006).

The under-30s have been identified as the most voracious users of the Internet, whereas the over-65s are the least adventurous (Cole et al., 2004). Younger users – having been earlier adopters – tend to be the more experienced users of online information tools (Lenhart et al., 2005). The youngest users of the Internet (aged under 30) tend to display the most diverse online behaviour patterns. This is manifest in the numbers of distinctive online applications in which they say they engage and the extent to which they do so compared with older Internet users (Lenhart et al., 2005). While older users – even up to 60 – may utilise online sources for specific purposes, they are less likely to be experimental in their online activities. Older users, for example, may turn to online sources for health information, while younger users may be more likely to engage actively in creating information content (Lenhart, 2007). Younger users also seek out online tools that facilitate speedier communications and information transmission (Shiu and Lenhart, 2004). What is without doubt is that more people across the generations go online to enhance their knowledge and understanding about a wide range of topics.

Despite these changes, traditional media still have an important part to play as information sources and learning tools. As Chapter 5 shows, students may have adopted online sources to locate course-related content, but many still also use and trust more traditional offline (hard copy) methods of content delivery (Kling and McKim, 2000). In fact, some evidence would suggest that there remain markets for both online and print content in educational settings, with different modes of conveying content preferred in different contexts (Bar-Ilan et al., 2003). As Chapter 6 finds, however, in an era of ever more advanced interactive online services and facilities, online tools can take centre stage in the learning process. Regular Internet users can display specific preferences for information formats, speed of presentation and creative engagement with content that Internet laggards or the less online literate are less keen on (Hay, 2000; Levin and Arafeh, 2002).

In sum, we have entered a period of dynamic change in which old and new forms of information search and delivery coexist and information seekers switch between these two modes. Gradually, for some, the new comes to dominate or supersede the old in respect of specific information access operations. Once adoption of such innovations has reached a critical mass of users – a 'tipping point' – then dramatic spread of penetration can follow.

Web 2.0

There has been an ongoing debate about whether there is a distinctive Internet generation that really got started in the mid-1990s, with different schools of thought on the issue. A solid evidence-based case has yet to emerge. The emergence of the concept of 'Web 2.0' has led to a closer investigation of the utility of a specific range of online applications in which users are more actively engaged not just in terms of advanced searches for information but also in the production of information. Age-related differences in the adoption of Web 2.0 applications have been consistently supported by empirical data (Madden and Fox, 2006). Even so, Web 2.0 activities are not the exclusive preserve of the under-30s.

Young people have been predominant among the early user groups for so-called Web 2.0 applications that embrace social networking and the production of user-generated content (Ofcom, 2007c, 2007d). Social networking sites have been mainly used for simple social interactions (Dutton and Helsper, 2007). Evidence has also emerged, however, that such online behaviour is sometimes linked to information searches (Horrigan, 2007).

It is not just Google Generation users who display adoption of advanced patterns of online behaviour. The next 'generation' above them, sometimes referred to as 'Generation Y' (aged up to 30 years) have also demonstrated an ability and willingness to use web technology to engage in complex online activities such as consumer and financial transactions and content creation (Madden, 2005). Web 2.0 developments – regardless of who uses them – have created an enhanced learning platform that carries many new tools for course construction, delivery and evaluation, for information storage and access, and for publishing content. As we will see in Chapter 7, these new tools have empowered students and tutors in different ways and created important professional and business issues for libraries and publishers concerning their future roles and modus operandi.

The Internet, learning and higher education

The tools and technologies associated with Web 2.0 have been acknowledged to carry significant implications for the future provision of higher education (as well as corporate training and lifelong learning – all of which represent educational activities in which universities might be engaged in the future) (Rainie and Tancer, 2007). These communications technologies may become especially pertinent in a world in which more people will study, but not necessarily in the traditional 'on-campus' mode. They will also become more significant in an educational context in a world in which students – young and older – are accustomed to utilising them in other aspects of their lives (see Raltivarakan, 2007).

Since 2004, the fastest growing online applications have been social networking sites. Sites such as MySpace, YouTube and Facebook have exhibited dramatic year-on-year growth and are especially popular among young people. The penetration of social networking sites disguises a variety of uses. Some of those registered use these sites almost routinely and in imaginative ways to disclose information about themselves, to seek new social and business contacts, and to create online communities with other individuals who share specific interests with them, while others lurk there deriving amusement from others but do not engage with these sites more actively. Social networking is certainly dominated by the Google Generation age group, though it is not used exclusively by them (Lenhart et al., 2005). For younger online networkers, however, these new tools have become integrated into their information searching repertoire, particularly in the context of their formal education (Rainie and Tancer, 2007).

Effective and advanced use of the Internet for information purposes can only be achieved once users have reached a certain level of competence. Despite reports that young people are adopting Web 2.0 applications enthusiastically and in large numbers, there is other evidence that casts doubt on the web literacy of many users, young and old alike.

There is no doubt though that among growing numbers of young people the Internet is an essential source of learning that helps them with their education and provides an on-tap electronic library. Online social networks are not only used to sustain friendships but also for educational purposes with online communications being used to discuss school or college work. Even by 2000, research from the USA indicated that over three-quarters of teenagers said they used the Internet for school-related work. Many uploaded study guides and used e-mail to contact teachers and fellow students about assignments (Horrigan, 2006).

There is no doubt that Web 2.0 is having an impact upon students and teachers. Blogs, wikis, podcasts, social networks and other new online features offer a range of new educational opportunities (New Media Consortium, 2007). While e-learning technologies have been available for a long time, the ways in which such technologies are applied in formal educational contexts is evolving. E-learning is about more than simply publishing content online. It represents a more dynamic learning environment in which students and tutors actively share knowledge and learning experiences. Both parties may have a creative role in finding and constructing content. Web 2.0 activities such as blogs, wikis and social networking condition this more dynamic and proactive engagement in the learning process on the part of students because these online facilities invite users to become content contributors and active participants.

Web 2.0 applications can serve as a textbook source, reference library, virtual tutor and guidance counsellor and virtual study group. For many experienced young Internet users, the web is a more reliable source than their real-world tutors. Through online social networks students can exchange information with an extensive array of contacts.

What does the future hold?

Predicting the speed and nature of these information and communication technology developments can be tackled by considering those innovations that have reached 'tipping points' in terms of penetration and which others are close to doing so. An important distinction that has been made in this context is that between 'transformative' and 'general-purpose' innovations.

A transformation occurs when a new technology enters the market that is unlike anything that has gone before and requires that users must discover what it is used for and how best to apply it. Alternatively, there is a range of general-purpose technologies with which many or most people may be familiar that continually undergo change. In these cases, new models may be produced that represent enhancements of earlier versions. Some new learning may be required on the part of their users, but the essential features and application protocols remain the same.

One can therefore debate whether the so-called Web 2.0 developments fall into the category of 'transformative' or 'general-purpose' changes. In most instances they can probably be considered exemplars of the latter rather than the former. What slightly confuses the issue is that the earlier versions upon which Web 2.0 applications are based have also had a short and changeable lifespan. In some cases, new upgrades occur even before the older models have reached a tipping point among the wider population.

One of the key problems holding back universal or near-universal penetration could be the centrality of the personal computer to accessing the Internet. The PC alone, however, does not make the Internet relevant for everyone. For some applications, such as video-conferencing, additional equipment must be obtained to enhance the functionality of the basic PC. The most popular online activities comprise e-mail, search, surfing, shopping, booking travel, messaging, listening to and downloading music, and playing games. Some of these activities are best handled by the PC with its full keyboard. Others could be effectively handled by other devices. E-mail and messaging, for example, could be appropriately handled by mobile devices.

Looking further at the expansion of Internet applications, social networking has emerged as the biggest success within the Web 2.0 context. This application has been widely adopted, especially by young people in the 15–30 age group. Providers of these services must consider how to construct effective and profitable business models.

The other major development identified with Web 2.0 is user-generated content. Video file sharing and blogging represent two phenomena that have grown rapidly since 2004. Even so, despite the volume of uploads and new sites, most of this content is consumed by very small user groups. Production skills remain limited in most cases at present. Yet, in terms of overall usage, social networking has already gone past the 'tipping point' among the under-30s and blogging is not far off.

Technology innovations must be considered alongside social and economic changes in considering what the future holds for higher education and learning. HE suppliers face tougher economic conditions and more competitive markets nationally and internationally. Students are increasingly regarded as customers who seek more choice and greater control over the scheduling of their own learning experiences. Remote study may increasingly become the choice of many. Growing information literacy levels will mean that electronic provision of information and learning must become more sophisticated and utilise the applications and techniques that draw young people to online systems already. Electronic publishing must and probably will attain the same professional status as offline publishing. Academic authors may then be less reliant on mainstream publishers. User-generated content will then be authored by scholars and students alike who will join in partnership to create and benefit from a creative and dynamic learning engagement.

The digital era is transforming the way universities and scholars disseminate knowledge content and the way that students engage with that content and learn from it. Hence in the future, all content may need to be available in electronic form, even though some or even much of it is also still available in hard copy. If and when this happens a genuinely new generation of information seekers will emerge – a Google Generation? What kind of roles will exist for libraries, publishers and universities in this rapidly changing digital scholarly world? How will they need to engage with new online tools and procedures to keep pace with the demands and expectations of their customers?

2

The rise of the information society

There is much interest in the rapidly evolving information and communications environment because of the implications it has for the way people live their lives. Information has always been important but the volume of information that flows around the world today is unprecedented as is the speed with which information can be widely disseminated. Such has been the dramatic rise in information and communication technologies and their centrality to many aspects of life, public and private, domestic and professional, that the world is seen by some observers to have evolved into an 'information society' (Bell, 1979; Castells, 1996–8; Webster, 2002).

Two hundred years ago, information still flowed but the ability of producers of information to disseminate what they knew far and wide was limited. Word of mouth was still a primary form of communication, though print communication was also available. Communicating to the 'mass', however, did not get underway until the early part of the nineteenth century with the emergence of the first newspapers, the rail transportation networks to convey them physically from one location to the next, and the telegraph that allowed messages to be transmitted virtually instantaneously across long distances, albeit only from one sender to one receiver.

Telephony permitted immediate and live information transmission on a one-to-one basis. Newspapers, magazines and newsreels shown in cinemas facilitated wider transmission of information to mass audiences, though not in real time. In other words, the information transmitted was time delayed. The emergence of radio in the early part of the twentieth century finally cracked the secret of immediate transmission of information in real time to the masses. The establishment of television in the 1950s added pictures to words and further enhanced the quality and richness of information transmission in real time to large audiences.

Even with these developments, there were still limitations to the flow of information. Communications technologies that targeted content at the mass audience were controlled centrally and elites determined the information agenda for their readers and audiences. There was no 'return path' through which information consumers could reply to information producers. Return path communications were available only for one-to-one messaging.

The emergence of computerised communications networks changed all this. Communications systems came on stream that allowed for the rapid transmission of large amounts of information on a one-to-one or one-to-many basis. Furthermore, these communications networks provided a return path allowing information recipients to contact information senders more readily in one-to-many settings. Initially, computerised communications networks were restricted to specialised user communities such as the military and academics. In the 1990s, however, all this changed with the development of new computer languages that facilitated worldwide communications online between virtually unlimited numbers of users. Furthermore, everyone could be an information sender – even in a one-to-many setting.

The birth of the Internet as a general communications phenomenon available to everyone at home by the mid-1990s opened up a multitude of new opportunities in diverse fields of business and commerce, government and public services, education and health, and entertainment and leisure. While founded upon computers linked to telecommunications networks, return path communications technology also moved across to older established media such as television. Television became digitised and then interactive. This led to radically new concepts about how this medium could operate in the future.

Wireless return path technology emerged in the form of mobile telephones or cell phones. These two became linked to the Internet and to broadcasting. Increased computerisation of these devices meant that they too could be used not just for voice messages but also to send and receive a wide range of other types of content.

All these communications technology developments have enhanced the flow of information. They have caused the amount of information that flows around the world to increase exponentially in the ten years since the Internet fully emerged as a 'mass' communications medium. They have increased the speed with which information flows. They have also called for users to develop new sets of skills in relation to these information devices because their effective use often requires a certain level of specialised competence.

One question that arises out of communication technology developments is whether the more packed information environment it has created has caused new forms of information processing and usage to evolve. Does the generation born into the Internet world behave and think differently from the generation born before online communications systems were widely available? The new generation has been variously labelled the 'net generation', the 'digital generation' or the 'Google Generation'. While there is no doubt that the emergence of the Internet has changed people's lives and that some people have been swifter than others to adopt it, are people who have little or no awareness of a world with no Internet different from older generations in their information-related behaviours? Does this 'Google Generation' adopt different information search strategies from earlier generations? Or have old information search and usage patterns survived in a different guise in the present information-rich world?

The concept of the 'information society' conveys a view that the world has changed fundamentally in the way it operates and that technology and the volume of 'information' flow have been driving forces behind this change. Whether an information society is a new type of society, however, is a view that has been challenged by some writers (Webster, 2002). Even if an information society does represent a new type of social functioning, it has not yet been effectively demonstrated by proponents of the information society because of their focus on the 'quantitative' rather than the 'qualitative'. That is, radical changes in the nature of societal functions and operations are linked to the overall (increased) volume of information in circulation. Much more might be learned about the social impact of this information by examining the different ways in which it is used and whether it is always used to good effect (Webster, 2006).

This volume may be unable conclusively to provide answers to all these important questions. What it does try to present, however, is an overview of how the communications and information environment has changed over time. It attempts to present profiles of the communications technologies and range of information content available to people over several decades up to the present day. It then looks beyond the present into the short- and medium-term future. What further developments can be expected to occur over the next 10–20 years in relation to information and communication technologies? What implications might these changes hold for the way people seek, handle and utilise information?

What does history teach us?

The history of information and communication technologies can be considered from a number of different angles covering developments of technologies, the way these technologies have been used, the regulatory implications and practices linked to communications technologies, and their emergence in different organisational fields. It is beyond the scope of this book to provide a detailed history of information and communication technology developments. It will be useful as background, however, to examine some of these developments, not least to establish whether innovation adoption patterns have taken on a consistent form over time. Furthermore, as the Google Generation has frequently been age-defined, that is a generation dominated by youth, does this factor – if true – represent a departure from technology adoption patterns that were already in place?

One of the major sources of debate has centred on whether the growth and establishment of information and communication technologies has been largely technology driven or socially driven. On this issue, different schools of thought have emerged. Without doubt, key technological developments in computing involving transistors and then microprocessors, other electronic components and latterly digitisation have provided the foundations upon which information and communication technologies have evolved. The application of these devices, however, takes place within a variety of social contexts – both public and private – and these applications and their settings can play an important part in determining design refinements to the technologies but also in defining their significance in the world.

The importance of studying the history of information and communication technology developments is to identify and distinguish between the successes and failures. Not all information and communication technologies have become successfully established. Some have done so only with a lot of effort and elite backing. Others have failed to take off or have done so temporarily only then to fall quickly by the wayside when new competitors emerge that are adopted more enthusiastically by end-users (Flichy, 2006). Examples here include the success of VHS over Betamax video tapes in the 1980s when home video recorders became widely adopted as household technology. Another illustration of this phenomenon is the more widespread adoption of e-mail over videotext, despite the fact that the latter received significant government backing in some countries, most notably France, and was introduced before the domestic Internet into European and North American consumer markets. Both technologies conveyed information, but with videotext information transmission was centrally determined and offered, in most systems, limited interactive interfaces for users.

Two models of analysis have also provided important insights into the growth and use of information and communication technologies. Diffusion of innovations theory has modelled the way new communications technologies become established (see Rogers, 1995). In addition, the social shaping of technology (SST) model has examined the extent to which social imperatives are critical to the development and utilisation of technologies (Mackay and Gillespie, 1992; Williams and Edge, 1996). These two models have sometimes been presented as oppositional in their orientations and explanations of technology adoption. However, they can be seen as complementary in many ways and both offer important insights into the emergence and establishment of information and communication technologies.

Despite being initially established as an information interrogation and sharing system for specialist groups in academia and the military, e-mail, in contrast, became quickly established on a wider scale internationally as networked computing systems spread to the general public. Its popular adoption was driven by its greater social versatility. Although used as a networked online information repository initially, its ability to enable easy site-to-site information transference among individuals opened up a wider range of applications for the Internet than videotext could offer. While the technology was not necessarily of higher quality, the social setting applications of the Internet, because of the popularity of e-mail and related services, meant it had greater social relevance to many end-users.

How to configure information and communication change

In examining the evolution of information and communications technologies, we are dealing with highly complex phenomena. Understanding how new information and communication technology forms become established is critical to making projections into the future. Work spanning more than 40 years into the adoption of innovations provides useful insights into how this phenomenon can be investigated.

Diffusion theory

The study of the diffusion of innovations is relevant to understanding the way new information and communication technologies are introduced and spread across a social system. The diffusion of innovations involves the study of social networks, the economics of information transmission and the role of communication in persuading people to adopt a new technology.

Everett Rogers developed a model of the innovation diffusion process. This model traced the speed with which new technologies became established. He found that innovations tended to display a similar development track which took the form of an S-shaped curve. This curve indicated that innovations would take off gradually and display a shallow slope initially. Once a critical mass in terms of penetration had been reached, adoption of that innovation would increase dramatically as large numbers of users adopted it. Then after a time the growth curve would slow down and flatten out again. The critical mass for rapid adoption was generally between 10 and 25 per cent of users.

Rogers (1995) distinguished five adopter categories. These were called innovators, early adopters, early majority, late majority and laggards. Innovators are people who experiment with new technologies as soon as they are launched and generally represent a tiny proportion of the total user population – no more than 3 per cent in Rogers' model. Early adopters are people who like to try out new things but prefer to see them trialled first by others. This group represents no more than 14 per cent of the user population. The early majority (33 per cent) represent the beginning of the steep slope of the S-curve. Once an innovation has been used by early adopters, a critical mass of usage is reached – sometimes known as a tipping point – following which market penetration of the innovation begins to accelerate. The late majority (33 per cent) represent individuals who only adopt once the innovation is no longer an 'innovation' but is rather an established technology. At this stage, they feel confident enough to adopt it as well. These individuals are slow to adopt anything that is new. At this stage, the growth in penetration of the innovation slows and the S-curve reaches its uppermost point and levels off or begins to decline. The last group, known as the laggards (16 per cent), tend to be suspicious of innovations and either use them very late or may never do so.

The adoption of innovations model can be used to track the rate at which new technologies become established and can also be used to indicate whether innovations are established yet in particular markets based on their existing penetration figures. For example, a country that records 50 per cent penetration of the Internet could be classified as moving from the early to late majority stage of development. Another country that records only 10 per cent penetration may still be in the early adopter phase and on the cusp of really taking off in a significant way.

Although the study of adoption of innovations has given rise to a standardised model of diffusion, the rates of penetration of new technologies are never exactly constant. Some technologies spread more rapidly than others. The speed with which a technology diffuses can be influenced by a range of social and economic factors. The ability of consumers to afford to adopt new technologies is one factor. This, as we see below, has been related to the extent to which an information and communication technology such as the Internet has become established in different countries. In addition, the presence of existing technologies and the degree of distinction between them and a technology innovation can affect the speed with which and extent to which that innovation becomes established in a social system. Existing technology networks that are widely and firmly established may erect barriers to delay the evolution of a new technology regarded as a competitor (Wellman, 1988).

Within specific international, national or local markets, the penetration of innovations may display a general pattern of development that disguises variations in penetration rates among sub-groups within those markets. Divides can develop in the rate and extent of adoption of new technologies that are associated with different demographic or behavioural segments within a population. In the context of modern information and communication technology developments, this phenomenon is frequently referred to as the 'digital divide'.

The political scientist, Pippa Norris (2001), has written extensively and informatively about this subject. She identified digital divides between countries and within countries in respect of the penetration and impact of digital technologies. She found that the rate of penetration of information and communication technology in different countries was linked to the status or strength of their economies, their level of social development (including levels of adult literacy and percentage of individuals with at least secondary education), their political development (level of democracy) and their location in the world. Countries in the northern hemisphere and in the West had the greatest penetration of information and communication technologies. This last factor, however, is probably also closely associated with economics and social and political circumstances.

The Human Development Report (UNDP, 1999) examined the time it took for different 'new technologies' to become established. A critical threshold of 'general acceptance' was whether they reached 50 million users worldwide. On this basis, major new communications technologies have displayed ever-increasing rates of penetration to that criterion level. From inception to 'acceptance', radio took 38 years, television 13 years, personal computers 16 years and the World Wide Web just four years.

These figures indicate that the Internet represents one of the fastest-growing technology innovations ever.

Some of its critics have challenged diffusion theory because it is regarded as too technologically deterministic. In other words, the mere presence of a new information and communication technology means that eventually it will spread, following the traditional S-shaped curve of diffusion. There is an assumption of inevitability to eventual widespread adoption and a presumption that all new technologies will display the same pattern of evolution. It has become clear, through empirical analysis, that not all technology innovations are equally successful in penetrating social systems and that the pace with which they do so can vary as well. Much can depend upon whether a technology innovation really is a genuine 'innovation' or simply a new version of an existing technology. In fact, many, if not most, information and communication technologies evolve over time and grow and develop into new forms. A new information and communication technology that is the spawn of an existing technology might benefit from the existing market presence of its 'parent' provided it is seen as adding something new and significant to what went before. If it does not add much that is new and relevant to users, and it involves a significant cost, then it may fail to achieve widespread adoption. It is in this context that the social shaping of technology comes into play.

Diffusion and social setting

The significance of social factors to the diffusion of information and communication technologies stems from the theoretical assumption that technologies succeed because of decisions and choices made by humans. Although technology can undoubtedly contribute to social change, the extreme notion of technological determinism has been challenged (Winner, 1986). Yet the language of technological determinism has continued to dominate discourses about information and communication technology penetration and adoption (MacKenzie and Wacjman, 1999).

An emphasis on the societal contexts of technology adoption introduces the idea that information and communication technologies often have a complex set of interrelationships with social factors and that society may shape technology as much as technology shapes society. Thus the SCOT (social construction of technology) model has argued that technology designers and developers must and often do take account of end-users' needs and of the settings in which technology will be applied. These social factors guide decisions about the construction of specific technologies because they must prove to be effective in specific application contexts and the latter are generally governed by social conventions and rules (Bijker and Law, 1992). The SCOT approach has been applied in the field of social informatics to investigate and understand the developing applications of computing and information systems across a range of organisational contexts (Star, 1995; Suchman, 1996).

How important is information access?

There has been much emphasis placed on information access, driven by technology access, particularly on the part of governments trying to drive forward the spread and adoption of public information systems and online public services. The spread of online information networks has been regarded by governments in developed countries as having critical social and economic significance. It is also regarded as enhancing democratic processes by bringing consumers as citizens closer to government and its services and by enhancing the transparency of government processes.

It is essential that everyone has equal opportunities to access key information systems. Indeed, information is critical to many sectors in business and industry with the effective flow of information representing the 'life blood' of many organisations. Information is important for effective management and marketing. It is important to the effective delivery of health care and education. Information has important personal, social and economic functions for individuals. Yet, as we have already seen, gaps exist in the availability and accessibility of information to different sectors of societies. Access to the Internet has become widespread, but not equally spread across different social sectors, particularly ones defined by location, socio-economic status and age. Even if specific groups have access to an ICT such as the Internet, they do not all use it with equal competence.

Internationally, developed countries enjoy a greater richness of information and communication technologies than developing countries. Nearly half of the world's Internet users (49 per cent), for example, live in Europe and North America where less than one in five (17 per cent) of the world's population live (*http://www.InternetWorldStats.com*, 10 June 2007). Without access to information and communication technologies such as the Internet, any social or economic benefits they might bring cannot be experienced. In the context of understanding whether there are new generations evolving defined by their use of communications technology, we need to establish whether there is empirical evidence for this phenomenon. More to the point, are new generations evolving that can be defined not just by the extent to which they access information and communication technologies, but also by the ways in which they do so? To answer this question, we need to find evidence that demonstrates not only differences in kind according to quantitative user indicators but also differences in kind according to qualitative usage indicators.

In relation to the current analysis, there are three cohorts that are the focus of attention, defined in terms of age in 2007. These groups are:

- Google Generation, born 1994 and later;
- Generation Y, born between 1978 and 1993;
- Generation X, born before 1978.

As later discussion will show, the pre-1978 population has been further divided by some researchers, especially in the United States, and Generation X is defined in terms of upper as well as lower age limits. In the current analysis, however, this threefold categorisation will be retained.

This study also set out to address several specific questions about the information-seeking habits of Generation Y and Generation X. Principally, this enquiry has investigated the information-seeking habits of Generations Y and X, how these might have changed over time and the impact of information and communication technology developments on information-seeking behaviour. Part of the initial analysis therefore will examine the information and communication technology environments at different points in time, identifying where possible the extent to which Generations Y and X availed themselves of specific information and communication technologies.

In later chapters, closer attention will be given to Internet and web developments, the impact of broadband and the growth of Web 2.0 features. The latter features, in many ways, define the Google Generation. To what extent though have they produced changes in the information-seeking behaviour of Generations Y and X?

Media landscape: pre-Google Generation era

This initial analysis will be structured in broad terms in relation to the pre- and post-Google Generation time periods. In other words, what were the key characteristics of the media landscape before and after 1994? The pre-1994 period was characterised by a media environment that was dominated by television, radio, newspapers and magazines as information sources, with evidence of book reading as well.

In terms of information and communication technology equipment, by the end of the 1980s, virtually all UK homes had TV and radio sets, most (70 per cent) had video recorders, while steadily growing minorities possessed teletext (30 per cent) and personal computers (26 per cent). One in ten (11 per cent) had computer or video games. Satellite television and cable television reception (2 per cent each) were still rare. The Internet had not yet surfaced. Home computer (43 per cent) and video games (21 per cent) penetration were much higher in households with children aged up to 15 years (Gunter and McLaughlin, 1992).

The dominant information source in 1990 for world news was television (69 per cent of UK TV viewers nominating it), with newspapers (18 per cent), radio (11 per cent) and magazines (<1 per cent) following on. In respect of local news information, newspapers ruled (51 per cent saying it was the main source), followed by television (21 per cent), radio (10 per cent) and magazines (1 per cent). Talking to people (12 per cent) was actually the third most important source of local news at this time (Gunter et al., 1994).

In the United Kingdom in the decade preceding the onset of the Internet era, television and radio were the dominant media. Television was more heavily used by older generations and radio was most used by young adults. From the mid-1980s to mid-1990s television viewing remained fairly stable, while radio listening increased in the 1990s across all age groups and particularly among older people.

Between 1984 and 1994, television viewing increased on average per week from 23 hours and 3 minutes to 25 hours and 41 minutes across all viewers aged 4 years and older (+11 per cent). Average weekly viewing levels rose by higher percentages among both children aged 4 to 15 years (+19 per cent) and among older viewers aged 65 and over (+20 per cent) (Griffin, 1998). Average weekly radio listening rose by 85 per cent between 1984 and 1994 among all listeners aged 4 years and over. Once again, as with viewing, listening levels increased by bigger margins among both children aged 4 to 15 years (+126 per cent) and among the oldest listeners aged 65 and over (+113 per cent).

Newspaper reading levels fell during this same pre-Internet period. Between 1986 and 1992, the percentage of all people in the UK aged 15 and over who claimed to read a daily newspaper fell from 67 per cent to 60 per cent. There was a slightly smaller fall for Sunday newspapers

(74 to 70 per cent). The drop in readership of daily newspapers over this time period was pronounced among those aged 15–24 years (69 to 59 per cent), but readership remained stable among those aged 65 and over (61 and 62 per cent) (Griffin, 1998).

The two youngest age groups (15–24s and 25–44s) here therefore are approximate age equivalents of Generations Y and X respectively. Within each time period, there was relatively limited variance in extent of claimed newspaper readership between age groups. There was, however, a notable drop-off in extent of newspaper reading between 1986 and 1992. This trend was most marked for daily newspaper reading and most strongly felt among the youngest readers, 15–24s and 25–44s – the Generations Y and X of their time (Griffin, 1998).

Despite the growth in numbers of radio stations and TV channels across the 1980s and early 1990s, book reading held its own. Females read more often than did males. Between 1980 and 1990, male book reading increased slightly (from 52 to 56 per cent saying they ever read a book), while female book reading increased by a greater margin over this period (61 to 68 per cent) (Matheson and Pullinger, 1999).

By 1994, book reading had reached 59 per cent among males and 72 per cent among females, but with the gap being wider than this among males and females aged 16–19 (55 versus 75 per cent). Whether this difference can be attributed to a greater studiousness of the part of teenage girls compared with teenage boys is not certain. Older Generation Y equivalents in their 20s exhibited a narrower gender divide in book reading (57 per cent of males and 70 per cent of females aged 20–29 saying they ever read a book).

Media landscape: Google Generation era

After 1994, media and communications experienced significant changes. The arrival of digital technology and the emergence of online data-carrying communications systems for everyone transformed the information and communications landscape. The Internet opened up a plethora of new opportunities for information transmission and the World Wide Web equally for information storage. Desktop computers became networked communications devices and access gateways to almost unlimited volumes of information content. Then enhancements to 'older' technologies such as television and telephony introduced a more diverse array of applications in each case whereby they could also be used to interface with the Internet and Web and provide alternative access points to massive quantities of information content. Further technological developments meant that technologies that formerly had exclusivity – such as television sets for television broadcast reception – found themselves in competition with other platforms such as computers and mobile telephones even in their own traditional markets.

By 1997, the media environment of the average household in the UK was much richer than it was at the end of the previous decade. Television and radio were virtually universal. An overwhelming majority of households now possessed a video recorder (88 per cent). A significant majority also possessed teletext TV sets (69 per cent). The prevalence of home computers (46 per cent) and computer/video games (31 per cent) had doubled since the end of the 1980s, while the spread of satellite TV (20 per cent) and cable TV (11 per cent) had grown by between five and ten times. Compact disc players, unheard of in 1989, were in nearly half of all homes (46 per cent). Video games (50 per cent) and home computers (43 per cent), again, were even more widespread in households with children (ITC, 1998).

In a sign that people who are early adopters of one new technology are also more likely to be early adopters of another, in 1997, households with multi-channel satellite TV reception were more likely than households with basic terrestrial TV reception to have teletext (89 versus 62 per cent), compact disc players (57 versus 41 per cent), home computers (50 versus 24 per cent), video games (37 versus 22 per cent) and video cameras (24 versus 10 per cent).

Television was still the premier source of world news in 1997 (67 per cent), followed by newspapers (20 per cent), radio (9 per cent), teletext (2 per cent) and magazines (<1 per cent). With regard to local news information, the gap between newspapers (40 per cent) and television (37 per cent) had narrowed since 1989/1990 (ITC, 1998).

Such developments, however, did not impact upon everyone in the same way or to an equal extent. Following traditionally observed patterns of innovation adoption, some sectors of society explored these information and communication technologies earlier and more enthusiastically than others.

By the end of the twentieth century significant variations existed between major regions of the world in terms of their media richness. This was demonstrated by Norris (2001) in her analysis of the proportions of the populations for different regions that used what she called 'new' and 'old' media. In this case, new media comprised the Internet and PCs. Old media comprised radio, television, newspapers, mainline telephones and mobile phones.

Norris examined data for radios from 1997, for TV sets from 1998, for landline and mobile phones from 1998 and for PCs from 1998. Daily newspaper data were from 1996. Data for Internet penetration (population online) were for 2000. The Information Society Index was calculated from an aggregation of old and new media penetration data.

A higher score on this index signified a region that was richer in terms of its media. Norris inter-correlated the use of old and new media and found that access to these various media was either high or low. Scandinavia emerged as the region most richly endowed with old and new media, followed by North America and then Western Europe. Africa was the poorest endowed region, followed by South America. There was, however, a large gap between Africa and the rest of the world.

In general, countries or regions of the world that provided poor accessibility to old media also provided poor accessibility to new media. Given that the spread of new technology was most powerfully predicted by per capita gross domestic product within a country, it is clear that economic wealth underpins the spread of information and communication technologies. The greatest supply and use of different media occurs in the wealthiest parts of the world (Norris, 2001).

The analysis by Norris was based on data that covered all new media users regardless of age. Other research has focused on the younger generation and the extent to which various 'new media' had been adopted by children and teenagers. Livingstone and Bovill (2001b) reported findings from a major survey of the media environment for children and teenagers in Europe. This survey provided data from 1997. Data were obtained about access to communications technologies at home and about the use of those technologies. Distinctions were made between different child and adolescent age groups. While this research does not allow us to examine wide generational differences in possession and utilisation of information and communication technologies, spanning all age-bands, it does provide significant data on the status of information and communication technologies in European households for the mid-1990s – and of their significance to Google Generation equivalents of that time. Moreover, the young people surveyed in this study comprise the Generation Y of 2007.

Livingstone and Bovill (2001b) presented data on the possession of selected information and communication technologies among different age groups surveyed across all the 12 participating EU countries. The penetration of television was universal and that of video recorders was almost as widespread, attaining over 90 per cent penetration for all child age groups examined (6–7s, 9–10s, 12–13s, 15–16s). Most age groups indicated that they had access to books (80+ per cent) and a telephone (90+ per cent).

A majority of each age group (64+ per cent) claimed to have access to electronic games that could be played through the TV set. Significant minorities had access to multi-channel television (cable and satellite – 37+ per cent) and to a personal computer (49+ per cent). At this time, however, PCs were stand-alone rather than networked. Many children with a PC could play CD-Roms on it (30+ per cent), but only small percentages had the technological capability to gain Internet access (6–9 per cent).

The most valued medium at this time was television. When children aged between 6 and 16 were asked what they would miss most if specific media were removed from their environment, television was most often mentioned by all age groups (6–7s: 46 per cent; 9–10s: 59 per cent; 12–13s: 58 per cent; 15–16s: 45 per cent).

Games machines (usually linked to the TV) were the next most likely to be mentioned – at least by three age groups: 6–7s: 33 per cent; 9–10s: 12 per cent; 12–13s: 10 per cent. The PC was mentioned quite often by 6–7s (25 per cent) and 9–10s (15 per cent). PCs did not feature in the top three 'most missed' media for the two older age groups. Among the two older age groups, the 12–13s (11 per cent) and 15–16s (27 per cent) said they would miss their hi-fi and the 15–16s would miss the phone (14 per cent). These differences may have reflected changing patterns of behaviour among these age groups and the importance of each medium to young people at different life stages. At this time, the Internet was still in its embryonic stage as a general public access medium. Internet access was indicated by respondents who said they possessed a PC with modem and had limited penetration.

The same children and teenagers were probed about their media aspirations with a question that asked them what they would like for their next birthday. For the oldest age group, in Britain, mobile phone was the communications device that finished top of their wish list (17 per cent) – ahead of a personal stereo (15 per cent) and a CD-Rom player (15 per cent). Among all three younger age groups, a TV was top of the birthday gift list (6–7s: 19 per cent; 9–10s: 16 per cent; 12–13s: 20 per cent). This was joined by games machine (15 per cent) and Gameboy (16 per cent) among 6–7s; games machine (16 per cent) and CD-Rom (15 per cent) for 9–10s, and CD-Rom (25 per cent) and hi-fi (17 per cent) for 12–13s.

Use of different media by young people

Further data on young people's use of various media and technologies during the early part of the Internet era in Europe indicated that television was used by everybody (99 per cent) and virtually all youngsters used radio (95 per cent) as well. A significant majority (89 per cent) used video (recorders). Across the 12 countries from which data were collected, books (79 per cent), magazines (78 per cent) and electronic games (74 per cent) were extensively used, while clear majorities also said they read newspapers (67 per cent) and comics (63 per cent). Six out of ten (60 per cent) across Europe said they used a personal computer for activities other than playing games. Only around one in three (32 per cent) used the Internet (Beentjes et al., 2001).

Age-related comparisons were made across all 12 countries, across the three age groups: 9–10s, 12–13s and 15–16s. There was little difference between them in terms of the extent to which they each used audio or audio-visual media. Use of print media changed with age but not always in the same direction for different media. Book (85 per cent of 9–10s, 82 per cent of 12–13s, 73 per cent of 15–16s) and comic reading (70 per cent of 9–10s and 12–13s, 61 per cent of 15–16s) declined somewhat with age, while magazine (60 per cent of 9–10s, 82 per cent of 12–13s, 88 per cent of 15–16s) and newspaper reading (44 per cent of 9–10s, 70 per cent of 12–13s, 84 per cent of 15–16s) increased. Use of PCs (48 per cent of 9–10s, 61 per cent of 12–13s, 65 per cent of 15–16s) and the Internet (14 per cent of 9–10s, 32 per cent of 12–13s, 41 per cent of 15–16s) both grew in prevalence with increased age (Beentjes et al., 2001). Thus use of new, interactive technologies and communications systems emerged most significantly during the teens. At the time of this research (1997), Internet use was fairly extensive among mid-teens but still fairly unusual among pre-teens. Given the low prevalence of PCs with modems at home, Internet access was facilitated mostly through schools in Europe in 1997.

The same research also examined the amount of time children and adolescents devoted to using different media (Beentjes et al., 2001). Averaged across the 12 participating countries, television emerged as the most used medium (136 minutes per day). Radio (90 mins/day) was the next most used medium, followed by TV-related electronic games (32 mins/day) and video (30 mins/day). Print media commanded far less time each day (magazines – 10 mins/day, newspapers – 7 mins/day) than did audio-visual media, but books (21 mins/day) were prominent among the print media.

The use of personal computers for activities (17 mins/day) other than game playing was almost at the level of book reading and finished ahead of time spent with other print media. Time devoted to use of the Internet (5 mins/day) was still limited, reflecting more restricted access at this time and perhaps also indicating that the embryonic Internet presented far less tempting content than at present.

The use of television and radio increased with age (118 mins/day at 9–10, 137 mins/day at 12–13, 136 mins/day at 15–16). Time devoted to electronic games (29 mins/day at 9–10, 34 mins/day at 12–13, 27 mins/day at 15–16) and video (30 mins/day at 9–10 and 12–13, 27 mins/day at 15–16), however, remained relatively unchanged across these age groups. Book reading declined not just in prevalence but also in terms of average amount of time devoted to reading among teenagers (25 mins/day at 9–10, 24 mins/day at 12–13, 16 mins/day at 15–16). The time spent with comics also declined with age (14 mins/day at 9–10, 12 mins/day at 12–13, 6 mins/day at 15–16), while teenagers spent more time than did pre-teens reading magazines (6 mins/day at 9–10, 11 mins/day at 12–13 and 15–16) and newspapers (3 mins/day at 9–10, 7 mins/day at 12–13, 11 mins/day at 15–16). Use of personal computers increased with age (11 mins/day at 9–10, 17 mins/day at 12–13, 21 mins/day at 15–16), as did that of the Internet. Internet usage, however, was generally at a low level (3 mins/day at 9–10, 5 mins/day at 12–13, 7 mins/day at 15–16).

The above data indicated that variations occurred across age groups in Europe in terms of access to different media and use of these media in the home. Use will also be determined in some degree by access. Taking the European young people's survey data further, Johnsson-Smaragdi (2001) produced a typology of media usage patterns linked to access for children and adolescents. The significance of this analysis is that it shows the degree to which different media are used or, perhaps more importantly, are not used even when readily available. Some media when available media may be widely used, while other available media may be less widely used. This analysis provides insights into the relative popularity of different media.

What Johnsson-Smaragdi (2001) found is that large proportions of those who had access to VCRs (81 per cent) and books (77 per cent) at home also used them. The percentages of use of other media such as electronic games (45 per cent), personal computers (27 per cent) and the Internet (13 per cent) among those who possessed them were much lower. In fact, at this time, it was clear that many Internet users were reliant on access sources outside their homes and that, in 1997, most child and teenage Internet users in Europe did not have home Internet access. Even among those young people who did not have such media at home, significant minorities nevertheless claimed to use a personal computer (36 per cent), electronic games (24 per cent) and the Internet

(21 per cent). In these cases, they were presumably gaining access to these media in other locations outside their home.

For VCRs, the biggest percentage was of those respondents who had home access and used this technology. One in ten of the sample (10 per cent) used VCRs but had no home access. Small percentages were non-users and these were equally divided between individuals who did and did not have access to a VCR at home (4 per cent in each case).

With regard to books, the largest percentage comprised young people who both had access to books at home and read books (77 per cent). One in 20 young people (5 per cent) read books even though they had no access to them at home. Among non-readers, more had home access to books than did not (15 versus 3 per cent).

In 1997, over half of young people in Europe did not use a personal computer. More PC users engaged with this technology outside their own home than within it. Among non-users, many more did not have home access than did. Hence, while home PC use was still becoming established ten years ago, once home access was in place, young people tended to use their PCs.

As we have already seen, Internet use among children and adolescents in 1997 Europe was at a fairly low level. Around two-thirds were non-users. More users used the Internet outside the home than inside it. However, few non-users had home access. Most youngsters in 1997 used electronic games and did so whether they had home access or not. Non-use was more prevalent among those with no home access than those who had such games at home (Johnsson-Smaragdi, 2001).

In 1997, therefore the world was dominated by video recorders and books with electronic games becoming firmly and widely established as well. Use of PCs was becoming established, reaching nearly two-thirds of young people in Europe. The Internet was still a minority pastime for around one-third of youngsters and still occurred outside the home more than inside it.

Johnsson-Smaragdi (2001) also differentiated a number of media use styles in 1997. She conducted an analysis of usage patterns of print media (books, newspapers, magazines and comics), screen media (television, video and electronic games) and ICT (computers). Eight types were identified:

1. *Low media users* – mostly consumed television and had generally low levels of media usage.

2. *Traditional media users* – low usage of new media and electronic games and average on other media.

3. *Specialists – 1: television specialist –* use mostly television; low on book reading and new media usage and average other print media and video.

4. *Specialists – 2: book specialists –* book fans who also read other print media but are lower than average on use of screen media and new media.

5. *Specialists – 3: PC specialists –* new media users specialising in PCs and the Internet; also high on electronic games and books but low on television.

6. *Specialists – 4: PC and games specialists –* strongly focused on PCs, electronic games and the Internet; above average on magazines and comics, less than average on books, television and video.

7. *Screen entertainment fans – television and video –* high on TV and video and low on games, computers and books.

8. *Screen entertainment fans – television and games –* spend equal amounts of time on electronic games and television and fairly high on videos and PCs, but low on books.

Johnsson-Smaragdi (2001) reported that young people with media preferences defined primarily by the use of audio-visual media read a lot less than did print specialists. This is neither surprising nor deeply insightful. Nonetheless, even fans of TV, electronic games and video still read. In fact, new media specialists, who used computers and computer games extensively, also read more than did young people whose media behaviour was dominated by television.

Turning to the use of information and communication technologies by different media usage types, PC and PC + games specialists devoted far more time overall than any other group to the use of computer technology (150 mins/day and 124 mins/day respectively) and the Internet (28 mins/day and 19 mins/day respectively). In 1997, however, the Internet was not as developed as it is today and therefore most computer use was not devoted to surfing the Web. At this time, young people whose media behaviours were dominated by the use of established media had not yet switched significantly to the use of computers (no more than 11 mins/day of use) or the Internet (no more than 3 mins/day).

Finally, turning to use of audio-visual media – electronic games, video and television – there was much heavier use of these media across all youth media behaviour types. This behaviour was largely driven by TV viewing. Children who exhibited a preference for watching videos

(104 mins/day on video and 21 mins/day on games) or playing with computer games (90 mins/day on games and 21 mins/day on video) as well as viewing TV devoted significant amounts of time to those media. Children who liked books also watched TV (110 mins/day) but to a much lesser extent than those youngsters who also showed a specific preference for audio-visual media (TV/video types watched 170 mins/day and TV/games types watched 168 mins/day).

Summary

The 1990s was an era of significant growth and expansion in communications media and information technologies. Until that time, traditional media such as radio and television were not only universal but also dominant. Television and related technologies such as video-recorders were widely used. The ownership and use of home computers also expanded significantly during this era. Although the technology had been available for many years, the Internet, as a general public information medium, came on stream during the second half of the 1990s, but initially children and teenagers were more likely to be introduced to online information searching at school than at home. Thus, despite the widespread entertainment-related appeals of the Internet, it has always been closely associated with informational and educational contexts.

The spread of private ownership of computers and computer/video games in the late 1990s, however, meant that youngsters did have increased opportunities to learn and practice essential computer-related skills at home as well as at school. Towards the end of the 1990s, the communications and media environment was much richer than it had been ten years earlier. Multi-channel television had reached a clear majority of the viewing population, more than half of homes had personal computers and the growth of compact disc players signalled further the appeal of electronic content. The real growth in the use of online digital networks for information, however, was still to come.

In beginning the search for the Google Generation, it is clear from the evidence discussed in this chapter that young people are quick to adopt new information and communication technologies. At the same time, this is not a universal trait. Even with the rapid emergence and spread of the Internet, some young people still exhibited preferences for more traditional audio-visual and print media. Book worms used the Internet but to a lesser extent than did same-age counterparts who had already exhibited a strong liking for new technologies such as computers and electronic games. Thus we cannot presume that if a new media generation is emerging that exhibits distinctively early or strong preferences for new interactive technologies that it can be age-defined. As later parts of this book will reveal, despite the youthful dominance of early Internet adopters, this age profile later exhibited equally rapid and profound change as the overall user demographic profile broadened out. This issue is explored further in the next chapter where we take a closer look at patterns of adoption and use specifically of the Internet.

3

The Internet era

Although the early origins of the Internet have been traced back to the 1960s, and certainly electronic mail was widely used by academics in the United States by the late 1980s, the 'Internet era', as defined by the widespread use of computerised electronic communications networks by the general public and by all major public and private organisations, did not begin until the mid-1990s. For the purposes of this analysis, the 'Google Generation' is defined as those individuals born in 1994 and later.

Evidence examined in the last section confirmed that the mid-1990s was the period during which computer-based media became established but when online activities involving the Internet were still in an embryonic stage of development. Since that time, and certainly from 2000, the Internet and related technologies have become more widespread in developed countries – and especially across Europe, North America and parts of the Far East. In this section, further evidence is examined that assesses not simply the extent of Internet use, but more importantly the nature of the applications to which it is put by users. This analysis also identifies emergent user classifications defined primarily by patterns of online behaviour. It is clear that age is an important variable in differentiating the way the Internet and online communications systems are used. However, with the dramatic growth in online innovations and their rapid penetration among user populations, most age groups display extensive adoption of new information and communication technologies (ICTs) and it is only the very oldest that lag significantly behind. More sophisticated analyses of ICT adoption are therefore needed to identify differences between age groups based on complex application patterns rather than simple access and use. Furthermore, non-age-related classifications provide further insights into the different types of online technology and application user.

The adoption of ICTs is often depicted as an S-shaped curve that has characterised patterns of penetration across many different innovations in many different communities and markets. This observation, while substantiated by innovation adoption research, disguises more complex patterns of growth and development that define the realities of new technology adoption and use.

ICTs are regarded as having the potential to change society and the way people live their lives. They are trumpeted as having significant implications for business and commerce, for the delivery of public services and for civic engagement. These technologies can make us more informed and can open up unlimited channels of knowledge and learning. It is often the case that governments that become excited by these prospects believe that the only thing that prevents the full potential of ICTs being realised is their lack of availability. Much emphasis has therefore been placed on technology roll-outs. Research into 'e-living', however, has revealed that it may be overly simplistic to talk about the 'impact' of ICTs purely in relation to their penetration. Instead, it is far more important to understand how people adapt these technologies and integrate them into different parts of their lives (Anderson et al., 2006).

It would be naive to presume that ICTs will automatically produce economic and social benefits merely as a result of their physical presence in people's lives. Benefits accrue as a consequence of the way technologies are utilised. This utilisation, in turn, will depend upon the degree to which people can conceive of useful and relevant ways in which technologies will fit into their lives. Even where benefits are identified for ICTs, it can be difficult to attribute sole causality to technology (Anderson, 2004; Anderson and Yttri, 2004). It is more likely that other factors have played a part in determining the value of technologies and in driving recognition on the part of users of where in their lives specific technologies might have relevance.

Thus ICT adoption is not a simple matter of unidirectional diffusion. Technology adoption occurs within a socio-economic context that may be further mediated by the psychological dispositions of individuals towards new experiences. Some people may be persistent new technology laggards or avoiders, while there are others who will experiment with innovations and stick with them and others who experiment and then give them up. Hence, some new technologies may experience 'churn' as well as gradual penetration. In this regard, Internet diffusion was found to display less smooth adoption patterns across Europe than mobile phone adoption. Drop-out rates were more prevalent for the Internet than mobile telephony (Anderson et al., 2004). One factor at play here could be the speed with which potential users identify the value of a technology to their lives. This may have become more readily apparent in the case of mobile phones than the Internet. Nonetheless, once people began to use the Internet and realise the potential it offered, they became committed adopters. Over time, technology churn becomes outweighed by committed adoption.

Media profiles

Across the Internet era the media environments of children have become enriched. By 2007, a clear majority of children aged up to 15 years in the UK had access to the Internet at home. Television remains ubiquitous across all child age groups from 5 to 15 years. In addition, other audio-visual entertainment media, most notably DVD players (92 per cent) and computer or video games (82 per cent) were also found in the great majority of households with children (Ofcom, 2007c). Possession of a laptop or personal computer with Internet connection became more prevalent with age (5–7s: 46 per cent; 8–11s: 63 per cent; 12–15s: 77 per cent). Likewise, having a webcam – although generally at a lower level across age groups (21 per cent) – increased significantly in prevalence with age (5–7s: 7 per cent; 8–11s: 18 per cent; 12–15s: 34 per cent).

Further questioning by the Ofcom survey of young media consumers explored the extent to which they own and possess different items of media equipment in their bedrooms. The percentages here were lower than for 'all household' media and communications equipment, but the findings nonetheless revealed that significant proportions of children and teenagers aged 5 to 15 years claimed to have their own TV sets (71 per cent), computer games consoles (62 per cent), DVD players (62 per cent), CD players (57 per cent), mobile phones (54 per cent) and mp3 players (41 per cent) in their bedrooms.

As a general rule, as children grow older they appear to acquire more items of media and communications equipment. Even among the youngest children (aged under 7 years) a majority had their own TV sets (55 per cent) and many reportedly had games consoles/players (45 per cent), with smaller minorities possessing other items. Between the ages of 8 and 11 years, majorities possessed their own TV sets (71 per cent), computer games consoles (67 per cent) and CD players (61 per cent), and one in two reportedly had their own mobile phone (50 per cent). By 12 to 15 years, clear majorities had all of the previously mentioned items of equipment (mobile phone – 87 per cent; TV – 82 per cent; DVD player – 80 per cent; games console/player – 69 per cent; CD players – 68 per cent) plus mp3s (69 per cent) and radio sets (55 per cent) in their bedrooms (Ofcom, 2007b).

Turning next to the media activities of young people, the Ofcom (2007c) *Young People's Media Usage Survey* probed the extent to which children and teenagers used different items of media and communications equipment on a regular basis. Watching television emerged as the most prevalent regular activity across all age groups (93 per cent). Playing computer games (50 per cent), using a mobile phone (43 per cent) and watching DVDs or videos (40 per cent) emerged as other prominent activities even from an early age, but in each case, all these audio-visual media activities tended to reach a fairly early plateau. By teenage years, while TV was widely used (92 per cent), the mobile phone (73 per cent) and Internet (64 per cent) emerged as highly prominent activities, initially taking off during the pre-teen years (8–11: Internet – 41 per cent; mobile phone – 32 per cent). Print media retained a fairly important position within young people's media consumption, with reading of comics, magazines or newspapers showing a gradual rise from 5 to 15 (5–7: 26 per cent; 8–11: 36 per cent; 12–15: 38 per cent), though not attaining the prominence of electronic media. Audio-only media, such as radio (24 per cent) and recorded music (mp3 use – 39 per cent), also formed part of a rich media portfolio of teens (12–15s).

Internet use by age

Early adopters of technological innovations have traditionally been dominated by younger members of the population. Younger generations have tended to be more open to new technological experiences. In the context of the current analysis, core interest centres on the young as learners. Before considering the impact of ICTs on the learning experience for young learners, however, it is relevant as background to consider the broader patterns of adoption and utilisation of digital and online communications that have characterised young people and to compare adoption patterns across age groups.

In the adoption of many new communications technologies, the United States has been a trendsetter. Internet use among Americans has been closely tracked by the Pew Institute. The Pew Internet and American Life Project has conducted a multitude of surveys since the late 1990s, usually by telephone, with large representative US samples of both Internet users and non-users. This project has tracked Internet penetration in general as well as among different age and other demographic groups. It has explored the different ways in which the Internet is used. It has also examined the way the Internet has spread across different technology platforms – wired and wireless – and how technological developments are linked to the evolving range of uses to which the Internet is put.

One thing that has become clear is that the Internet has emerged as a major source of information for the American public. In this regard, its users seek out information on a wide range of topics and for an equally wide range of reasons. The Internet has become a news source of growing significance, challenging longer established media in terms of the extent to which it is used. It also provides access to online knowledge repositories that can be and are used in contexts such as education and health, travel, finance and consumerism. It also provides access to much government-generated information that citizens can benefit from.

In the context of the Google Generation project, the value of the Pew research lies in the extent to which it has made comparisons between generations, operationally defined by age groups (18–29s, 30–49s, 50–64s, 65+s), in respect of Internet penetration and use. Its extensive surveys have produced consistent evidence that age is one of the critical differentiating characteristics among Internet-using populations. Young people have adopted the Internet as an innovation more quickly and more extensively than have older people. This observation was most clearly visible during the early days of this new communications medium, between 1995 and 2000, when Internet penetration among the 18–29s in the USA grew from 21 to 61 per cent. Over the same period, there was dramatic growth in Internet penetration among the 30–49s as well (from 18 to 57 per cent).

Since 2000, however, the adoption of the Internet by younger generations – aged under 40 – has levelled off while penetration among older generations (often called the Baby Boomers, aged 40–65) has continued to grow and they are catching up with the younger age groups. By 2001, Internet penetration had reach 73 per cent among the 18–29s, and then grew to 81 per cent by 2005. While Internet penetration in 1995 was low among the 50–64s (9 per cent) and 65+s (2 per cent), by 2005, Internet adoption had grown to 63 per cent among the 50–64s. Across the same ten-year period, it remained at a fairly low level among the 65+s, however, reaching one in four (26 per cent) by 2005.

In 1995, just 14 per cent of Americans were online. This had grown to 38 per cent by 1998, 47 per cent by 2000, 53 per cent by 2001, 58 per cent by 2002, 61 per cent by 2003, 63 per cent by 2004 and 66 per cent by 2005. One significant technology change that had an impact on the way the Internet could be used was the development of broadband. In 2000, just 6 per cent of Americans had broadband connections, but over the next few years a spurt of growth in broadband occurred. By the end of 2001, 18 per cent had broadband and this increased to 28 per cent in 2002 and 39 per cent in 2003.

Another major tracking study in the United States is the Digital Futures project run by the Center for the Digital Future at the Annenberg School, University of Southern California (Cole et al., 2004). This research confirmed that Internet use became increasingly prevalent between 2000 and 2003 in the United States, and was almost universal among teenagers and young adults and widespread among older age groups up to 65. The over 65s also exhibited growth in Internet use across this time period but lagged far behind young age groups in their uptake of this information source. By 2000, overwhelming percentages of 12–15 year olds (83 per cent) and 16–18 year olds (91 per cent) registered at least some use of the Internet, with both figures growing still further by 2003 (98 per cent and 97 per cent respectively). Among people aged 56–65 years, however, just over one in two (55 per cent) had used the Internet in 2000, growing to two out of three (67 per cent) by 2003. It was the over 65s, however, who lagged farthest behind with fewer than three in ten (29 per cent) having reportedly used the Internet in 2000, and still fewer than four in ten (38 per cent) having done so by 2003 (Cole et al., 2004).

The adoption of information and communication technologies, and in particular the ownership and use of personal computers and the Internet, in Europe have been found to display patterns that have some similarity to those observed in North America. Age has emerged as a factor that differentiates adoption of ICTs, though the relationship is not always straightforward, nor is it exactly the same between countries (Brynin et al., 2004). Some age distributions can be poor differentiators of ICT adoption. One reason for this is that adoption of new technologies such as PCs and the Internet may be relatively more prevalent among younger age groups, but is not totally the preserve of those age groups. Older age groups can display significant adoption profiles as well, and it is only among the really old (70+) that ICT adoption dramatically tails off. Even among the over 70s, there are active users of new technologies. Where adoption and usage is much lower than average, however, among those individuals at the 'very old' end of the age spectrum, other factors such as economic constraints and diminishing social networks may play a significant part in affecting adoption levels (Brynin et al., 2004).

Research across six countries (the UK, Italy, Germany, Norway, Bulgaria and Israel) for the *e-Living: Life in a Digital Europe* project reported that adoption of ICTs such as personal computers and the Internet was age-related, but that once adoption had occurred age was a much weaker predictor of levels of use (Brynin et al., 2004). Further research from this programme found that younger men were the dominant users of ICTs such as PCs, the Internet and e-mail, though younger women tended to be the main users of mobile phones. The use of text messaging was also dominated by young people, but it was still unclear as to whether the patterns of ICT utilisation observed could be regarded as a life-phase or a cohort phenomenon (Ling, 2004). In other words, was there evidence here of a long-term generational effect or of a phased adoption effect with gradual penetration occurring across age groups but more quickly among some than others?

Across age groups, adoption of ICTs was related to economic and resource factors and also level of interest. Adoption was less likely to be present where interest levels were lower, even among young age groups. Further, economic constraints could act to limit uptake of ICTs regardless of age group. Nonetheless, these other limitations, though independent of age, were more prevalent among the very oldest age groups (Brynin et al., 2004).

The penetration and use of telecommunications-linked and computer technologies in the UK have been tracked by the communications regulator, the Office of Communications (see Ofcom, 2006, 2007a–e), by the Oxford Internet Institute (see Dutton and Helsper, 2007) and by the Office for National Statistics in Britain (see Avery et al., 2007).

Ofcom (2006) reported a growth in personal computer ownership from 48 per cent in the UK population in 2000 to 68 per cent in 2006. Internet take-up also increased over this period from 30 to 61 per cent. By 2006, nearly four in ten (39 per cent) of the UK population had acquired broadband Internet. Personal computer penetration (76 to 78 per cent) varied little across different age groups (15–24s, 25–44s, 45–64s) and a similar finding emerged in respect of Internet take-up (67–71 per cent range across these age groups). Both PC take-up (32 per cent) and Internet take-up (28 per cent) were significantly lower among people aged over 65 years. Over seven in ten Internet users aged 15–64 years (average 77 per cent) had broadband access, but the highest percentage penetration was registered among the 15 to 24s (81 per cent of Internet users in that age group).

The Oxford Internet Institute surveyed Internet access and use in the United Kingdom in three surveys conducted in 2003, 2005 and 2007 (see Dutton and Helsper, 2007). Internet access was recorded to have continued an upward track between 2003 (58 per cent of UK households) to 2007 (66 per cent). There was a parallel increase in the percentages of people saying they used the Internet over this time (59 to 67 per cent).

During the first quarter (January–April) of 2006, the ONS reported that more than a half of households in Great Britain (56 per cent) contained personal or desktop computers (Avery et al., 2007). Three in ten households contained portable or laptop computers, and 7 per cent contained palmtop or handheld computers. Around three-quarters of adults in Britain (76 per cent) said they had ever used a computer and two-thirds (67 per cent) had reportedly used one during the previous three months. Recent claimed computer usage was more widespread among young adults aged 16–30 (87 per cent) than it was among those aged 50+ (45 per cent). By 2006, over half of British adults (52 per cent) had used the Internet within the previous three months and lived in a household with Internet access, up from 37 per cent in 2001/2. Just over three in ten British adults surveyed (31 per cent) were not Internet users and lived in a household without Internet access – down from 43 per cent in 2001/2.

The ONS research also tracked the penetration of mobile phones. The first digital mobile phones were introduced to the UK in 1991. By 1996–7 17 per cent of households owned a mobile phone, with this figure increasing significantly to 65 per cent by 2001–2 and to 79 per cent in 2005–6. Another survey by communications regulator, Ofcom, in its Media Literacy Audit, found that different age groups had different primary reasons for owning a mobile phone. People aged 55+ owned one for emergencies. Individuals aged under 35 owned one for keeping in touch with friends and those aged under 25 owned one for texting. There were significant differences between the youngest and oldest in the population in the kinds of uses to which mobile phones were put. An overwhelming majority of 16–24s (94 per cent) sent personal or business messages compared with a minority (17 per cent) of those aged 65+. More 16–24s (93 per cent) were likely to make business or personal calls on their mobile telephones than were 65+s (58 per cent). More 16–24s (58 per cent) than 65+s (2 per cent) were likely to take photos with their mobile phones.

By the first quarter of 2006 nearly two-thirds (64 per cent) of British adults had ever used the Internet. This figure showed a significant increase on the position five years earlier when under half of adults (48 per cent) said they had used the Internet. Research from 2004–5, reported that most British adults (94 per cent) who were current users of the Internet went online using a desktop computer, while much smaller proportions used a portable computer (29 per cent), a mobile phone (14 per cent), a palmtop or handheld computer (3 per cent) or digital TV (2 per cent). At that time, 84 per cent of current Internet users went online only using a computer, while 15 per cent used more than one device to go online.

Despite the dominance of a PC interface with the Internet, there was a growth in use of mobile phones to go online, from just 3 per cent in 2002 to 14 per cent in early 2006. There has been slower growth in the use of digital television to go online. In 2002–3, 3 per cent of households had digital TV equipment through which they could go online; by 2006, this number had grown to 5 per cent (Avery et al., 2007).

Age differences were clearly apparent in prevalence of Internet use in Britain, just as has been observed in other countries such as the United States (Avery et al., 2007). ONS statistics for the British government showed a growth in Internet penetration among 16–24 year olds between 2001 and 2006 (from 75 to 84 per cent), with similar growth albeit at a lower level for 45–54 year olds (51 to 64 per cent), but more modest growth at a much lower level for the over 65s (10 to 15 per cent). Other research confirmed the widespread use of the Internet among the under 20s in Britain by the middle of the first decade of the new millennium, confirming government statistics (Livingstone and Bober, 2005).

Turning to the use of the Internet by the under 16s, Ofcom (2007d) reported that time spent with the Internet gradually increases across childhood. Ofcom found that children aged 8–11 years increased their time online from 1.8 hours to 5.0 hours per week, while 12–15 year olds exhibited an increase from 4.6 hours to 10.5 hours per week. Thus there is a progressive increase in online behaviour as children grow older, and for all age groups, Internet usage has increased in volume over time.

The broadband effect

One of the key developments in relation to the Internet in the post-2000 era has been the growth of broadband technology. This has occurred worldwide. The adoption of broadband is also associated with different patterns of Internet use. The always-on mode and greater data-handling capacity of broadband makes the Internet run faster and facilitates more sophisticated online applications. In the earliest days of the Internet in the UK, in 1996–7, access was available only via a dial-up connection. Digital television had not yet become established and second-generation mobile phones with greater interactive capability and more diverse functionality were just starting to be rolled out. Text messaging was in its infancy as were audio and video streaming. Significant developments then occurred over the next ten years and the development of broadband online connections has played a central part in driving forward the communications revolution that has taken place during that period.

In 2003–4, 50 per cent of UK households had an Internet connection of any kind. By 2006, this had grown to 57 per cent. In 2003–4, 38 per cent of households with Internet access had dial-up narrowband connections. This percentage fell to 17 per cent by the first quarter of 2006. Over the same period, broadband connections grew from 11 per cent of those with Internet access in 2002–3 to 40 per cent in 2006. In 2006, 62 per cent of broadband users used the Internet everyday or almost every day, compared with 35 per cent of narrowband users (Avery et al., 2007).

Research in the UK by the Oxford Internet Institute reported a rapidly increasing range of types of Internet access emerging between 2003 and 2007. Access to the Internet was still most popularly achieved in the UK in 2007 via a telephone line (80 per cent of Internet users), but this number represented a drop on 2003 (92 per cent). In 2007, however, growing numbers of Internet users reported obtaining Internet access via WiFi (29 per cent), a mobile phone (21 per cent), cable television (19 per cent) and digital television (15 per cent) (Dutton and Helsper, 2007).

Research with Internet users in the UK in 2003 found that one in three users (33 per cent) at that time said they had a broadband connection. Interestingly, broadband users had an older profile than narrowband or dial-up modem users. A larger proportion of broadband users (44 per cent) than narrowband users (27 per cent) were aged over 45 (Gunter et al., 2004). While both broadband and narrowband Internet users almost universally utilised the Internet for e-mail and looking up information about news events, hobbies, products, weather and travel (over 92 per cent throughout), there were other online activities in which broadband users were much more likely than dial-up users to engage: sending instant messages (65.5 per cent versus 46.3 per cent); obtaining music recordings (49.7 per cent versus 30.8 per cent); and sharing files from own computer with others (38.5 per cent versus 11.2 per cent).

Research by the Pew Institute in the mid-2000s further indicated how broadband had affected the way the Internet is used. It also showed, once again, the generational differences in the way this online innovation was used (Fox, 2005). Fox reported a survey of 2001 adults aged 18+ conducted in May and June 2005 by telephone interviews. Age differences were reported in the penetration of the Internet. In all, 84 per cent of 18–29s went online compared with 67 per cent of 30–49s and 26 per cent of Americans aged 65+. Twenty two per cent of people aged 70 and over went online. There were also marked age differences in use of a computer: 87 per cent of 18–28s used a computer on a regular basis compared with 24 per cent of those aged over 70 years. Fox reported that 79 per cent of Internet users had four or more years of online experience, with just 6 per cent of Internet users claiming to have less than one year's experience online.

Different access speeds were observed to create a divide among Internet users. Connection speed emerged as a more important factor in Internet use than personal experience online. Broadband connections in the US increased from 21 per cent of Internet users in 2002 to 53 per cent by 2005. Broadband access also varied with age. Younger age groups were more likely to have a broadband connection: 18–29s 50 per cent; 30–49s 40 per cent; 50–64 36 per cent; 65+ 9 per cent.

A number of differences were observed between dial-up and broadband Internet users in terms of the way they used the Internet (Fox, 2005). Broadband users were much more likely than dial-up users to use online sources for news (82 versus 68 per cent), to conduct online transactions such as purchases (81 versus 59 per cent) and banking (59 versus 35 per cent), to download content for entertainment such as computer games (47 versus 35 per cent) and music (33 versus 17 per cent), and to get creative with their own blogs (11 versus 4 per cent).

Further Pew research continued to examine the penetration of broadband in the USA (Madden, 2005). By the middle of the first decade in the twenty-first century, the Internet was being used at all by a majority of most age groups. At 80 per cent of under 40s, at least 68 per cent of 40s to 60s and over half of 60–69s had home Internet access in the United states. Only among the over 70s had the online world failed to penetrate very far. Here no more than one in four had Internet access. The emergence of broadband has meant increased capacity for transmitting content and for engaging in complex transactions online. Broadband, as an innovation, has spread quickly, but it has been taken up most rapidly by the younger generations. The most significant early in-roads of broadband in the USA occurred among teenagers and adults in their 20s (40 per cent and over), followed by those in their 30s (36 per cent and over), 40s (36 per cent and over) and 50s (27 per cent and over). Nearly one in four of those in their early 60s (23 per cent) had home broadband access, but far fewer of those in their late 60s (13 per cent) or 70s (8 per cent) did (Madden, 2005).

Subsequent research conducted by the Pew Institute for its Internet and American Life Project confirmed these age differences in broadband connectedness, but also showed that the greatest growth in new adoption occurred among the oldest Internet users (aged 65+). While 18–29s, 30–49s and 50–64s showed year-on-year growth in broadband penetration that averaged 42 per cent between 2005 and 2006, among the 65 and overs, year-on-year growth reached 63 per cent (Horrigan, 2006b).

Within the UK, broadband access was more commonly reported among younger than older Internet users. Data produced by the Oxford Internet Institute showed a steady growth in broadband adoption across most age groups and most of the older age groups have been gaining on younger ones in this respect (Dutton and Helsper, 2007). By 2005, nine out of ten (90 per cent) of under 18s had broadband access in the UK, a figure that remained at this level by 2007. Nearly as many of those aged 18–24 years (86 per cent) and a significant majority of those aged 25–54 years (78 per cent) also reported home broadband access in 2007. In each case, this figure had risen by between 8 and 13 per cent since 2005. Among the 55–64s, over half (58 per cent) had home broadband in 2007, while among the 65–74s (37 per cent) and over 75s (24 per cent) this figure got progressively smaller. Even among these oldest age groups, however, broadband access showed a clear upward trend.

Generations and Internet use

Evidence has emerged, mostly from the United States, that variations in the way the Internet is used are associated with different generations of user. In addition, there are many commonalities in the online behaviour patterns of different age groups. The data from this study revealed some significant age differences in the way the Internet is used. While majorities of all but the oldest age group use the Internet, it is clear that younger users utilise the Internet for a wider array of things than do older users.

Virtually all online users, regardless of their age, use the Internet for e-mail purposes. This is true even among the oldest Internet users. Older users as much as younger users use the Internet to get health information, news and information about products. In most age groups, by this time, a majority of Internet users went online to make actual purchases.

The very youngest and very oldest users were least likely to do this. Although the survey did not explore the reasons for not making purchases, one might surmise that the reasons for not doing so may have differed among the youngest and oldest Internet users. In both cases, financial limitations may have affected their purchase levels, But one also wonders whether there is a confidence issue at play among the oldest Internet users (i.e. those aged 70 and over).

The most pronounced generational differences in Internet use concern the extent to which users engage in online activities such as text messaging, downloading music and video entertainment, and reading or creating blogs. Indeed, the creation of own sites – though occurring at a relatively low level across all age bands – was twice as likely to occur among online teens (12–17s) and Generation Y (18–30s).

Use of the Internet for school research was also most prevalent among the younger age groups, but was not just the preserve of the teens and Generation Y users. The Generation X and Trailing Boomers also made use of online sources for school-related information. Of course, school research might mean different things. It could involve searching for information about schools which is something both students and parents might do. It might also mean searching for information linked to school work, which is more likely to be carried out by students. The Digital Future research project provided confirmation that young people regard the Internet as an important learning resource. Over six in ten young people aged under 18 years (62 per cent) claimed that the Internet was very or extremely important to their schoolwork. In the meantime, parents cautiously agreed that the Internet improved the school grades of their children (16 per cent saying this in 2003), with most (80 per cent) believing that it made no difference (Cole et al., 2004).

What is apparent is that in some respects the older generations of Internet users are catching up with younger users in terms of some interactive and transactional online behaviours, but not in the case of others. Use of online banking, travel reservations services and photo services occur to similar degrees across a range of age groups. Downloading and blogging is predominantly found among the youngest Internet users.

Internet access can be achieved through a number of different technologies. Research by the Pew Institute found that 28 per cent of Americans and 41 per cent of all Internet users said they had, within the past month, used a laptop that could connect wirelessly to the Internet or a cell phone that let them send or receive e-mail. Nearly one in five Internet users (18 per cent) had used a wireless-enabled laptop and nearly three in ten cell phone users (29 per cent) had used a cell phone that could handle e-mail (Horrigan, 2001).

Age differences emerged in the way Internet users got online. Young adults were more likely than older Americans to have wireless-ready computers and Internet-connected cell phones. The research found that 22 per cent of Internet users in Generation Y (18–29s) had used laptops with wireless connections in the previous month compared to 17 per cent of Baby Boomers (40–58s). There were bigger differences with cell phones. Here, 45 per cent of Generation Y had cell phones linked to the Internet, compared with 25 per cent of Baby Boomers.

By 2005, there were clear age-related profile differences in the way that the Internet was used. Evidence from the United States from the Pew Institute provided a clear indication of these age differences (Madden, 2005). Virtually all Internet users (91 per cent) used e-mail. Age differences here among Internet users were small (range 88–94 per cent across 12+s). Internet use for information purposes had also become widespread even among the oldest age groups. Even among Internet users aged 69+, most went online to get health-related information (72 per cent), news information (68 per cent), product information (60 per cent) and even to make travel reservations (60 per cent). Web 2.0 applications, however, were much more widely used among the youngest Internet users than by the oldest. Thus the 12–17s (38 per cent and 18–28s (45 per cent) were much more likely in 2005 to read blogs than were the 60–68s (19 per cent) or 69+s (16 per cent). The 12–28s (20 per cent) were also much more likely to create their own blogs than were the 60+s (4 per cent).

Another Pew Institute survey examined the way young people used the Internet. At the time of this survey in October–November 2004, 87 per cent of 12–17s in the US said they used the Internet at this time. Of those, 78 per cent said they used the Internet for school. In 2000, 73 per cent of 12–17s used the Internet; 47 per cent of these used it for school (Hitlin and Rainie, 2005).

Among American teens who went online from school, the percentages who said they also go online from additional locations were: home – 87 per cent; someone else's house – 75 per cent; a library – 61 per cent; and a community centre – 11 per cent. In all, 86 per cent of teens and 88 per cent of online teens believed that the Internet helps teenagers to do better in school. In addition, 80 per cent of parents and 83 per cent of parents of online teens agreed with this view. Further findings showed that 75 per cent of online teens used instant messaging. Of those, 78 per cent said they used IM to talk about homework, tests or schoolwork.

Online girls were more likely to do this than online boys. In addition, 57 per cent of online teens had gone online to get information about a college, university or other school they were thinking about attending. Girls were more likely to search for schools on the Internet than were boys (61 versus 53 per cent). Again age differences emerged: 27 per cent of 12 year olds had done this as had 59 per cent of 17 year olds.

A further report on this research explored the kinds of online activities in which teenagers engaged (Lenhart et al., 2005). In 2005, 51 per cent of 12–17s went online every day (up from 42 per cent in 2000). At this time, 81 per cent of teen Internet users played games online, 76 per cent got news online, 43 per cent made purchases online and 31 per cent got health information online. There were still some teenagers at this time that did not use the Internet (13 per cent). The survey reported that among US teens:

- 84 per cent reported owning at least one personal media device such as a desktop or laptop computer, a cell phone or a PDA;
- 44 per cent had two or more of these devices;
- 12 per cent had three or more such devices;
- 45 per cent of teens owned a cell phone;
- 33 per cent had used a cell phone to send a text message;
- 75 per cent of online teens used instant messaging compared to 42 per cent of online adults;
- 50 per cent of instant messaging-using teens had included a link to an interesting or funny article or website in an instant message;
- 45 per cent had used IM to send photos or documents; 31 per cent had sent music or video files over IM.

The Internet has emerged as an important site for socialising. Pew research found that 55 per cent of online American 12–17s use online social networking sites. Users can create profiles and build a personal network to link to others (Lenhart, 2007). A telephone survey of 935 12–17s carried out in October–November 2006 found that 55 per cent had used social networking sites such as MySpace or Facebook; 55 per cent had created personal profiles; 48 per cent visited social networking sites daily; 70 per cent of 15–17 year old girls and 54 per cent of 15–17 year old boys said they had used social networking sites.

In all, 91 per cent of all social networking teens said they used the sites to stay in touch with friends they saw frequently. In addition, 81 per cent used sites to stay in touch with friends they rarely saw in person. Boys aged 15–17 (60 per cent) were more likely than same age girls (46 per cent) to say they used social networking sites to make new friends.

Further insights into generational differences across the full spectrum of age bands emerged from a survey by Pew of the use of instant messaging (Shiu and Lenhart, 2004). The research found that 46 per cent of Generation Y (18–27 years) reported using IM more frequently than e-mail. In comparison, 18 per cent of Generation X (28–39 years) said they used IM more than e-mail. Among respondents who claimed to use instant messaging several times a day, young users did this more often than older ones: 21 per cent Generation Y (18–27); 21 per cent Generation X (28–39); 17 per cent Trailing Boomers (40–49); 15 per cent Leading Boomers (50–59); 10 per cent Matures (60–68); and 9 per cent After work (69+).

Further research from the Pew Institute focused on older Internet users or 'seniors' as they were called by Pew's researchers. Although most people aged over 65 in the United States are not yet online, growing numbers of them are gradually becoming Internet users. Pew reported that at the beginning of 2006, around one third of Americans aged 65 and older (34 per cent) used the Internet. This figure represented a year-on-year increase of five percentage points from 29 per cent. Among those aged 70 and over, however, fewer than three in ten (28 per cent) went online. This figure had shown a much slower year-on-year increase (from 26 per cent in 2005).

Among younger age groups, Internet use was much more widespread: 18–28s – 89 per cent; 29–40s – 86 per cent; 41–50s – 78 per cent; 51–59s – 72 per cent. Even among 60–69s, over half (54 per cent) went online. What we have then is a pattern of widespread Internet adoption by a number of age groups and generations. Not only the X and Y Generations but also the middle aged and 'young' elderly had taken to going online. Only the mature retired market was lagging in terms of its adoption of online technology (Fox, 2006).

There are differences between young and middle-aged Internet users, however, in the way they use the Internet. Hence, it is not enough to know that all these age groups have widely adopted this innovation. We also need to know whether there are critical differences in the nature of their adoption of this communications medium.

Fox (2006) reported that Generation Y users (18–28s) were more likely than those aged 51–59 to report having spyware on their computers (45 versus 27 per cent). Younger Internet users aged 18–28 were also more likely than those aged in their 50s to change their online behaviour to avoid getting unwanted software programs on their computers. Generation Y users were more likely than those in their 50s to switch the browser they used (29 versus 14 per cent), to stop peer-to-peer activities (35 versus 17 per cent), to stop downloading software (44 versus 29 per cent) and to stop visiting certain sites (54 versus 43 per cent).

Pew conduced research with US college students to investigate the websites that attracted the most traffic from them. The findings indicated that music downloading and file-sharing services were the most popularly visited sites (Rainie et al., 2002). Among the top 20 websites used by college students, many catered to interests in music, movies and fashion. Other popular sites focused on posters and artwork, video games and consumer electronics.

The items US college students most often bought online were: event tickets (10.5 per cent of dollar sales attributed to spending by college students), sports and fitness (9.6 per cent), movies and video (7.1 per cent), books (6.4 per cent), music (6.1 per cent), apparel and accessories (5.7 per cent), consumer electronics (5.1 per cent), computer hardware (5.1 per cent), flowers and gifts (4.4 per cent) and health and beauty products (4.0 per cent).

Within the UK, Internet use was found to vary across age groups (Ofcom, 2007a). Younger users aged 15–24 engaged more often than 45–54s or 65+s in content downloading (55 versus 34/16 per cent), online game playing (40 versus 24/19 per cent), social networking online (31 versus 24/10 per cent) and watching webcasts or video clips online (27 versus 15/8 per cent). Age-related differences were less pronounced for other applications such as watching TV programmes or listening to radio online. In fact, Internet users in the UK aged 45–54 (22 per cent) were more likely than those aged 15–24 (18 per cent) to listen to radio online.

Additional findings published by Ofcom (2007a) indicated that young people in the UK have access to a wide range of communications technologies with the most significant growth between 2005 and 2007 occurring in the use of laptops with Internet links (up 24 to 70 per cent) and mp3 players (up 35 to 61 per cent) by 8–15 year olds. There were movements in varying directions in terms of 'regular' use of different media. Nearly all 8–15 year olds (93 per cent) watched television in 2007 (down 3 per cent from 2005), but only a minority (22 per cent) listened to radio (down by 18 per cent on 2005). Regular listening to mp3 players (28 per cent, up from 20 per cent in 2005) may have partially displaced radio listening. Regular mobile phone usage increased marginally (53 per cent, up by 3 per cent from 2005). Another interesting finding was that reading of magazines, comics and newspapers rose very slightly in 2007 (37 per cent up 2 per cent from 2005).

Further research by Ofcom (2007c, 2007d) focused on the media habits of children aged 5–15 years old. The youngest children, aged 5–7 years, reportedly used the Internet far more for playing games online than for anything else. There was some evidence of going online for information as well, including the use of online sources in support of school or homework. At primary school age (8–11 years), children still used the Internet extensively for playing games, but also exhibited increased use for schoolwork and homework and for looking up other information. Young teens, aged 12–15 years, used the Internet in more diverse ways, but most often for school/homework and for communications via instant messaging.

Among children with Internet access, TV remained the medium they said they would be most likely to miss the most if it was taken away for children between the ages of 5 and 7 (63 per cent) and 8 and 11 years (47 per cent). For those aged 12 to 15 years with Internet access, the Internet was the medium they most often said they would miss the most (30 per cent), with mobile phones in second place (26 per cent) and TV in third place (24 per cent).

Further findings indicated the significance of the Internet as an entertainment medium initially among young children (Ofcom, 2007c, 2007d). While this reason remained firmly positioned as a prevalent motive for going online across age groups, as children grow older they also turned to the Internet increasingly for informational and educational applications. The use of the Internet in relation to schoolwork and homework becomes most prominent during teenage years. While just one in four children aged 5–7 years (24 per cent) reported using the Internet for school homework at least weekly, this use became much more widespread among those aged 8–11 years (60 per cent) and 12–15 years (80 per cent). During this period also, the social contact function dramatically emerges as well, as evidenced by the rapid growth in percentages of young Internet users who report engaging in instant messaging (31 per cent at 8–11 years and 70 per cent at 12–15 years doing this at least once a week) and visiting social network websites during their early teens (27 per cent do this at 8–11 years and 70 per cent at 12–15 years doing this at least once a week).

One interesting pattern of behaviour that has emerged among children in the UK is the use of the Internet to engage with audio-visual material online. Ofcom (2007d) reported that among those aged 12–15 years who used the Internet at home, more than half (53 per cent) watched or downloaded music videos, more than four in ten (44 per cent) watched or downloaded videos made by ordinary people and placed on sites such as YouTube, more than three in ten (33 per cent) watched or downloaded clips from films or TV programmes), and over one in four (26 per cent) watched or downloaded whole films or TV programmes. More than six in ten of these children (63 per cent) did any of these things. It is apparent from these findings, that the Internet has become established as a significant source of entertainment for children.

Consumption of modern media – including the Internet – varies among children with socio-economic class. Children aged 12–15 years who lived in professional and middle-class households (ABC1) used the Internet more than did same-age counterparts from working-class households (C2DE). The former averaged 7.3 hours of Internet use per week and the latter averaged 5.4 hours. ABC1s (50 per cent) were also more likely than C2DEs (37 per cent) to say they used the Internet almost every day. This finding should not be taken, however, as evidence of greater familiarity with computers among ABC1 children. C2DEs (53 per cent) were more likely than ABC1s (47 per cent) to say they played computer or video games almost every day (Ofcom, 2007d).

Online information searching

From 2000, the Internet rapidly emerged as a primary information source. In the United States, more than one out of two Internet users (56 per cent) stated that they read news online (UCLA Center for Communication Policy, 2003). In Europe, the Internet also emerged as a news source during this period, though at a slower pace than in North America. Just one in ten Europeans (10 per cent) said they used the Web for news in 2000 and this figure reached one in seven (14 per cent) two years later (European Commission, 2000, 2002). There were nation-by-nation differences. Sweden emerged as the leading online news consuming country at this time, with one third of the population saying they read online newspapers in 2003 (Reitsma, 2003). By 2002, the Internet remained behind television, newspapers and magazines, radio and informed discussions with other people as an information source, but it had moved ahead of books, brochures and information leaflets (European Commission, 2003).

It was not simply the use of online news that signalled its significance, but also how much online users said they relied upon it. By 2002, one in five Americans (20 per cent) rated the Internet as the 'most essential' medium in their lives, ahead of newspapers (11 per cent) but behind television (39 per cent) and radio (26 per cent). Most significant here, perhaps, was the further finding that among those aged 12–24 years, the Internet (33 per cent) was more widely endorsed in this respect than either television (30 per cent) or radio (27 per cent) (Rose and Rosin, 2002).

The rise of broadband penetration further promoted the significance of the Internet as a news source. Broadband adopters were found to utilise the Internet for a wider range of applications, and this included news searching (Findahl, 2001). Broadband adopters were found to be more avid readers of online newspapers (Coats, 2001) and they were more likely to use the Internet as a source of breaking news (MSNBC, 2001).

Pew research has revealed that the Internet has emerged as a major source of information about science. Horrigan (2006) reported that one in five Americans (20 per cent) turned to the Internet for most of their science news. Newspapers and magazines were cited as the main source for science news by one in seven each (14 per cent). TV remained the number one source overall (41 per cent).

Broadband users cited the Internet (34 per cent) as often as TV (33 per cent) as their main source of science news. Among adult home broadband users aged under 30, the Internet was the most popular science news source (44 per cent), even more widely supported than TV (32 per cent).

Overall, 70 per cent of Internet users used the Internet to look up the meaning of a scientific concept; 68 per cent used it to answer a question about a scientific concept or theory; 65 per cent used it to learn more about a science story or discovery first heard of in the offline world; 55 per cent used the Internet to complete a science assignment for school; and 52 per cent used the Internet to check the accuracy of a scientific fact or statistic.

Over six in ten (62 per cent) of those who got science information online used other online information to check the reliability of scientific facts. Over half (54 per cent) of online science consumers used offline resources like a journal or encyclopaedia to assess the reliability of science information. Over half (54 per cent) of online science consumers went to the original source of the information or the original study it was based upon. More than seven in ten (71 per cent) of those who got science information online turned to the Internet because it was a convenient information source. A few (13 per cent) said they turned to the Internet because they believed information there was more accurate than other sources. Others (12 per cent) said they turned to the Internet because information is available online that is not available elsewhere.

There were age differences in the searching for science information online. Over seven in ten (71 per cent) of those aged under 30 said they had come upon science information when they went online for another reason compared to an overall percentage of 65 per cent. The percentages saying they had done this progressively declined with increased age: 30–49 – 70 per cent; 50–64 – 60 per cent; and 65+ – 43 per cent. Horrigan (2006a) provided an age profile for those who relied most on the Internet for their science news and information. The 30–49s (43 per cent) and 18–29s (36 per cent) were most likely to identify the Internet as their main science news source, while the 50–64s (17 per cent) and 65+s (4 per cent) were much less likely to say this.

The presence of broadband made a difference to the extent to which the Internet was used to obtain science news and information (Horrigan, 2006a). Among this category of committed Internet users, the Internet emerged as a major information source for all age groups. For those aged 18–29 years, the Internet finished ahead of television (44 versus 32 per cent), while among those aged 30–49 years it was on level pegging with television (33 versus 32 per cent). Even among those aged 50 and over, the gap between television and the Internet was significantly narrowed (29 versus 25 per cent) compared with data for all Americans. What these data indicate is that while there is a younger generation that has adopted new ICTs enthusiastically as information sources, there are committed ICT enthusiasts even among older generations.

Further research produced by the Pew Internet and American Life Project has sought to identify distinct groups of users of information and communication technology and has produced a typology based on the kinds of ICT equipment people possessed, the activities in which they engaged using these technologies and their attitudes towards different ICTs and their applications (Horrigan, 2007). A telephone survey was conducted with over 4,000 American adults aged 18 and over between February and April 2006. Ten groups were identified that slotted into 'high end', 'medium users' and 'low-level adopters'. In others words, the Pew research distinguished between 'elite users' of ICTs, 'middle-of-the-road users' and individuals with 'few technology assets'.

Omnivores, Connectors, Lacklustre Veterans and Productivity Enhancers which comprised 'Elite Technology Users' covered 31 per cent of American adults. Mobile Centrics and Connected But Hassled were 'Middle-of-the-Road Technology Users' comprising 20 per cent of the adult population. Finally, Light But Satisfied, Indifferents and Off the Network comprised those with 'Few Technology Assets' (49 per cent of the population).

The elite technology users were characterised by being information technology-rich and were regular users of these technologies, though their enthusiasm for ICTs varied from high (Omnivores, Connectors) to moderate (Lacklustre Veterans). The middle-of-the-road users were regular users of new technologies – including the Internet and cell phones – but usage was functional (especially for the Productivity Enhancers) and not always welcomed with enthusiasm (e.g. Connected But Hassled). The low-end users with few technology assets were not necessarily disconnected but new communications technologies were not central to their lives.

Horrigan (2007) reported that these types illustrate the variations among ICT users. Distinctions can be made not just in terms of who has access and who does not, but also in relation to patterns of utility of ICTs and attitudes towards ICT applications. A focus on who is connected to the Internet, for example, may disguise a diverse array of variations in the way it is used and in the experiences that users have. This research also found that the ICT user types displayed different age profiles.

These profiles confirm earlier ones in showing that the unconnected (Off the Network) had an older profile than all the other types. One in two of these individuals were aged 65 or over, while few (8 per cent) were aged under 30. The elite technology-using categories – Omnivores, Connectors, Lacklustre Veterans and Productivity Enhancers – all had younger profiles. The most voracious users of ICTs (Omnivores) were the 18–29s (53 per cent), while this group was virtually not-existent among the 65+s (1 per cent). Among other groups that used ICTs regularly and for specific tried and tested functional purposes were many users from older age groups. Productivity Enhancers – perhaps the most clear-cut functional-user group – was comprised most prominently of 30–49s (51 per cent), with far fewer 18–29s (23 per cent), 50–64s (23 per cent) and over 65s (14 per cent) being found in this new technology cluster. Cell phone use (MobileCentrics) was dominated by 30–49s (45 per cent) and 18–29s (40 per cent), but there were few over 65s (1 per cent) in this group. However, the early signs that the oldest age group was starting to jump on board the new technology bandwagon derived from the profile of the Light But Satisfied users, which had a somewhat older profile than other user groups (18–29s: 7 per cent; 30–49s: 36 per cent; 50–64s: 33 per cent; 65+s: 25 per cent). Thus, once again, this research provided evidence that advanced ICT use, though often dominated by younger people, is beginning to occur among people in their 40, 50s and even early 60s.

Nor was it invariably the case that young people were elite technology users. Among the middle-of-the-road user types, especially those defined by cell phone-dominated behaviour, the under 30s were prominently represented. The less experienced ICT user groups were dominated by people from the over 30 age bands. What is interesting here is that the key age thresholds occur at around 30 and early 60s. Advanced ICT utility that embraces all new ICTs and a complex array of usage patterns is predominantly (though not exclusively) the preserve of the under 30s. At the other end of the spectrum, disconnectedness is most significantly present among those beyond their mid-60s. In between, we have a number of generations that are connected and engaged in varying degrees. What is perhaps most significant among these 'generations' is not simply whether they are connected to modern ICTs at all, but the ways in which they use them. Here there seems to be a critical age threshold at around 50 years. While many over 50s are connected to online and mobile technologies, they tend to adopt a simpler usage profile than the under 50s.

Within the UK, further evidence has emerged that the Internet has become an important information source and that it has a distinctive role to play, for some users, in the context of learning activities. In 2007, clear majorities of Internet users said they used the Internet for travel information (84 per cent), information about local events (77 per cent), news (69 per cent) and health and medical information (68 per cent), and almost half used it when looking for jobs (48 per cent). Within a learning context, significant majorities of UK Internet users in 2007 said they went online to find or check on a fact (82 per cent) and investigate a topic of personal interest (78 per cent). More than one in two said they went online to look up the definition of a word (56 per cent) or to find out about opportunities for further study of specified topics (52 per cent). More than one in five (22 per cent) said they used the Internet in relation to distance learning for an academic degree course or job training (Dutton and Helsper, 2007).

Concluding remarks

This chapter has examined evidence for the emergence of the Internet in the modern world. Within the space of ten years the Internet has grown from a narrow niche activity to a normative phenomenon that has reached into all sectors of the population. The early adopters of the Internet and a range of online applications and activities were dominated by young people. Over time, this position has rapidly changed with majorities of people aged in their 30s, 40s and 50s adopting online technology for a wide variety of purposes and even significant and ever growing percentages of people in their 60s and 70s doing likewise.

In addressing the question of whether a new online generation, variously termed the 'net', 'digital or 'Google' generation, has emerged is less clear-cut. Although young people have been quick to move into the online world and to integrate its new technologies and their communication, information search and transactional applications into their lives, such behaviours do not make them a distinctive generation. The emergence of the older, 'grey market' users or 'silver surfers' has meant that if there is a 'Google Generation', it is not defined by youth. Nonetheless, what emergence of online technologies has achieved is a change in the way people of all ages can now engage with each other and carry out many different transactions in their lives. Everyone has access to huge quantities of information through one very convenient access route – the Internet – and, through this device, has been empowered in so many ways.

The key theme of this book is to determine whether a new generation of information seeker has emerged within formal learning contexts and, if so, what implications might this development have for those involved in learning provision and support. So far, the scene has been set through an examination of the emergence of the so-called 'information society' and the Internet. The current chapter has examined the adoption and penetration of the Internet. The next chapter focuses in more detail on the way the Internet is used as an information source (as well as for other applications) and the competencies and skills it demands of its users. If access and adoption alone cannot identify a Google Generation, can it be differentiated through patterns of online application behaviour and online user competence?

4

'Google Generation': what is the evidence?

This chapter will explore the concept of the 'Google Generation' in a wider societal context, although in doing so it will still consider the idea of a distinctive generation of individuals defined by their information-related behaviours in the online world. While analyses presented earlier in this book focused on access to information and communication technologies, 'access' alone is not sufficient to define a new 'generation'. We must look further into the nature of online behaviour, examine the different competencies required to be an efficacious information searcher and establish to what extent these abilities or skills are demonstrated by different sectors of society, and in particular sectors defined by age. Chapters 5 and 6 will take the analysis further, narrowing down the focus to within a learning context and a higher education context.

The idea that there is a specific and distinguishable generation that can be defined by being born during an era when they have never known a world without the Internet has been championed by a number of writers. Tapscott (1998) wrote about the 'digital generation' or the 'net' generation. He differentiated between this 'Internet' generation and the previous 'television' generation. He identified a number of population categories by birth date: the Boomers (born between 1946 and 1964), the Bust (1965–76) and the Boom Echo (1977–97). Those born after 1997 (mostly the children of the Boom Echo) represent the Net generation. The Boomers represent the TV generation.

Tapscott argued that there are important differences between the ways these different communications media engage their users that may create differences between these generations other than the periods during which they happened to be born. Television is a passive medium whereas the Internet is an active medium. TV viewers allow its content to wash over them whereas Internet users seek out content and may even engage in creating content. Television is controlled by elites whereas the Internet is democratic and open to anyone. Television thus contributed towards the establishment of a conservative generation while the Internet has produced an adventurous and more open-minded generation.

According to Tapscott, the young generation has taken to the Internet and online technologies whereas the older generations have not done so as readily and in consequence are being left behind. The 'net' generation is characterised as being computer literate and accustomed to using the Internet for information, sending e-mail and creating websites for themselves. They watch less TV and spend more time with more dynamic interactive media. The Internet is an information and entertainment source and also a communications device used for social networking. Not everyone would agree with Tapscott's (1998) analysis even though it did draw attention to some relevant distinctions that existed at that time. Ten years on, the Internet has evolved and so has the way it is used.

Some writers have reflected on the meaning of the term 'generation' and how it might be defined in relation to the use of information and communications technologies (Buckingham, 2006). So, what is a 'generation'? It has been defined in age-delimited terms together with having some kind of common cultural identity (Edmunds and Turner, 2003). Often it is associated with particular eras in time when specific fashions dominated the social and cultural scene. These fashions could be manifested in terms of popular clothing styles, music styles, celebrity icons and so on. Generational identity can also be defined according to tastes, beliefs and values.

The media play a significant role in the shaping of cultural identities and their significance has grown over time. Mass media have expanded and diversified and become more pervasive. Communication technology advances have also come to play an increasingly powerful role in defining generations. A distinction has been drawn between the newer Internet generation and the older TV generation. This may be a simplistic distinction and one that may not effectively define different generations as older technologies such as TV evolve and take on many of the functionalities of newer media such as personal computers. For some writers, there is a firm view that younger people who have grown up with the Internet differ from those who came to it later in their lives in their use of the online world. Furthermore, experience with the Internet can change the way people relate to it and to other longer-established media (Bakker and Sadaba, 2008; Dimmick et al., 2004).

Whether such observations are true or not, it is undeniable that newer media forms are more dynamic than older ones and operate with non-linear content configurations. There has been increased discussion about the new generation of web technology under the so-called 'Web 2.0' label. The growing volume of analysis of 'Web 2.0' has not necessarily produced a greater clarity of meaning and understanding about this technological phenomenon (Madden and Fox, 2006). 'Web 2.0' is often conceived as a defining aspect of the Google Generation. It represents a more advanced portfolio of online behaviours that set the Google Generation apart from other online users because they are more likely to be the early adopters of these activities. Before 'Web 2.0' can serve us well in this defining role, however, it also needs to be clearly articulated.

Web 2.0

The broad concept of 'Web 2.0' has tended to embrace online applications such as blogs, wikis, podcasts, really simple syndication and live social networking. These are applications that have in many instances grown organically from earlier, simpler applications. They reflect a web environment in which more advanced forms of user content creation and dynamic interaction can be found. The Web was initially a vast library of content and searching for the information needed posed the growing challenge for users. It has since moved on to embrace a range of information-driven social interactions or conversations among users. Such facilities provide accelerated access to information sources, sources that are alternatives to the mainstream and sources to which users can contribute content.

The tools and technologies associated with Web 2.0 have been acknowledged to carry significant implications for the future provision of higher education (as well as corporate training and lifelong learning – all of which represent educational activities in which universities might be engaged in the future). These communications technologies may become especially pertinent in a world in which more people will study, but not necessarily in the traditional 'on-campus' mode. They will also become more significant in an educational context in a world in which students – young and older – are accustomed to utilising them in other aspects of their lives (New Media Consortium, 2007).

Online phenomena including user-generated content, social networking, virtual worlds and multi-player gaming and technologies such as enhanced mobile telephony will not only become normative but will trigger new forms of e-learning that could transform the way education is delivered in the future. The technologies that underpin the 'social web' pre-date the era during which the Internet moved from being an elitist tool to one adopted by all. Some commentators have observed that the social web will fundamentally change the way we connect to other people. Further, making 'public' much of what we currently do in 'private' may not only keep us more closely connected to others but could also 'even make us more civil and tolerant' (Jarvis, 2007: 6).

The earliest computer networking software using standard telephone connections emerged in the 1960s. The first online social networks that laid the foundations of those that have been so widely adopted today were the Usenet newsgroups that emerged at the turn of the 1980s. Users could read and post e-mail-like messages that could then be distributed to closed user groups. Usenet can effectively lay claim to be the first Internet community (Reid, 2007). Within three years of the launch of the World Wide Web, Usenet posts were archived on the Web by Deja News, from 1995. Later, this archive was purchased by Google. Eventually, Usenet services were superseded by Web 2.0 phenomena such as blogging and the later online social networks.

Each of these technologies and related applications exist and have exhibited significant growth in terms of their adoption and continual evolution. User-generated content and social networking tools will create more dynamic learning environments in which students and tutors interact asynchronously and in real time jointly to create relevant learning resources and a valuable learning experience. Virtual worlds such as Second Life will create environments in which new learning techniques can be trialled at relatively little expense as well as producing settings within which virtual resources can be constructed for learning tasks and exercises where the real physical space to house them is unavailable (New Media Consortium, 2007).

There has been mounting evidence that 'Web 2.0' activities have displayed rapid growth. In some cases, they have come close to reaching a 'tipping point' as their use has reached between 10 and 25 per cent of Internet users. In many instances, they have already become preferred to more traditional media activities among those who use them.

Pew Institute researchers reviewed a number of surveys conducted in 2005 and 2006 that provided data on the proportions of Internet users who had ever engaged in various activities that could be taken as illustrative of 'Web 2.0' (Madden and Fox, 2006). While some of these activities had been adopted by significant minorities of Internet users (e.g. online development or display of photographs (34 per cent); online ratings of products, services or persons (30 per cent); computer-to-computer file sharing (27 per cent)), other activities were still relatively rare (e.g. use of online social networks (11 per cent); creating own web journal or blog (8 per cent)).

These Pew researchers observed that despite the claims of its proponents that 'Web 2.0' suited those who preferred a more dynamic web environment, static, asynchronous e-mail remained the most prevalent online activity. Between 2005 and 2000 there was hardly any change at all in the percentages of Internet users who said they sent or read e-mail on a typical day (Madden and Fox, 2006). However, research elsewhere showed that new users of the Internet (less than one year of online experience) were twice as likely as very experienced users (seven or more years) to say that e-mail should be checked as soon as possible (30 versus 15 per cent). New users were far less likely than very experienced users to agree that it is appropriate to wait one to three days before responding to e-mail (46 versus 65 per cent). Such findings indicate that while e-mail may prevail as the most widespread online activity, the new breed of Internet user expects it to be used at a far faster pace than longer-established Internet users (Cole et al., 2004).

Online research conducted in the United States with a sample of over 2,200 Internet users found that social networking sites that allowed user-generated content such as comments, reviews, feedback, ratings or own dedicated pages were attracting steadily growing traffic. Visits to these social search engine sites, however, were not replacing the use of major traditional search engines. The most visited sites in the previous 12 months were the market leaders, Google (85 per cent ever visited), Yahoo! (84 per cent) and MSN (64 per cent). These search engines were also the ones most likely to be used everyday (40 per cent, 32 per cent and 22 per cent respectively). Even so, sites operated by MySpace (38 per cent) and YouTube (37 per cent) were widely used across the year, though much less likely to be used daily (12 per cent and 2 per cent respectively). Facebook (8 per cent annual users) lagged further behind (iProspect, 2007).

On many social search engines, however, visitors did not perform a search at all. This was true of between one in five and one in four visitors to MySpace (23 per cent) and Facebook (22 per cent). This means that significant minorities of visitors to these sites fail to utilise them to their full potential. A generational profile is clearly apparent with the leading social networking sites. MySpace (68 per cent), YouTube (65 per cent) and Facebook (42 per cent) are all visited by greater percentages of 16–24 year olds than by any other age group. This age group is also more likely than any other to post comments on sites such as MySpace (56 per cent of young visitors) or YouTube (31 per cent) (iProspect, 2007).

In Europe, research by the European Interactive Advertising Association (2007) involved random telephone interviews with a sample of over 7,000 respondents in the UK, Belgium, France, Germany, Italy, the Netherlands, Spain and the Scandinavian countries. Nearly one in four (23 per cent) of online Europeans said they visited social networking sites at least once a month, with this figure being significantly higher for 16–24 year olds (32 per cent).

The Oxford Internet Institute reported research that revealed widespread use of the Internet in the UK for interactive communications reasons, many of which had a social dimension. More creative uses of the Web for networking purposes, however, tended to be undertaken by minorities of Internet users (Dutton and Helsper, 2007). Thus virtually all UK Internet users questioned in 2007 said they checked e-mail (93 per cent) and a clear majority (60 per cent) said they engaged in instant messaging. Far fewer said they participated in chat rooms (29 per cent) and even fewer still said they wrote a blog (12 per cent). Posting pictures or photos online was again a minority activity, but one that was on the increase (28 per cent in 2007, up from 18 per cent in 2005). Only minorities of current Internet users said they tried to set up a website for personal or other purposes (16 per cent) or actually maintained a personal website (15 per cent).

The Oxford research reported generational differences in the prevalence of some online social activities. Comparisons here were made between 'students', 'employed' and 'retired'. Students (46 per cent) were far more likely than either the employed (27 per cent) or retired (14 per cent) to say they had posted pictures or photos on the Internet. Students (43 per cent) were also more likely than the employed (26 per cent) or retired (13 per cent) to say they had posted messages or contributed to discussions on message boards. Finally, students (28 per cent) were also more likely than the employed (13 per cent) or retired (3 per cent) to say they had designed or maintained a website (Dutton and Helsper, 2007).

Further research on UK Internet users found that four in ten adults in Britain said they used the Internet to keep in touch with their friends on networking sites such as Bebo, Facebook or MySpace. In this respect, Britain was ahead of other major Western European countries such as Italy (22 per cent), Germany (17 per cent) and France (12 per cent). British users of social networking sites reported making an average of 23 visits and spending an average of five hours a month there (Judge and Sabbagh, 2007).

User literacy

To use these technologies effectively, media consumers must acquire a new form of media literacy. Different kinds of competencies are needed to utilise interactive media from those deployed when using older non-interactive media. However, the position adopted by writers such as Tapscott represents a form of technological determinism which, as explored in an earlier chapter of this book, presumes that technology has a force all of its own which drives its adoption. Yet there is compelling evidence that technology does not become adopted in this simplistic fashion. 'Adoption' of technology is not a unitary concept and cannot be operationally defined simply in terms of access penetration. How a technology is used for information and communication purposes is determined significantly by the social contexts in which it is utilised.

We cannot consider 'new media literacy', however, as something that is quite distinct from 'old media literacy'. While the competence or literacy to use new online developments is crucial to their eventual successful and willing adoption, what does this concept of 'literacy' really mean? Some writers have observed that it is not the case that 'media literacy' is a phenomenon that has just arisen alongside the dramatic emergence of interactive, multi-modal online forms of communication (Graham and Goodrum, 2007).

The first initiatives that underpinned the literacy-related concerns associated with new ICTs occurred several centuries ago. As the early printed texts emerged, usually linked to religious discourses, it became imperative that the clergy acquire minimal literacy skills. These developments laid the foundations for the establishment of the earliest universities. For a long time, 'literacy' was defined in terms of the ability to use printed language – to read and write it. The emergence of film and electronic broadcast media, such as radio and television, in the twentieth century led to a widening concept of literacy that embraced spoken words and images.

The new ICTs that emerged towards the end of the twentieth century utilised all these forms of communication in 'multi-modal' formats (Kress, 2003; Kress and van Leeuwen, 1996). Although written and spoken text and images already existed and were long established in distinctive media, digital technologies provided new transmission opportunities that facilitated the packaging together of information in these different forms. Text literacy was still needed to apprehend information presented in writing and image literacy to apprehend information presented as pictures. In addition, there was a further layer of competencies needed effectively to cope with streams of information presented simultaneously or in quick succession through varying modalities and in diverse formats.

The emergence of digital technologies has enhanced the rate at which information or knowledge is produced. These technologies have also facilitated the development and use of more compact forms of information storage and more advanced and speedier search systems through which targeted information can be readily accessed from vast information stores. Such technological developments have also affected the position and role of traditional repositories of knowledge – libraries and museums – and of traditional packagers and disseminators of knowledge – publishing houses, schools and universities (Graham and Goodrum, 2007).

In the light of findings that show large proportions of adults even in advanced western nations who cannot fill out application forms or read warning labels on commodities, there remains a need for basic literacy training as supplied by the traditional institutions of education. In addition, with the increased prevalence and utilisation of digital communications media in all walks of life, another layer of 'literacy' has surfaced with which ordinary people need increasingly to contend (American Library Association, 2001).

Adopting a technologically determinist perspective may lead us to ignore the more gradual changes that are taking place in the utilisation of communications media. While the Internet – accessed via a computer – potentially opens up a significantly different media world from that characterised by traditional forms of broadcasting, very often many early users of the Internet use it in a fairly simplistic fashion for basic forms of information retrieval. In other words, information search strategies that are adopted in the old media environment migrate into the new media environment.

Qualitative research among a small sample of UK families that focused on the use children and teenagers aged 8 to 16 years made of the Internet in 2001 found two dominant search strategies. Young Internet users most often searched the web either by using a specified address (URL) or simply by surfing that involved starting with one page and following links to others that looked interesting (Livingstone and Bovill, 2001a). Searching via URLs often relied on word-of-mouth recommendations about websites. This method was not always successful as web addresses could be mis-recalled or typed incorrectly. Search engines and search directories were also used though again not always effectively or successfully. One interesting observation from this research was that children and teenagers at this time were especially attracted by visually pleasing websites and found greater appeal in pictures than text while online. Reluctance to use text undermined the effectiveness of search engines and search directories because essential information indicating the success of a search tends to be text-based.

Research has emerged that challenges the notion that the young invariably adopt the latest technology with enthusiasm whether the purpose for doing so is information or entertainment oriented. One recent survey of 18–24 year olds in 11 European countries considered their use of the Internet within the wider context of use of leisure time (Synovate, 2007). The Planet Edge project found that relatively few of the people in this age group that were surveyed said they bought the latest technology as soon as it became available (11 per cent). On the other hand, this percentage would fit with the percentages of any population customarily found to fall into the category of 'innovators', that is the first to adopt an innovation. A clear majority (74 per cent), however, reported that they regularly surfed the Web, outstripping the percentage (72 per cent) who said they regularly watched television. What is not clear in this case is whether the term 'regularly' means the same thing in relation to use of these two media. Only around one in ten British respondents (11 per cent) said they had ever blogged.

Although more than one in four young adult Europeans (28 per cent) said they could not live without their laptop and their computer was the most popular device for listening to music (for 81 per cent), many Internet users still regularly read books (49 per cent) and magazines (41 per cent). Hence the traditional text media appear to remain reasonably popular even among this digital generation.

The Planet Edge project found that not all young people are equally 'techno-savvy'. Three distinct categories of young adult ICT user were differentiated. The first category was labelled as 'cybernauts' and represented a minority (27 per cent) that comprised innovators and early adopters of new technology. These individuals tended to be ahead of the game and were always eager to try out new innovations. The second category labelled 'average Joes' comprised a majority (53 per cent) that took a more functional view of technology. Although they would adopt, they were not among the first to do so. Technology was not a badge to be worn, but something that had value once its functional usefulness had been amply demonstrated. A third category, called the 'digital dissidents' comprised a minority (20 per cent) that tended to hold an aversion to technology and were generally slow to adopt and then did so in only a very limited way (Synovate, 2007).

Larger-scale research on 3,000+ British Internet users by the Oxford Internet Institute found that over six in ten (62 per cent) surveyed in 2007 thought that their Internet skills were excellent or good. This represented a slight fall on 2005 (66 per cent) but an increase on 2003 (60 per cent). There were some generation-related differences as indicated by the differing proportions of students (86 per cent), employed (63 per cent) and retired (40 per cent) respondents in this survey who rated their Internet-using capabilities as excellent or good. Younger users displayed greater confidence in their abilities online (Dutton and Helsper, 2007).

If users did experience problems with using the Internet, most (78 per cent) said they would work out for themselves how to resolve them, while many (62 per cent) would also seek help from friends and people they knew. Around one in five (21 per cent) said they would seek out training courses on Internet use. The retired (26 per cent) were especially likely to say they would seek out formal training (Dutton and Helsper, 2007).

The evidence from surveys of ICT innovation adopters has consistently indicated that not everyone utilises new technologies in the same way or with the same level of competence. It has been recognised that those who lack technology-related skills may be placed at a disadvantage. This is a problem that will not be resolved simply through mere adoption of technologies encouraged through the achievement of universal technology penetration. It may be more important to place an emphasis on understanding technology applications and the needs of potential users. The solution to the lack of adoption of technologies among some social communities may lie in the failure to perceive the relevance of technologies and related applications to their own lives (Brynin and Lichtwardt, 2004).

Cognitive skills and interactive technologies

'Literacy' is a term that represents the cognitive abilities of users to utilise information sources, whether these appear as written texts, static pictures, video sequences or multimedia presentations. The concept of user literacy in the context of the Internet has been investigated in terms of the reported experiences of Internet users and self-attributed competencies to use the 'net'. Computer literacy is closely associated with the use of the Internet and a minimal level of competence must have been acquired before online technologies and the information services to which they provide access can be effectively utilised. Some consideration has also been given to the qualitative nature of cognitive abilities and competencies in this context. One important question that has been asked is whether the use of new media cultivates new kinds of mental skills or promotes specific classes of pre-existing skills more so than the use of old media such as print.

Research evidence has emerged that playing with computer or video games can exercise and cultivate specific cognitive abilities that not only have value in terms of game-playing competence but might also be transferable to other information processing or learning settings. These effects can derive both from playing electronic games that are designed to promote educational benefits and from games produced for entertainment purposes. Whether such abilities can be identified as defining attributes of a 'Google Generation' of young new media users is an open question. Nevertheless, if playing with computer or video games is associated with use of online media more generally and with specific age bands, it could play a part in establishing a distinctive generation defined in part in terms of cognitive competencies and associated information technology literacy that could, in turn, mediate information search strategies.

Cognitive benefits of computer and video games

The cognitive benefits of playing with computer or video games are manifest in terms of generic cognitive skills development and more specific forms of educational performance enhancement. Computer-assisted instruction has been used in educational settings for many years (Atkinson and Wilson, 1968). This form of tuition has been regarded as superior to other technology-based instruction such as educational television because students are more actively engaged in learning tasks (Papert, 1980). Similar benefits can also emerge from playing entertainment-oriented computer or video games. While these games are developed predominantly for entertainment purposes, they engage players' cognitive faculties in ways that condition mental skills that not only enhance game-playing success but may also be transferable to other settings (Greenfield, 1994).

Electronic games developed for the leisure and entertainment markets have generally required players to acquire specific cognitive competencies that are essential to making progress in terms of game-playing expertise. Such games may require players to develop forms of hand–eye coordination, be able to process information rapidly through more than one modality and use logical problem-solving strategies. In other words, there is a range of cognitive skills that computer or video game players must develop to attain a high level of game-playing competence (Forsyth and Lancy, 1987; Hayes et al., 1985; Lancy and Hayes, 1988). With experience, players may learn to anticipate outcomes on screen and therefore to take appropriate courses of action in sufficient time to avoid elimination (Roberts and Ondrejko, 1995). There is further evidence that with repeated experience, electronic game players commit to memory the narrative of events that comprise specific computer or video games and that their anticipation of on-screen episodes can be manifest in physical movements on the part of players. Thus children will physically jump the moment before a critical incident in an electronic game with which they are familiar (Calvert, 1999). This phenomenon has been referred to as 'enactive representation' of events (Calvert and Tan, 1994; Calvert, 2005).

Playing computer/video games can enhance young children's abilities to remember pictures when those pictures form an integral part of the game (Oyen and Bebko, 1996). Some video games have been developed from the outset with educational principles and outcomes in mind. Some games involve word identification tasks played competitively (Fredericksen et al., 1982). Others, such as Sim City, involve players in designing their own virtual community (Friedman, 1995). Video game simulations have been used to train military personnel in the application of specific psycho-motor skills (Nawrocki and Winner, 1983; Trachtman, 1981).

Playing computer or video games effectively requires the acquisition of specific sets of cognitive skills and this process has been regarded by some scholars who have worked in the field as a new form of 'literacy'. These electronic games can teach physical coordination skills such as hand–eye coordination, increase attention spans, improve spatial visualisation skills and enhance the ability to process parallel streams of information in multimodal presentation formats (Greenfield, de Winstanley et al., 1994). For one writer, video games may be conceived as 'cultural artifacts' with their own distinctive symbol system and grammar. A specific type of cognitive competence must therefore be acquired by players to be successful exponents of this game playing (Greenfield, 1994).

The impact of computer or video games on players' cognitive abilities is not just restricted to childhood. It has also been observed to occur among adults. One study found that playing a non-violent video game called *Evolution* that presented players with a number of levels of difficulty enabled them to practise skills that benefited their later performance in tests of their computer literacy abilities (Greenfield, Camaioni et al., 1994).

It is the significance of early computer game play for the development of essential computer-related skills that underlines the potentially positive outcomes that can derive from engagement with these games. The immediate effect of regular playing with computer games is increased competence with those games which generally means learning advanced strategies to be successful (Kawashima et al., 1991). While these skills can be developed by playing alone, there is evidence that when children play electronic games together their performance can be even further enhanced (Littleton et al., 1992).

Being good at playing computer/video games is one thing, but can they produce wider cognitive or intellectual benefits for children beyond the game playing environment? There is empirical evidence that playing these games can exercise specific categories of cognitive abilities that represent important intellectual foundations for other kinds of learning in more formal educational contexts. Some computer/video games, for example, require players to use visual-spatial skills that involve identifying spatial relations between objects in virtual space, predicting their movements, and being able to create three-dimensional mental configurations from two-dimensional displays (Linn and Peterson, 1985; Pellegrino et al., 1987; Subrahmanyam and Greenfield, 1994). These skills can be important for other computer applications that include basic functions such as word processing, use of spreadsheets, application of desktop publishing and multimedia presentation software (Tierney et al., 1992; Greenfield, Camaioni et al., 1994).

Some computer/video games have been constructed specifically for instructional or training purposes, but even popular action games manufactured for the leisure and entertainment market can require players to develop sophisticated game-playing skills to reach the highest levels of competence. Such games cultivate in young players especially the abilities to mentally map the likely outcomes of events on screen and to strategise movements of virtual characters to achieve specific end-goals (Roberts and Ondrejko, 1995). Although players can receive instruction in advance of playing to support their performance, self-directed playing can produce inductive learning that is just as powerful and that can subsequently be transferred successfully to non-computer game-playing tasks (Greenfield, Camaioni et al., 1994). One example of this was a study in which young video game players were found able to transfer skills acquired to a mental paper-folding task (Greenfield, Branton et al., 1994).

Use of computer or video games

From their earliest days, computer games have been adopted and played by people of all ages. In developed countries where electronic games achieved initial widespread market penetration, however, evidence has emerged that they attracted more attention from children, teenagers and young adults than older age groups. Arcade video game playing was initially very popular. Over time, home-based playing has overtaken arcades. Early surveys in the United States reported that nine out of ten teenagers played video games (Gallup, 1982). By the end of the 1980s, American computer/video game players reportedly spent anything from two hours a week to two hours or even more per day playing these games (Funk, 1993). The amount of time spent playing these games, however, could depend on how long specific individuals had been playing. Some game players would display significant investment of time with computer/video games, but only for a limited period after which time devoted to these games could drop off significantly (Creasey and Myers, 1986).

Recently, Ofcom (2007d) reported that more than eight in ten (82 per cent) children aged 5 to 15 years in the UK reportedly used a computer games console at home and more than six in ten (62 per cent) said they had one of these devices in their bedroom. One out of two 5 to 15 year olds said they played computer/video games almost every day. Playing computer/video games almost everyday was most prevalent among children aged 8 to 11 years (56 per cent). The latter age group was also the one most likely to play games online at least once a week (65 per cent), with significant proportions of older (12–15s, 58 per cent) and younger (5–7s, 47 per cent) making a similar claim.

Differences across generations in playing computer and video games have been confirmed by further Ofcom data which showed that online interactive game playing became progressively less prevalent across age groups. While three in ten (30 per cent) of people with home Internet access said they played these games, this activity was more prevalent among the 15–24s (40 per cent) and 25–44s (32 per cent) than among the 45–64s (24 per cent) and over 65s (19 per cent) (Ofcom, 2007c). No data were provided for the amount of time spent playing electronic games which is likely to be a more insightful measure in relation to the cultivation of specific types of cognitive skills as a function of involvement with computer games. Even so, these statistics reveal that even though computer game playing occurs over all age groups, electronic games attract the attention of younger generations more widely than that of older generations.

Early evidence about electronic game playing indicated that boys tended to play computer or video games more frequently than girls and that boys devoted more time to playing these games (Dominick, 1984; Griffiths, 1991; Kubey and Larson, 1990; Loftus and Loftus, 1983). Girls were found to be part of the game playing scene, for example in arcades, but more often watched boys p lay than played themselves (Kiesler et al., 1983). In general, boys have consistently been found to spend much more time playing computer or video games than girls, both inside and outside the home. Although home-based game playing declined as children grew older, arcade-based playing increased particularly among teenagers as they spent more time with peers outside the home (Buchman and Funk, 1996). Boys have been found generally to prefer action-oriented games while girls prefer games that test visual-spatial competence or games with educational or feminine themes (Buchman and Funk, 1996; Funk et al., 1997; Wright et al., 2001).

In examining the reasons for computer or video game playing, we need to consider why young people say they play these games and what gratifications they derive from them. Popular computer or video game playing can be traced back over more than 30 years. In the earliest years of game playing, they represented the first introduction for many youngsters to computers. These games were initially marketed not just as a new form of home entertainment but also as one with educational side benefits (Murdock et al., 1992). Children and teenagers have been found to report that computer or video games have a variety of appeals that include offering surrogate companionship that is fun, a form of escape from life's problems and worries, and a personal challenge in achieving a high level of game-playing competence (Selnow, 1984). These attractions were confirmed in a survey of arcade video game players in the UK (Griffiths, 1995).

In summary, computer or video games have attained widespread market penetration across age groups but have been especially popular among children, teenagers and young adults. They often represent the first point of entry for many children into the world of computers and interactive technology. These games require players to acquire specific cognitive skills in order to become competent as players. Electronic game playing is therefore not simply a leisure activity; it also exercises specific classes of mental faculties that are important in a world where computer literacy skills are so important. Thus computer and video games require players to practise cognitive skills that are relevant to the wider use of computer technology. Furthermore, playing these games can cultivate generic cognitive spatial skills that can be important beyond the computer environment.

Whether these games can and do work alongside other new information and communications technologies to contribute towards the establishment of a distinctive new generation – a Google Generation – that not only has a distinctive orientation towards new technologies but also towards information search is a question that remains open to debate. Computer and video games have the ability to promote certain cognitive faculties (Dorval and Pepin, 1986). Their application in cognitive rehabilitation settings has demonstrated their effectiveness in this respect (Lawrence, 1986; Skilbeck, 1991; see also, Griffiths, 2005).

Not all players demonstrate the same degrees of improvement in specific cognitive competencies as a result of playing with computer or video games. Much seems to depend upon how well developed specific competencies are to begin with (Subrahmanyan and Greenfield, 1994). This observation would suggest therefore that the blueprints of cognitive skills developed through playing electronic games may already be installed in the human brain and that computer or video games represent one type of experience (among others) that can help individuals to realise their cognitive potential.

A generational perspective

This 'generational' model and what it implies about the role of patterns of media behaviour in defining the identity of different generational groups has received some support from empirical evidence about the way new media and old media are used. However, generational differences are also gradually being eroded as the use of ICTs spreads across all age groups.

A generational distinction is certainly reinforced by the rate at which Internet penetration was achieved among different age groups. Young people took to using this new medium far more quickly than older people. Yet, once they have switched on, Internet users whatever their age utilise this medium for an increasingly diverse range of purposes. All age groups use e-mail and all use the Internet as an information source. Information needs vary, of course, and understandably the Internet is used as an educational information source more often by the young than the old. Nonetheless, even older Internet users turn increasingly to the Internet for the types of information of greatest value to them. Hence older Internet users turn to it extensively for health and travel information. Internet users of all age groups and generations use the 'net' as a news medium (Madden, 2005). In some respects older Internet users have exhibited signs of catching up with their younger counterparts perhaps as they gain experience and confidence on the 'net'. Increasingly, the older generations are engaging not just in basic information searches online but also in more complex transactions.

Although significant proportions of all age groups of Internet users report turning to the Internet for news, when asked which is their most important news source, generational differences still tend to emerge. In this case, the younger generations are much more likely than older generations to nominate the Internet not just as a news source, but as their number one source. For older generations, television remains the primary news source (Horrigan, 2006). But in a further twist, which again provides evidence of the erosion of generational differences, broadband Internet subscribers have displayed much narrower generational differences in relation to the importance of online news. Across young, middle-aged and older age bands, broadband users regard the Internet as having either superior or equal status to television as a news source (Horrigan, 2006).

There is no doubt though that among growing numbers of young people the Internet is an essential source of learning that helps them with their education and provides an on-tap electronic library. Teenagers go online a lot and help older members of their family to use the Internet. The Internet is also an important social networking medium. It is used to maintain existing friendships as well as to meet new people (UCLA, 2000). Thus active Internet users do not generally use this medium as a substitute for real social contact or companionship. Moreover, network contacts may be utilised for educational purposes with online communications being used to discuss school or college work.

An attempt at developing an ICT-user typology has revealed age distinctions that confirm generational divisions in the use of new information and communication technologies. While access to these technologies is spreading across most age bands, usage profiles indicate age-related differences in the complexity of interactive media behaviour. The most advanced users of ICTs tend to be aged under 30, the disconnected at over 65. In between there are distinctions to be made between ICT users who are under and over 50. While the over 50s may use ICTs as widely as the under 50s, they tend to have simpler user behaviour patterns and are less likely than the under 50s to engage in more complex interactive applications (Horrigan, 2007).

Google Generation and learning scenarios

Overall trends have revealed growing numbers of people across generations becoming increasingly engaged with ICTs. This has been illustrated not least by trends in the use of the Internet. One key issue in debates about the growing significance of new ICTs has focused on the extent to which this phenomenon has occurred equally across different segments of societies. There are dramatic differences in the degree to which Internet use has become established in developed and developing countries. Even within developed countries, however, divides have opened up between ICT 'haves' and 'have nots'.

One such divide is age or 'generation' related. Age, however, is not the only differentiating variable in the context of the spread of Internet access and use. Level of education is another critical factor. In the United States educational level has been observed as a factor that differentiates between Internet users and non-users for a number of years.

Research published in 2000 found that less than one in three Americans who had not graduated from high school (31 per cent) used the Internet compared with over eight out of ten college graduates (86 per cent) (UCLA, 2000). These findings were confirmed by the Pew Institute (Horrigan and Rainie, 2002), with the gap between individuals with no more than high school graduation (32 per cent) and those with college graduation (88 per cent) again being very pronounced.

While the Internet adoption divide associated with educational attainment level might also be linked to socio-economic circumstances, it could also signal different relative degrees of relevance of the Internet to people with varying amounts of full-time education. This interpretation is supported by findings from the United States from young people who believed that having access to and then actually using the Internet benefited them as students. Over half of a national youth sample (56 per cent) said that they went online to help with their homework, which was double the proportion (26 per cent) who said they used a library (AOL, 2000).

The growing relevance of online information and communication technologies for all young people was underlined by Pew Institute research in the United States that showed that even though Internet users with no more than high school education were much less likely than those who were college graduates to possess broadband at home, year on year between 2005 and 2006 the least well educated group showed the biggest growth in broadband uptake (+70 per cent, compared with +32 per cent for college graduates). Such data reveal that while a digital divide persists in relation to societal groups defined by education attainment level, the gap is gradually closing (Horrigan, 2006a, 2006b).

Research conducted at the start of the new millennium in the United States underlined the growing significance of the Internet in the context of education. A survey among online teenagers aged 12–17 years conducted in November and December 2000 revealed that virtually all of them (94 per cent) reported using the Internet for school-related research and over three-quarters (78 per cent) regarded the Internet as a valuable resource that could help them with their school work. Over seven in ten online teenagers (71 per cent) stated that they had used the Internet in connection with their latest school assignment (Lenhart et al., 2001).

What was even more interesting in this survey was what it revealed about the way in which online resources are used and why. A significant minority of online American teenagers (41 per cent) used e-mail and instant messaging to contact teachers or classmates about schoolwork. Around one in three (34 per cent) said they had downloaded study guides from the Internet (Lenhart et al., 2001).

On a more negative note, nearly one in five (18 per cent) online teens said they knew of someone who had used the Internet to cheat on a paper or test. Online teenage boys (21 per cent) were more likely to make this admission than were online teenager girls (15 per cent). Older teens aged 15–17 years (23 per cent) were twice as likely to acknowledge this use of the Internet as were younger teens aged 12–14 years (12 per cent). Experience on the Internet was also associated with knowledge of online cheating. Teens with three or more years' online experience (28 per cent) were three times as likely as those with no more than one year's experience (9 per cent) to say they knew about online cheating.

Online learning: conventional versus innovative styles

Evidence has continued to emerge from different parts of the world that young people are turning to the Internet for educational purposes. Technology innovations are presenting learners – young and old – with many different alternatives to conventional learning styles. As observed earlier in this volume, however, the mere presence of an innovation does not guarantee its widespread adoption. Potential users must be able to conceive the personal relevance of an online technology to their own needs and they must acquire the skills required to utilise new technologies and their applications. These factors are prerequisites to widespread technology utilisation. If online learning represents a totally different style of learning, how readily will learners be prepared to accommodate the demands of this new 'literacy'? If online learning represents a different mode of delivering conventional learning styles, what incentives are there for learners to abandon traditional forms of delivery in favour of moving online?

Digital technology developments embrace both the conventional and innovative in relation to learning styles. While some technology platforms offer a fresh departure from earlier forms of learning, others largely imitate traditional forms in a new way. The success of these two types of development will ultimately rest not on their mere availability, but on demonstrating enhanced functionality of real value to learner-consumers.

'Conventional' digital learning

The idea of 'conventional learning' conjures up images of reading and writing. Traditional learning has relied heavily on oral communication by teachers and written communication via texts. Texts have traditionally been produced in hard-copy forms such as books and journals through print on paper. Increasingly, publishers have migrated onto the online environment. Text lives on, but in electronic form. Electronic publishing is already starting to transform the media landscape. The Internet and World Wide Web have provided a new infrastructure through which published content can be transported to consumers. This innovation was catalysed by best-selling authors such as Stephen King deciding to release new works only via the Internet. Over half a million people tried to download his novella, *Riding the Bullet*, within one week of online-only publication. At a charge of $2, it cost much less than a standard hard copy. A subsequent novel by King called *The Plant* was published electronically in instalments starting from June 2000. After a few months, however, King stopped posting new chapters as the market ran out of steam and less than half those interested in the story wanted to pay for it this way. Clearly, there is an important lesson to be learned here. There may be a market for e-books, but the right business model must be adopted if this type of innovation is to be successful.

The potential of electronic books is underlined by the growing number of publishing houses that now operate and distribute books and journals in this way. It is further reinforced by the investments being made in new technologies that allow readers to download e-books onto a portable device that displays pages of text on a screen that resembles the size of a standard paperback book. Indeed, it was recognised early on in this context that there is more than one e-book market and that the consumer base can be differentiated in terms of content tastes and preferred reception technology (Spiselman, 2001).

Major publishing houses such as Random House and Hachette have rolled out more titles electronically, including those produced by mainstream popular fiction and non-fiction authors. Such business strategies have been motivated by the emergence of technology innovations such as Sony's 'Reader' and Amazon's 'Kindle' that can allow readers to download hundreds of books from publisher's websites onto pocket-sized portable electronic devices (Brooks, 2008). Such devices represent the iPods of the book world. These products are available at affordable prices and give readers the option to carry around a far greater number of titles than they could possibly manage in hard copy form. The critical question posed by these devices is how popular they will prove to be with readers.

A number of market analysts have provided estimates of the future prospects of e-books, with some predicting significant revenue growth during the first decade of the twenty-first century (Romano, 2001; Spiselman, 2001) and others being more cautiously optimistic (Mayfield, 2001). Certainly, confident market forecasts were encouraged in the United States by impressive year-on-year market growth in sales figures for e-books during the first two to three years of the new millennium (Blough, 2003; Writenews.com, 2003).

Sales growth trends may provide encouraging signs that e-books have a future, but to understand the market better it is important to understand where the appeal of e-books lies. If the marketplace is heterogeneous as suggested by some observers (e.g. Spiselman, 2001), then it is possible that this will be reflected in the types of e-books readers most prefer and in the way they choose to consume them.

Research in the UK conducted in 2005 found that most established Internet users (85 per cent) had heard of e-books (Gunter, 2005). Around half (49 per cent) said they had ever accessed one online on a trial basis and nearly four in ten (38 per cent) said they had ever purchased an e-book. The most popular purchases among those who had made any at all were technical manuals (39 per cent), popular non-fiction related to a hobby or interest (34 per cent), followed some distance behind by a popular novel (18 per cent), an academic textbook (15 per cent) and specialised research monograph (14 per cent), a dictionary (8 per cent) and an encyclopaedia (8 per cent).

In the same survey, e-book buyers were asked whether the e-book they had last purchased had also been available in hard copy. This question is important because it could provide evidence that a market will only exist for e-books that are not also available in a traditional non-digital format. One in three e-book purchasers (33 per cent) said that the last e-book they had bought had also been available in hard copy, while nearly four in ten (38 per cent) said that it was not. The remainder (28 per cent) did not know (Gunter, 2005).

So what is it that motivates readers to obtain e-books? The UK survey revealed that the three most widely endorsed reasons given by e-book purchasers were that it was more convenient to buy a book online than walk to a bookstore (28 per cent), that the electronic version was cheaper than the hard-copy version (24 per cent) and that it was easier to search the content of an e-book (17 per cent).

Innovative learning styles

The rapidly growing phenomenon of social networking has been implicated in the context of online learning developments. Social networking was the fastest growing online phenomenon from 2003 with rapid adoption of early networking sites giving encouragement to many others. Although established primarily for social purposes, some of the most significant of these networks were initially developed by students within higher education contexts.

Research by the National School Boards Associations (NSBA) and Grunwald Associates LLC found that virtually all teens and pre-teens with Internet access (96 per cent) claimed to use social networking technologies such as online chatting and blogging and visiting online communities such as Facebook, MySpace and Webkinz. A clear majority (60 per cent) also said they use the 'social web' to discuss education-related topics. Further, more than eight in ten (81 per cent) claimed to have visited a social networking site in the past three months and over seven in ten (71 per cent) claimed to use these sites at least once a week. In fact, teens claimed to spend almost as much time with social networking sites (nine hours a week on average) as they did watching television (10 hours a week). In virtually all school districts surveyed (96 per cent), at least some teachers reported that they set homework exercises that required the use of the Internet (NSBA, 2007).

Evidence of the importance of Internet sources in an educational context has also emerged from analyses of traffic for and reported use of Wikipedia. Earlier in this report, the use of wikis was included within the operational definition of 'Web 2.0'. Wikipedia has a youthful user profile (Rainie and Tancer, 2007). Use of this information resource was found progressively to decline with age: 18–29s (44 per cent had ever used it); 30–49s (38 per cent); 50–64s (31 per cent); and over 65s (26 per cent). Education level was also associated with use of Wikipedia, with college graduates (50 per cent) being more likely to have used it than either those with some college education (36 per cent) or those with only a high school diploma (22 per cent).

Wikipedia has emerged as a market leader. While it has progressively attracted more Internet traffic, other competitors such as Encarta have lost market share. Online traffic monitoring has revealed that users of Wikipedia have a more youthful profile than those of Encarta. In particular a significantly larger percentage of Wikipedia users (24 per cent) than of Encarta users (15 per cent) are aged 18–24 (Madden and Fox, 2006).

There is no doubt that Web 2.0 is having an impact upon students and teachers. Blogs, wikis, podcasts, social networks and other new online features offer a range of new educational opportunities. While e-learning technologies have been available for a long time, the ways in which such technologies are applied in formal educational contexts is evolving. E-learning is about more than simply publishing content online. It represents a more dynamic learning environment in which students and tutors actively share knowledge and learning experiences. Both parties may have a creative role in finding and constructing content. Web 2.0 activities such as blogs, wikis and social networking condition this more dynamic and proactive engagement in the learning process on the part of students because these online facilities invite users to become content contributors and active participants (see Raltivarakan, 2007).

Further insights into the way online sources are utilised in an educational context emerged from a qualitative study sponsored by the Pew Internet and American Life Project at around the same time as the survey just referred to. In this instance, focus group interviews were carried out with young people aged 12–19 years. Fourteen group discussions were held in all involving 136 participants (Levin and Arafeh, 2002).

Five metaphors emerged to explain the use of the Internet for school work. These referred to the Internet as:

- a virtual textbook or reference library;
- a virtual tutor and study shortcut;
- a virtual study group;
- a virtual guidance counsellor;
- a virtual locker, backpack and notebook.

In relation to the idea of the Internet as a virtual textbook or library, school and college-age respondents reported using online sources for course assignments. It was often perceived as more convenient to look up information on the Internet than from a textbook or a reference library. There was also a view that printed textbooks quickly become stagnant whereas online reference content was seen as more dynamic and more frequently updated. Libraries often had limited facilities whereas the Internet was seen as offering a virtually unlimited resource.

The Internet also occupied a role as a virtual tutor in that it could provide sources of instruction that provided shortcuts to completion of assignments. These teens said they could locate online tutorials and study guides that provided quick fixes to assignment problems. They could also engage in online discussions with tutors and other students to exchange ideas and get advice about course work.

The Internet served as a virtual study group because it facilitated collaboration with other students who could be readily located online via e-mail or better still in real time via instant messaging. The concept of the Internet as virtual guidance counsellor emerged from reports that online teens turned to it as a source of careers advice or advice about how to further their education beyond their present position. Teens reported using websites to check out details about jobs and careers.

Finally, the fifth metaphor of the Internet as locker, backpack or notebook underlined the convenience of the online facilities as storage devices. It was found to be much easier and more convenient to carry around large quantities of content in electronic form than in hard copy form.

This research indicated that a generation of Internet-savvy teenagers was emerging that had high expectations about the use of online technologies and resources in the context of their education. They often felt let down by their schools and their teachers because of a shortfall in facilities and professional skilled tutors who could help them to make more of online resources to support their learning.

A growing 'social' orientation to learning mirrors the increasingly social networking orientation of Web 2.0. Blogs and wikis, for instance, encourage group or community content generation. Online networks such as MySpace and Facebook facilitate contact between users that can again be used to generate content or to share links to information sources (Alexander, 2006).

For some commentators, the adoption of social software tools and techniques of the sort currently being trialled on the Internet will represent a key element of emerging education approaches over the next few years (New Media Consortium, 2007). The social nature of Web 2.0 technologies has led to their use being labelled as 'emerging humanity'. The always switched-on world of broadband has encouraged and facilitated the development of more dynamic online behaviour in which people increasingly go online to share ideas with others (Bryant, 2007).

For the Web 2.0 technologies to be fully established, they must be sufficiently widely adopted. They must become mainstream and not just the preserve of 'innovators' or a few early adopters. Although e-learning techniques are being developed increasingly in higher education circles, their success as educational applications requires a change of mindset towards teaching and course construction. The simple transference of traditional course content to an electronic environment will not suffice. In Web 2.0, users are dynamic and creative participants. This must be reflected in the e-learning setting. This may mean that, at times, the normally distinctive roles of tutor and student could become blurred. Both will be engaged in the use of online tools to find or create content, course structure, forms of learning assessment and modes of knowledge delivery. To embrace the 'social software' of Web 2.0 will create a different learning culture. It will invoke a range of new learning principles and require tutors to think in more detail about the dynamics of the learning process within the context of the stated learning objectives of a course.

Understanding the way learning scenarios and related information requirements may evolve in a Web 2.0 environment therefore requires an examination not simply of the penetration of adoption of relevant ICTs, it must also embrace an analysis of learning styles. Even before the concept of Web 2.0 emerged young people, within the Google Generation age range as defined in this volume, exhibited specific styles and preferences in relation to the way they engaged with information online. The initiation into use of the Internet was found to take place within an entertainment or leisure context for many children and teenagers. They were attracted by features that enabled them to personalise screen displays through the use of fonts, colours, symbolic components such as emoticons and the use of pictures (Livingstone and Bovill, 2001a).

As they acquired 'net literacy', young people realised that it was fashionable to have a distinctive Internet identity, to use shorthand expressions associated with chat rooms and to be able to take full advantage of the multimodal capabilities of online technologies such as utilisation of multiple-window formats. It emerged also that valuable informal learning experiences could be accrued through the use of the Internet for entertainment or social purposes, particularly in relation to enhanced competencies in understanding and using the 'grammar' of online scenarios to navigate websites and find content. What was often missing, however, was any evaluation of the authority of online information sources which is particularly crucial when using the Internet as a learning resource. One important aspect of Internet use is that it must be fun and it would seem that this ethos must be imbued in any formal learning applications with young people.

Concluding remarks

It has been established that a 'Google Generation' is not simply a convenient marketing category or a label to hang on a group born after a certain year. There is evidence of a young generation that has grown up with a range of online information and communication technologies and has never known a world without them. The pace of technology change, especially within the ICT domain, has appeared to take an upward curve. This change has also been felt within higher education. What then is the likely future scenario in higher education as far as the shape of the typical learning environment is concerned? Can we map innovation rates and predict the kinds of learning techniques that will prevail and the types of learning resources that will be needed?

Making future predictions is not always straightforward. Old innovation adoption trends may not always provide accurate predictive models. This is because the economic, political, social and cultural circumstances within which innovations appear and that can mediate adoption rates can change over time. Furthermore, no two innovations are necessarily the same, even when they may appear to have certain similarities.

Rates of innovation have certainly varied among older and newer established ICTs, but it is important to ensure comparisons of 'like with like' are being made before jumping to conclusions about how learning environments might change in the next decade or two. It has been noted earlier that in relation to innovation adoption, a critical stage is often reached – sometimes called a 'tipping point' – when a new technology reaches 10 per cent penetration. That is the point at which its penetration can take off dramatically. It took five decades for telephone technology to reach that level of penetration in the early part of the twentieth century and just five years for the World Wide Web to do the same at the end of the same century (Chen and Crowston, 1997). In this case, however, we are not comparing like with like. When it was first introduced the telephone was a totally new concept unlike any that people had encountered before. Although it represented an exciting new development for some, it gave rise to doubts and uncertainties among many people about the usefulness, relevance and safety of the device.

With the World Wide Web, the technology and the concept of electronically linked computer networks had been around for many years before it became a popular public phenomenon. For instance, an initial 'Internet' was extensively used in the 1980s by academic and military institutions in the United States. In addition, many people outside these sectors had already become familiar with computer-mediated communications networks within their workplaces (so-called intranets). The popular Internet therefore represented a repurposing of existing technology rather than the introduction of a brand new one.

An important distinction that has been made in this context is that between 'transformative' and 'general-purpose' innovations (Liebenau, 2007). A transformation occurs when a new technology enters the market that is unlike anything that has gone before and requires that users must discover what it is used for and how best to apply it. Alternatively, there is a range of general-purpose technologies with which many or most people may be familiar that continually undergo change. In these cases, new models may be produced that represent enhancements of earlier versions. Some new learning may be required on the part of their users, but the essential features and application protocols remain the same. One can therefore debate whether the so-called Web 2.0 developments fall into the category of 'transformative' or 'general-purpose' changes. In most instances they can probably be considered exemplars of the latter rather than the former. What slightly confuses the issue is that the earlier versions upon which Web 2.0 applications are based have also had a short and changeable lifespan. In some cases, new upgrades occur even before the older models have reached a tipping point among the wider population.

Despite the debate about whether it represented a genuinely new or transformative innovation, the growth of the Internet and World Wide Web has been astounding. The first web server was introduced in 1991 and by early 1993 there were only around 50 websites in the world. By the end of the same year, more than 600 servers had been established, growing to 2,700 by mid-1994 and 230,000 by mid-1996. The numbers of servers and websites have continued to grow rapidly and the inventiveness of users has, as much as anything, driven the development of applications that now define Web 2.0 (Liebenau, 2007). Whether innovations will exhibit an accelerated pattern of growth in the future has been disputed by some writers and rates of innovations were calculated to have fallen away even in the second half of the twentieth century compared with the unrelenting upward track identified over the previous 500 years (Huebner, 2005).

One observation about innovations is that it has become increasingly expensive to produce them and bring them successfully to market. This observation has been made, in particular, in relation to the telecommunications market (Liebenau, 2007). The shortage of adequate investment in innovations could therefore be a critical factor that underpins future developments and their rate of adoption. Turning this spotlight on future developments in the context of higher education, the reduction in industry funding of research and development in universities and the failure of successive governments to provide basic funding for the higher education sector commensurate with the growth in student numbers could slow down even 'general-purpose' innovations adoption if the latter incur a cost to users – whether this cost is borne by institutions or students. At the same time, such financial barriers might be offset by the increased availability of open-source information and communication technologies that incur little or no initial adoption costs. The open source trend is not universal but has been sufficiently widespread that many online tools for user content creation and social networking are economical, while others such as virtual worlds have low entry costs.

In the next two chapters, we turn our attention in a more focused way to the information searching behaviours that occur in more formal learning contexts in higher education. To begin with we need to consider the change implications that information and communication technologies have for that sector. Then we examine evidence from a range of empirical sources to find out whether there are signs of an emergent Google Generation in formal educational settings.

5

Emergence of new forms of knowledge production, search and acquisition

This chapter focuses attention on more specialised information-searching behaviour associated with formal learning situations, especially those found in higher education, and considers whether the emergence of the Internet has produced a new generation of scholarly searchers who seek out information differently from older generations. Previous chapters have examined wider public uses of new communications technologies and, in particular, the Internet, to identify defining attributes of the Google generation or 'Net Generation' (see Tapscott, 2009). The next two chapters narrow the focus down to the study of information needs and information-seeking practices. This chapter considers the implications of digital technology advances for the production and distribution of content in the scholarly context. The next chapter attempts to define the 'digital scholar' by focusing more on the behaviour of scholars themselves in finding information relevant to their studies. Both sets of analyses have relevance to the overall aims and objectives of this book, namely to determine whether those brought up in the Internet era display qualitatively different approaches to the location and use of information and different expectations about how information should be made available from earlier generations.

Online search engines, such as Google, provide a continually expanding range of information search facilities and applications. Some digital developments occurred with the scholarly community in mind (e.g. new digital library services), while others that were initially developed for more general purposes have been adapted as support systems in formal learning environments (e.g. online social networking). Most publishers are publishing texts (books and journals) electronically. Universities and other education institutions utilise electronic learning facilities increasingly in their courses. This chapter examines published evidence from different parts of the world on how people obtain information in the scholarly world.

Earlier chapters have indicated that the world of information seeking and knowledge acquisition has evolved rapidly in response to the opportunities created by new information and communications technologies that have now permeated modern and developing societies. These changes have been felt in the scholarly world where researchers, teachers and students have all recognised the advantages and benefits that some of these information and communication technology (ICT) applications can bring to the learning process. Such developments have given rise to important questions about whether a new generation of learners has emerged that seek out qualitatively different styles of information provision from previous generations and what implications this change process has for the way academic institutions, publishers and libraries operate in the future. Do new kinds of expectations exist among students and scholars concerning the availability and packaging of information? Exploring such questions also gives rise to further questions about the roles of publishers and libraries. Do (traditional) publishers and librarians have a role at all? If they do, in what ways must their roles evolve to keep up with the opportunities presented by ICT developments and the changing demands of new ICT users, especially in learning contexts?

Changing contexts for scholarly output production and use

Change is already with us. To understand where it might take us, we need to examine what is already happening in the world where information finding and knowledge acquisition are primary objectives. In considering learning processes, of course, we must also examine knowledge production and distribution activities and how these, too, have been changed by the penetration of new ICTs. Hence, we need to look at some of the larger-scale trends that are shaping the research landscape and patterns of scholarly communication.

Changing research needs and practices

The world of the researcher is changing. This is not simply a reaction to the availability of new ICTs. It also reflects wider cultural changes in the research community driven by new political and associated economic imperatives for research as an activity in developed countries. Research conducted in Australia, for instance, showed that societal and economic needs are driving forward research-related policies from government that encourage more applied, cross-discipline research (Houghton et al., 2003, 2004). Such policies encourage researchers to collaborate more, which could mean the establishment of geographically dispersed networks that may seldom enjoy face-to-face contact. Such developments increasingly bring into play electronic communications systems through which these virtual research communities are able to engage, maintain contact and transfer information between members. The use of such networking infrastructures also requires users to acquire new technical skills.

Further evidence has emerged from the United States of the increasingly collaborative nature of the research enterprise. Liu's (2003) study comprised a longitudinal analysis of three journals (*Journal of the American Chemical Society, American Journal of Mathematics, American Journal of Sociology*) using a century's worth of data, 1900–2000. This showed an increase in the average number of authors per published research paper from 1.36 to 4.30 in chemistry (+216 per cent), from 1.04 to 1.45 (+38 per cent) in mathematics, and from 1.00 to 1.58 (+58 per cent) in sociology. One prediction (Price, 1965) that the single-authored paper was on its way out was not borne out by other data that showed, for sociology (5 per cent) and mathematics (57 per cent) in particular, most published papers were produced by single authors.

A further significant change within the academy is an increase in the sheer volume of published research, which has been driven by evolving academic assessment policies that place emphasis on key metrics such as published outputs and on the increased availability of publications outlets. The growth in volume of published research places a strain on researchers, teachers and students in being able to keep abreast of all the latest developments that may be relevant to their needs. It has been observed that academics are reading across a wider range of sources and appear to be reading more articles than ever before (Boyce et al., 2004; Houghton et al., 2003; King et al., 2003). Libraries and library-provided databases are a major source of reading materials as personal subscriptions to journals have declined (King et al., 2003). The increased breadth of reading seems also to have been supported by the wider availability of end-user electronic search tools (Boyce et al., 2004). While technological determinism has certainly driven the increased use of digital information sources, they also enhance the convenience with which large amounts of information from diverse sources and disciplines can be located (Houghton et al., 2003). The problem posed by growth in the quantity of information while the time available to read it remains finite for users is that attempts to read more widely may result in less depth of reading. The price of trying to retain a depth of reading must be that the reader consumes a smaller proportion of the totality of content available (King and Tenopir, 1999; King et al., 2003; Tenopir et al., 2004).

The digital transition

As online technologies have achieved wider penetration, more computer power and greater diversity of applications, users' engagement with these technologies has also evolved. The impact of this phenomenon has been felt among individuals as consumers and citizens and across many different types of organisation – public and commercial. The scholarly world has not escaped these changes and a number of key groups within that world, including academic publishers, librarians, academics and their students, have been presented with new opportunities for producing, storing, distributing and utilising knowledge. These opportunities have also thrown up challenges for some, if not all of these groups that have signalled the need to review business and working practices. Within the thematic context of this book, an examination of these changes could provide further insights into whether new and distinctive information-related behaviour practices are emerging that define a Google Generation.

Early studies

The 'digital transition' has been manifest within the academic world most distinctively in the migration of hard copy content into electronic forms. Herman (2001) examined the transition from print to electronic information sources from research published between 1981 and 2000. Early studies focused on the evolution of the digital library (Lancaster and Sandore, 1997) and changes deriving from the development of electronic networks to support the growth in desktop access to the Internet, bibliographic and full-text databases and the significant use of e-mail as a means of scholarly communication (Adams and Bonk, 1995; Budd and Connaway, 1997). Disciplinary variations were noted, with the scientific community adopting electronic information sources more enthusiastically than those in the arts and humanities (Liebscher et al., 1997; Mehta and Young, 1995; Pullinger, 1999; Noble and Coughlin, 1997; Lazinger et al., 1997; Milne, 1999). The Superjournal project (Eason et al., 2000a) identified social scientists as frequent users.

Barriers to the acceptance of electronic resources contributed to low usage on the part of academics and researchers. These barriers were often technological as well as factors such as a lack of reliability, incomplete content, imperfect search engines, shortcomings in hardware, software and network access from home and the workplace, authentication and lack of integrated access across systems, onscreen readability and reproduction (page integrity), and a perceived lack of attention by publishers to readers' needs such as browsing (Adams and Bonk, 1995; Rowland et al., 1997; Budd and Connaway, 1997; Zhang, 2001; Rusch-Feja and Siebecky, 1999). Despite the popularity of electronic resources on the one hand, a reluctance to abandon print formats on the other was to some extent fuelled by the low regard in which electronic journals were held and a reluctance by promotion committees to recognise their value, with peer review and archiving being frequently cited as issues (Cronin, 1995).

Herman (2001) identifies a trend throughout the 1990s for younger academics to make greater use of electronic resources (Lazinger et al., 1997; Milne, 1999; Zhang, 1999). Whitmire (2001) also provides evidence of increasing engagement with electronic resources during undergraduates' academic careers. Projects such as Superjournal (Eason et al., 2000a; Pullinger, 1999), an e-Lib programme which investigated the use of electronic journals in UK academic libraries, and TULIP (The University Licensing Project) (Borghuis, 1997; Hunter, 1996), a collaborative study between Elsevier Science and nine universities in the USA, identified issues relating to technical matters, user behaviour and organisational and economic questions. TULIP's primary focus was on e-journal delivery and usability issues in Materials Science titles, and log file analysis yielded data showing that graduate students viewed more abstracts and searched electronic journals more actively and with a broader focus than faculty. While undergraduate usage was not examined in depth, log data also indicated a significant degree of activity by this group (Borghuis, 1997). Superjournal, which examined the breadth and depth of use of e-journals, found variations according to subject discipline and user status and identified social scientists as enthusiastic users, partly due the ability to browse broadly (Eason et al., 2000a: 493).

Tenopir (2003a) undertook a comprehensive review of research into electronic library resource usage published between 1995 and 2003, which brought together major (Tier 1) and smaller-scale (Tier 2) studies. A highly selective approach identified eight Tier 1 studies, or groups of studies, defined as large-scale, multifaceted and generating complex findings described in many publications by different authors. The studies used a variety of research methods, including surveys, focus groups and digital log analyses, which can introduce contradiction and limit the ability for cross-study comparison. Tier 2 studies typically involved fewer participants in a specific environment or are one-time projects of similar quality to those designated Tier 1 status.

The purpose of Tenopir's review was to identify reliable research studies for librarians and analyse their findings, although she acknowledged that research methods would influence the conclusions that could be drawn from each study. Part of her work here also included analysis of the way electronic resources were used. From her review of both large-scale and small-scale studies, while there were some differences between researchers from different disciplines, other more generic patterns of behaviour and preference emerged in the way electronic resources were utilised. Electronic resources could be advantageous when used in content browsing mode and yielded economies of effort and time. Disadvantages associated with electronic resources concerned user friendliness of archives, ease of navigation, format readability of text displays and availability of appropriate technology for access.

Evolutionary processes

Electronic journals have not simply and suddenly emerged. They have become established through a number of stages over time. One model has identified three phases in the evolution of the electronic journal (Mahé, 2004; Boyce et al., 2004):

- *An early, pre-1993, pre-Web, phase* where electronic full texts were confined to CD-Rom and a few online services and article readings were almost entirely confined to print. This phase was characterised by low levels of electronic use, a preference for low-technology resources, and a lack of recognition of e-journals which were anyway only accessible through limited experimental platforms.

- *An evolving phase*, beginning in the late 1990s and continuing into the present, marked by the availability of print and electronic alternatives. In this phase electronic use has increased but has failed to reach critical mass. Research attention focuses on readers and on the socio-cognitive factors that enable or inhibit take-up (technical barriers, lack of knowledge, peer pressure and the fact that prestige is still associated with print rather than virtual journals).

- *An advanced phase*, already arrived at in some disciplines, marked by sophisticated information systems designed specifically to enhance the way that scientists work (e.g. NASA's Astrophysics Data System). Research attention becomes increasingly user-focused as critical mass develops. Knowledge on use becomes more specific and detailed and greater sensitivity is shown to differences between disciplines.

Another perspective is a diffusion theory approach that some researchers have deployed in research into use of and attitudes towards electronic scholarly resources (Brennan et al., 2002). This research has identified a number of content and functional factors linked to e-journals that drive their adoption. Content factors include: critical mass of issues and volumes for a given title; critical mass of titles in a subject collection; full equivalence to print issues; timeliness of appearance. Functionality attributes comprise: searching facilities that support browsing, locating known articles and subject/author retrieval; ease of navigation; links to other articles; high-quality printing; and seamless movement among related resources.

By 2005, of course, practically all these elements were in place. Based on a series of longitudinal surveys, Boyce et al. (2004) asked the question, 'How have electronic journals changed patterns of use?' They then related their data to the three evolutionary phases noted earlier. Their data revealed the extent to which electronic formats have displaced print and illustrate a significant shift from journals to separates, all in a remarkably short space of time. Among scholars who read papers from journals to which they made personal subscriptions, all of these were print journals in 1990–3, while just over half were from print journals (55 per cent) in 2001–2. Similarly, with library subscriptions that were used as sources, while virtually all of these (99 per cent) were print sources in 1990–3, the overwhelming majority (87 per cent) were electronic sources in 2001–2.

For Odlyzko (2002), as for many other writers, this is a sign of the electronic journal as a revolutionary, disruptive technology. What went before is history. According to this author, 'the real issue is that, in this new electronic age, if it isn't online, for many purposes it might as well not exist. Further, even if it is online, it might not matter if it is not easy to access or timely' (Odlyzko, 2002: 10). With the use of e-scholarly resources growing at 50–100 per cent per annum and print use static or declining, Odlyzko predicted that electronic formats will become the completely dominant medium in less than a decade.

Flaxbart (2001) reported that electronic access has taken over more completely and more rapidly in chemistry than anyone could have predicted in the mid-1990s, with faculty leading the way. Much less use is being made of the physical library because of the convenience and time-savings that are possible: 'As a new generation of graduate students moves into the faculty, it is very possible that their attitudes, coupled with market forces, will virtually eliminate the traditional printed journal from the radar screens of most practicing chemists' (Flaxbart, 2001: 24).

Obst (2003) compared print and electronic use of 270 matched journals in the context of a German academic medical sciences library using reshelving statistics and online user metrics.[1] He found that print usage declined dramatically between 1999 and 2001, that electronic journal usage accelerating rapidly (nearly tripling over the same period), and that journals published in both formats lost 30.4 per cent of their print use within approximately two years (the total loss for print-only titles was 45.8 per cent). In effect there was a gradual shift towards using a manageable number of information access channels and that ease of access was a critical factor that determined preferred access routes.

Within two years of their introduction, electronic accesses were exceeding print uses for matched pairs of journals by a factor of nearly eight (although this figure disguises wide variation between different publishers). Obst noted a strong correlation (0.6 for 1999–2001) between the frequencies of use of a journal title in both formats: in other words, journals that are heavily consulted in digital libraries are often the same titles as those most often consulted in print. Walter (1996) found that usage increases with frequency of publication: titles published irregularly or less than four times a year have distinctly lower levels of use.

In contrast to the above studies, other researchers have concluded that most print journals at Washington State University's Owen Science and Engineering Library in 2003 were actually being used *more* than they were prior to the introduction of electronic journals (Siebenberg et al., 2004). The view here was that the availability of electronic formats has in fact greatly enhanced the total use of all titles.[2] According to Siebenberg and his colleagues:

> The popular lore/common wisdom that people are changing from using print journals to electronic journals is not true across the board. This study suggests that users' migration from paper to

e-use is dependent on subject area ... It may be worth noting that [other] studies reporting e-use as more than ten times the paper use were conducted at medical libraries where the time-sensitive nature of many queries may have been a factor. (p. 436)

Surveys of ARL academic library members in 1991, 1995, 1997 and 2001 by Tenopir and Ennis (2002) offer another insight into the impact of the transition to electronic journal formats from a library professional perspective. They found a big shift from mediated searches to self-service searching, with nearly 20 per cent of libraries reporting that mediated services would be withdrawn within two years. They also noted that reference staff dependency on electronic materials to service patrons' requests is now 'virtually total' and that these developments are more complex than might at first be recognised.

As most of the reported trends seemed to point towards the imminent demise of print, Vaughan (2003) posed the research question: 'In a hybrid print/electronic journal environment, what data are needed to decide when print is no longer needed?' and undertook a study to look at the short-term effects of online availability (Elsevier ScienceDirect was introduced in February 2000) of journals on print use at Duke University Chemistry Library. He compared the use of three groups of journals from 1999 to 2002: 'Elsevier' (44 journals available in print and online), 'electronic' (84 journals available in print and online before the introduction of ScienceDirect) and 125 print only titles. Vaughan noted a big drop in print use across all categories (down 47.5 per cent), even among print-only titles (down by 31 per cent – nearly a third). Even e-journals exhibited a fall in usage (down 48 per cent) over this period. This finding was echoed by De Groote and Dorsch (2001) who also found that the introduction of online services impacted on the use of print-only subscriptions at the University of Chicago Health Sciences Library.[3] They point out that library patrons may assume that all journals are available in both formats and that librarians may have an important awareness-raising role to carry out.

In spite of the obvious convenience and attractiveness of electronic formats, these are disturbing findings and are 'clearly a source of concern to information specialists, especially in light of the recent research study at John Hopkins University where drug toxicity information available from print sources was not used, resulting in the death of a study subject' (Vaughan, 2003: 1151). In an article that seemed designed to inflame the debate about the impact of electronic access, Odlyzko (2002) questioned some fundamental assumptions at the heart of formal scholarly communication, especially the view of journals as the 'minutes of science'. According to this writer, 'authors like to think of their articles as precious resources that are absolutely unique and for which no substitutes can be found. Yet a more accurate picture is that any one article is just one item in a river of knowledge ... substitutes exist for almost anything' (Odlyzko, 2002: 12).

This is an extreme example of the convenience argument and one that finds some support in the self-reported views of authors in a UK survey (Rowlands et al., 2004) and in a detailed analysis of web logs (Nicholas et al., 2003). Odlyzko's position is certainly iconoclastic, especially in relation to his views on the non-unique, substitutable, nature of much that is currently published. On a more positive note for publishers, however, Odlyzko did highlight the importance of 'digital visibility': 'Whether they like it or not, scholars are engaged in a "war for the eyeballs" just as much as commercial outfits, and ease of access will be seen as vital' (Odlyzko, 2002: 18). This last point found empirical support from a series of UK studies (Nicholas et al., 2003, 2004, 2005) where parallels were developed between scholarly information-seeking and general consumerist behaviour.

Print versus electronic journals

A number of studies have reported on the relative advantages and disadvantages of electronic and print formats. For example, Bar-Ilan et al. (2003) undertook a large-scale questionnaire survey of senior academic staff in eight Israeli universities, exploring their use of electronic journals and databases (2000/2001). They found that e-journals and databases have found wide acceptance across the academy with more than three-quarters of faculty making regular use and reporting very high levels of satisfaction. There are major differences between broad disciplines, with life sciences and medicine the heaviest users, humanities the lightest. Age appears to be a big factor: older faculty members were much less likely to use e-journals than their younger colleagues. Users themselves may be contradictory, perhaps indicating some inner confusion, in terms of their personal competence in coping with online information sources. Bar-Ilan et al. (2003) observed that an overwhelming majority of researchers they surveyed (85 per cent) felt they were either perfectly competent online or else needed only a little help from time to time. Yet, a clear majority (62 per cent) also expressed a firm interest in receiving more training about use of online sources.

The most frequently endorsed advantage of electronic services was the speed and ease of information access they afforded (58 per cent). At the same time, speed and ease of access were the most often mentioned disadvantages or problems (22 per cent). What such findings reveal is that ease of access is a critical factor and can, depending upon whether it works well or not, be a source of great satisfaction or frustration to online information searchers.

General conclusions of the Bar-Ilan et al. (2003) study were that print was the preferred medium for use in teaching and for catching up with developments in other fields. Most of the researchers who were interviewed held firmly to the view that electronic materials are supplementing print, not supplanting it (but note the relatively early date during which this research was carried out in terms of the format revolution). The inherently conservative nature of many academics is reinforced by Houghton et al. (2003) whose respondents also made the point that things had not changed very much, that they were doing the same kinds of things, only quicker.

Electronic books

Information-seeking behaviour in a digital environment is not limited to the Internet and use of scholarly journals. Electronic books are increasingly available, although studies of e-book usage using transaction log data are limited. Connaway and Snyder (2005) undertook an analysis of netLibrary logs for a specific day over each of three years. The primary aim of the study was to establish system loadings, but the logs also yielded data about the number of books and pages viewed. Social science, science and technology titles were most consistently accessed and users viewed, on a single day, an average of 14.1 unique pages per book in 2002, 16.4 in 2003 and 18.1 in 2004. The average time per session was approximately 11 minutes, suggesting that e-books were used as a reference collection rather than being read in their entirety. Downloading functions were not available.

A more recent survey carried out at the University of Strathclyde (Abdullah and Gibb, 2006) which investigated awareness of e-books among students, found that although usage and awareness of e-books was limited, textbooks were most commonly used, with the majority of users (94 per cent) reading them on screen despite the disadvantages of eyestrain. Printing was also popular with 35 per cent of respondents. A study carried out at the Indian Institute of Science (Anuradha and Usha,

2006) also identified low usage levels, but found that students used e-books more than faculty members and staff and used mainly technical and reference material. Bennett and Landoni (2005) also found limited awareness and low usage of e-books among students.

Further research was carried out by Roesnita and Zainab (2005) at the University of Malaysia, who found that students preferred to read e-books online (82 per cent), rather than in print format (16 per cent); however, reasons for non-use include preferring paper books and difficulties in browsing and reading. This confirms the tension identified by Abdulla and Gibb (2006) between use by enthusiastic readers who read on screen despite the disadvantages which deter non-users. As with other studies a low level of usage of e-books was identified and promotion is suggested to increase take-up. An analysis of subject-specific e-book usage was undertaken by Hernon et al. (2007), who examined undergraduate use in nursing, economics and literature. Participants in the study tended to look at tables of contents before proceeding to relevant chapters. Printing was preferred to downloading, although expense was a deterrent; an alternative strategy was to cut and paste relevant sections into a Word document. Resistance to electronic books by faculty was also found by Palmer and Sandler (2003). The limited take-up suggests that more promotion of e-books is necessary to increase awareness.

The digital transition: some theoretical perspectives

The transformation in scholarly communication has naturally attracted the attention of theorists as well as empirical researchers. Jacobs (2001) used discourse analysis to characterise the utterances of researchers and librarians and found that technological determinism is a deeply entrenched position in both cases. Bohlin (2004) argued that the publication of research results serves three fundamental functions for scholars: quality control, distribution and archiving.[4] These functions set it apart from informal communication. In this respect, his arguments were broadly similar to those of Mabe (2001), acting as an antidote to the excesses of the technology determinists by returning to the fundamental communicative and other functions of journals and how these need to be maintained in the digital universe, although his conclusions were very different.

Bohlin's basic argument is that the changes taking place in journal publishing and use are much more significant than they currently appear and that the whole system is about to implode completely. According to this writer, 'The significance of the Internet to academic publishing is comparable with that of the printing press and and the scholarly journal: in the course of the process thus set in motion, the nature of the learned journal, as well as of scholarly communication in general, may well be reconfigured altogether' (Bohlin, 2004: 366).

Like many on the Left, Bohlin appeared to welcome such disruption as a way of returning control to scholars. Fyffe (2002) reviewed the scholarly communications crisis from a social theoretic point of view, drawing on the work of Castells and Giddens, and argued that we should understand the fragility of digital systems (his concerns are very much to do with issues of preservation and the continuity of the scholarly record) and the resulting possibility of cultural loss.

Fyffe offers an essentially alarmist argument that bewails the increasing dependence of scholarship on business, systems and networks, leaving academia potentially subject to massive disruptive change outside of its control. He therefore called for libraries and administrators to engage in risk management planning *now*. These arguments were largely informed by the idea that what is technologically possible will inevitably be realised in the social and economic sphere ('technological determinism').

Kling and McKim (2000) offer a very different perspective in a conceptual paper that argues strongly against the proposition that we are in the early stages of a communications revolution in which it is only a matter of time before all academic fields converge on a stable set of electronic forums. Using a social shaping of technology (SST) perspective, they argue that notions of trust and legitimate communication pull against this tendency to convergence and that communications plurality will both persist and indeed become more sharply defined. Using the examples of high-energy physics, molecular biology and information systems as examples, the authors note stark differences in communication patterns and preferences between disciplines, which they believe to be persistent features.

Kling and McKim (2000) observed:

> We expect that considerations of trust will continue to shape the kinds of scholarly communication that are seen as legitimate in a specific field. The divide between fields where researchers share non-refereed articles quite freely ('open flow fields') and those where peer reviewing creates a kind of chastity belt ('restricted flow fields') is likely to change slowly, if at all. Thus, for example, Ginsparg's

> non-refereed and (largely) unrestricted working article server includes some areas of physics, and a few cognate mathematical and chemical subfields ... but we expect few biological or chemical specialties to join forces with this venture. (p. 6)

Kling and McKim argued that the electronic publishing reform movement was being energised by a core group of highly vocal enthusiasts (e.g. Harnad, Ginsparg, Odlyzko) and that these activists promoted a shared ideology (briefly that electronic materials were less expensive, distribution was easier and wider and that these aspects would in and of themselves speed up scientific communication). The tenets of inevitability and convergence to a common set of tools flowed from these arguments. These factors homogenised the debate and left contestable areas (like the fact that disciplines are different) as uncontested.

In a related study, Kling et al. (2003) explored scholarly communication from a socio-technical interaction networks (STIN) perspective. They referred to a broad spectrum of scholarly communication forums (SCFs) such as e-print servers, e-journals and collaboratories and argued that a regrettable tendency in scholarly communication is to try to understand it primarily in terms of information processing and rationality (thus higher speed networks, Internet access, etc., necessarily imply certain models). Instead they suggested that more emphasis should be given to issues like resources, incentive structures and stakeholder perspectives.

> ... some scientists believe that the high-energy physics working article (e-print) server at the Los Alamos National Laboratory (now called arXiv.org) is the model of publishing that will sooner or later be followed by all of the sciences: it is 'just a matter of time' ... [but] empirical research studies have found that 'almost identical technologies' are often configured very differently in practice, and that these configurational differences can influence their use and uses. (Kling et al., 2003: 51).

Subject domains and information use

That disciplines vary widely in their communication habits and preferences has been a 'given' in bibliometric studies for many years. What is new, perhaps, is the emergence of recent studies which try to model and explain this commonly observed if unexplained phenomenon.

This strand of research might be coined the 'Nordic School' since the authors are largely of Danish and Finnish origin, no doubt inspired by the earlier conceptual work of Birger Hjørland at the Royal School of Librarianship at Copenhagen.

Fry and Talja (2004) observed that most studies of journal behaviour tend to focus on the following factors:

- the use, usefulness and value of the articles read;
- how scientists learn about the articles they read;
- from where scientists obtain the articles they read;
- the format of the articles obtained;
- the age of the articles read.

This approach is of limited value, however, since it fails to explain the reasons underlying use and non-use, especially between disciplines. Most of the studies Fry and Talja cited in their argument were limited to a single institution or discipline or were comparative across very broad disciplinary groupings (e.g. physical sciences, health sciences). Furthermore, they focused on use rather than non-use, thus skewing perceptions further.

Fry and Talja argued that we should embed journal use studies within a specific theoretical framework: we should be more aware of the organisational and cultural context of users and their domains, with specialties, preferably, or disciplines as the unit of analysis. Moreover, we should conceptualise the epistemic and social organisation of disciplines along two dimensions: the axes of 'task uncertainty' and 'mutual dependence'. Mutual dependence refers to the degree to which a specialty depends on knowledge produced elsewhere (environmental studies would be a good example) and the extent to which researchers are required to show how their work is connected to others. This varies enormously. Task uncertainty refers to the degree to which task outcomes and research processes are predictable, visible and clearly connected to general goals. This model revealed why, for example, 'topic' and 'systematic review' can be understood as almost entirely different concepts in different disciplines.

Talja and Maula (2003) also noted major differences in the use of electronic networked resources between disciplines and argued that these should be related to factors such as the size of the domain, the degree of literature scatter and domain-specific relevance criteria. This led them to the following conjectures:

- Research areas with high numbers of topically relevant materials are best searched by browsing.

- Research areas with middling numbers of topically relevant materials are best searched by directed subject searches.

- Areas with very sparse ('needle in a haystack') numbers of relevant items are best searched by linking (citation chaining from known documents).

- In high scatter domains, access to e-journal services and databases covering several domains helps in countering scatter.

- E-journals and databases are likely to be used more heavily in fields in which topical relevance is the primary relevance criterion and less in fields where paradigmatic relevance is the primary relevance criterion.

Further, issues such as professional orientation (e.g. teaching versus research, local versus international, basic versus applied) can have a major influence on information-seeking strategies and journal use. The implications of these issues for digital library design should be obvious and include the fact that the usefulness of e-journals and aggregated services may be limited in fields which are low in mutual dependence and high in respect of task uncertainty (Talja and Maula, 2003).

Domain differences offer a valuable corrective to the technologically determinist thinking of authors like Odlyzko (2002) who seem to assume that the ease, speed and seamless experience offered by electronic journals mean that all fields will eventually settle on a stable set of common electronic fora: preprint servers, discussion lists and e-journals. This is effectively projecting the physics arXiv model[5] onto all disciplines as a technological inevitability, and is an example of thinking which is implicit in a whole range of debates, from open access publishing to institutional repositories.

While the domain perspective advocated by Fry, Talja and Malua are intellectually appealing, there are few empirical studies which explore disciplinary and organisational differences systematically. One exception, and a good example of trying to make these concepts work out in practice, is a study of disciplinary differences in the use of digital journal materials in the Finnish National Electronic Library (FinELib) by means of nationwide survey data by Torma and Vakkari (2004) and Kortelainnen (2004). Discipline was the independent variable in their analysis: frequency of use and satisfaction were dependent variables scored on a Likert scale.

A key finding here was that the perceived availability of relevant materials in the FinELib digital library was a better predictor of use than the users' discipline. In addition, regardless of discipline, a perception of the resources as being 'good' led to more frequent use. Finally, satisfaction also did not vary with discipline and, again, perceived relevance was the key predictor. If these results seem somewhat surprising in the context of this section on the primacy of domain differences, the authors are the first to admit that the six disciplinary categories they used (e.g. humanities, natural sciences) were simply too broad to be useful and that these categories mask substantial within-group variation. Here lies the real challenge: how to design studies at a meaningful (and definable) level of disciplinary aggregation?

Changing user behaviour

In this section, we are concerned with how users interact with journal collections: how they find articles, what they read and how they integrate journal materials into their working practices. Much of the research in this section stresses the need for studies in scholarly communication to provide insights into motivation and behaviour, not just to crunch performance indicators. According to Tenopir (2003b), 'We are finding that all aspects of human behaviour – affective, cognitive, and sensorimotor – have an influence on how people interact with information' (p. 17).

Writing and researching articles

A major gap in the literature during the period under consideration relates to author behaviour in respect of how electronic tools are influencing writing practices: this is particularly surprising given the arrival of online manuscript submission and peer review mechanisms. The last major study appears to be that of McKnight and Price (1999), based on research at an early juncture in the evolution of the electronic journal, although Borgman (2000) covers a range of author-related issues in her 2000 article. She set out a research agenda for scholarly communication and digital libraries:

- studying how researchers disaggregate documents and reaggregate them in different ways;
- studying the 'social life' of documents;

- incorporating the criteria by which scholars choose publication outlets which could better inform the design of digital libraries.

Borgman also noted: 'Scholarly publishing is inherently a social process, in which authors choose their publication outlet based on characteristics such as prestige, perceived quality of reviewing, ability to reach the intended audience and availability to the target readership' (Borgman, 2000: 419).

Finding articles

How do authors identify and retrieve the articles they want to read, especially in electronic networked environments? Eason, Yu and Harker (2000) analysed the value to users of a range of functionality in electronic journals, arising out of insights from the SuperJournal project and thus an early benchmark. Their key findings were, first, that the core (indispensable) functions of digital libraries are basic browsing, printing and search facilities; second, that directed searching is used less intensively than browsing features: researchers are not very good at searching; and third, that features such as alerting, saving, customising and communications functions are peripheral (i.e. dispensable) for most users.

An interesting observational study by Worel (2004) examined the form in which patrons presented specific bibliographic references to the reference desks at an academic health sciences library (University of Minnesota Bio-Med Library) and a governmental library (the RN Barr Library at the Minnesota Department of Health). Despite major differences in the size and orientation of the two libraries (one academic, one practitioner-focused) a very similar profile was found in both cases. This study provided evidence that library users seem to place considerable reliance on large databases like PubMed and on chaining from one document to earlier documents by following up references.

If we return to the work of Boyce et al. (2004) and their summary of survey data collected over a long period, evidence emerged of a very substantial shift from the early 1990s to early 2000s towards directed online searching and away from browsing behaviours. Nominated methods of learning about articles dropped from 58 per cent in 1990–3 to 21 per cent in 2001–2. Online search grew from 9 per cent in 1990–3 to 39 per cent in 2001–2. It was also noted, however, that colleagues retained importance as information gatekeepers (16 per cent of sources in 1990–3; 21 per cent in 2001–2). In addition, the use of citations grew as a source (6 to 16 per cent).

In digital libraries, referral logs offer a very useful resource for helping us to understand how users navigate to the documents they deem worth downloading or printing (Nicholas and Huntington, 2003). A study by Davis (2004a) starts from the proposition that although we may think we know quite a lot about the information-seeking behaviour of chemists, the networked information environment throws up new challenges and knowledge. Specifically, what pathways do researchers at Cornell take to get to American Chemical Society servers? Davis's findings suggest that users employ a wide range of strategies to find chemistry articles. Table 5.1 aggregates the behaviour of a large number of individuals and is misleading in one very important respect: despite the range of strategies exhibited across a whole population, most individuals tend to rely consistently on a small sub-set of these methods. This has implications for librarians and publishers.

Implications for librarians

Duplication should be encouraged: Davis's findings support the view that it is not necessarily a duplication of librarians' efforts, for instance,

Table 5.1 Types of referral

	Total referrals	% total referrals	Unique IPs	Referrals per IP
Library catalogue	2,482	24.9	552	4.5
Bib database	2,372	23.8	324	7.3
E-journal list	1,813	18.2	405	4.5
Web page	1,108	11.1	190	5.8
Web search	996	10.0	491	2.0
E-mail (web based)	592	6.0	79	7.5
Article link	571	5.7	204	2.8
Other	15	0.2	9	1.7
Total referrals	**9,949**	**100.0**	**1,591**	**6.3**

Source: Davis (2004a).

to maintain links to journal URLs from the library catalogue as well as having the same information on a university e-journal list.

Implications for publishers

According to Davis (2004a), 'from the perspective of scientists, it is in their interest to have the electronic literature linked to as many types of information referral as possible. A publisher's rationale for limiting direct linking from other databases and full-text products may be as much political as technical' (p. 331). The complexity of the issues and the difficulty of making sweeping generalisations in this area are underlined by the work of Bontrhon et al. (2003). This was a small-scale investigation of 35 faculty and 500 students at Edinburgh University into their use of electronic journals. The starting premise was that the move to electronic formats is affecting serials management practices in libraries and it explores what this means for the ways that faculty and students incorporate electronic journal usage into their working patterns.

The study found that faculty made very little use of the library's electronic journals web page and its subject trees, preferring to go directly to (bookmarked) tools such as the Web of Science, Beilstein or PubMed to find relevant articles. Staff generally seemed to make very little use of the value-added features of electronic journals such as tables of contents or mailing features. Most got their articles by bookmarking Internet sites or using links from databases such as the Web of Science. The library web page was used as a call of last resort.

Several studies underline the convenience of electronic journal services for off-site users. Jacoby and Laskowski (2004) found that the majority of use of e-journals at the University of Illinois, Urbana-Champaign, takes place off campus (69 per cent in 2002, 83 per cent in 2003) or on campus but not in the library (library use accounted for 7 per cent and 4.5 per cent respectively). At any time of the day, extramural usage is an order of magnitude greater than in the library: e-reserves were used more heavily off campus at 04:00 than at any time during the library's working day!

Further evidence of the popularity and convenience of electronic networked services came from de Groote and Dorsch (2003) at the University of Chicago who found very high levels of electronic access among medical faculty and students. However, take-up varied enormously between different journal platforms, suggesting a lack of awareness of the richness of provision on offer: patrons strongly prefer to use services with which they are already familiar.

Both Davis (2002 and 2004a) and Ke et al. (2002) reported on the highly asymmetric patterns of digital library use as reflected in their logs. In the case of ScienceDirect, Ke et al. report that nearly 50 per cent of full text downloads came from the 100 most active IP addresses out of a total population of more than 30,000. In a later paper, Davis explored these patterns more systematically, using monthly COUNTER full-text download reports from 16 HighWire participating institutions (Davis, 2004b). The other primary variable was the number of unique IP addresses (a surrogate for the number of users). Multivariate statistical methods revealed a very strong linear relationship between quantities of downloads and unique IP addresses. Davis posited that article downloads are therefore a good predictor of the number of unique reader proxies (IP addresses), constant across time and institutions.

Further evidence was produced by Sandstrom (2001) who offered some intriguing new thinking about information search behaviour. She used the metaphor of animals foraging for food to explain some of the dynamics of information searching. According to Sandstrom (2001):

> Resource-selection decisions about where and how long to search, what to pursue and what to ignore, and whether to forage alone or in groups are similar, whether the decision-makers are animal subsistence foragers, human hunter-gatherers or scholarly information seekers … Scholars as subsistence foragers are constrained by the density and distribution of resources, which affect encounter rates, and by limits on skills, technology, knowledge of the environment, availability of foraging partners, opportunity costs and other factors that affect their decision-making and processing abilities. (p. 598)

This might be a highly appropriate new model for helping us to understand information-seeking behaviour across multidisciplinary journal platforms like ScienceDirect.

Reading articles

How is the reading behaviour of researchers changing in relation to electronic access and the 'journals crisis'? A good starting point for tackling this question is the work of Belefant-Miller and King (2003) who profiled reading behaviour at a medium-sized US university (the University of Tennessee at Knoxville). This was a re-examination of a

1993 study so it presents the situation at the cusp of the paper and electronic eras and is a useful benchmark for subsequent studies. Belefant-Miller and King found that faculty read 384 documents per annum of which 161 were journal articles, had 4.2 personal journal subscriptions and published three articles per annum.

Tenopir et al. (2003) provided a rich synthesis of earlier surveys and literature on reading behaviour. They found that the number of personal subscriptions per scientist decreased steadily from 5.8 (1977) to 2.2 (2003), signalling a shift from a journal economy to an article economy.[6] It was also reported that author websites had not caught on, accounting for less than one per cent of readings in both the early and advanced phases. Even so, there was a massive increase in electronic formats for reading. An important finding for publishers was that the journal publisher makes a big contribution to knowledge creation: average readings per scientist have increased from 87 (1977) to 148 per annum, the large majority of which are readings supplied from library collections in print or digital form. Finally, the usefulness of the articles read and indicators of their value suggested that information content had not changed much, but its overall value to the scientific community had increased as more articles are read and can be accessed more conveniently.

These data accorded reasonably well with Mabe and Amin's (2002) study which concluded that the average researcher read 97 articles, 204 abstracts, 1,142 titles and gave 21 citations each year. Of course, disciplinary differences will show considerable variation within these global figures. Jones et al. (2004) also made the point that there is a significant difference (within the context of British psychologists working in the NHS) in the median number of journals read annually between those with academic commitments and those without.

What role do electronic journals play in the weekly reading behaviour of researchers in the sciences and social sciences? Smith (2003) reported on a survey at the University of Georgia (carried out in 2001) and found that print has a much higher profile in terms of weekly reading habits than might have been expected and that personal subscriptions are still an integral part of scholarly pursuits. A higher proportion of scholars across the sciences and social sciences reported weekly use of print journals (95 per cent) than electronic journals (74 per cent). While there was widespread use of personal subscriptions to journals in the case of print, this was much less widespread in the case of e-journals (29 per cent). Use of library subscriptions to print (73 per cent) and e-journals (67 per cent) occurred to a similar extent.

Interestingly, the profiles of science and social science researchers were very similar (although this might simply be because these disciplinary categories are too broad to be useful, disguising within-group variation). Print accounted for more than half of the articles read each week (54 per cent), ahead of e-journals (42 per cent). Personal collections of journals still played a vital role in researchers' working practices, with just over one in two scholars (51 per cent) reporting use of these as their first-choice resource. Full text e-journals were first choice sources in around one in five cases (19 per cent) (Smith, 2003).

Smith was clearly of the view that print is alive and well:

> [Various authors] have predicted the end of traditional paper journals and embraced electronic journals as the panacea for the ills of scholarly communication. They foresaw this technology taking scholarly communication out of the hands of commercial publishers, and in doing so decreasing publication delays, eliminating editorial cronyism, and, perhaps most importantly, drastically reducing subscription costs. Empirical research into electronic journal use also revealed that the majority of faculty members were not as enthralled with the idea of a paperless society. (Smith, 2003: 162)

Using articles

An emerging trend in the literature, albeit slight and from a low base, is an increase in bigger picture studies which attempt to capture something of the value of journals in increasing the efficiency and effectiveness of research. Drawing on experience and data from the pharmaceuticals sector, Koenig (2001) advances the argument that research productivity is a direct function of organisational information culture. Environments characterised by openness, richness (of information resources and communication tools) and serendipity are more productive and creative places to work.

Many of the authors cited in this study have emphasised the convenience that attaches to electronic desktop access. Indeed, it is easy to overlook the frustrations and sometimes harsh realities of using printed journal collections. Shaw-Kokot and de la Varre (2001) offer one of a surprisingly low number of journal availability studies in a print-based collection, the context being an academic health sciences library at the University of North Carolina. They showed that user groups found locating journal articles to be problematic: finding and photocopying items takes a long time out of busy schedules. User errors (bad citations, lack of understanding of the way journals are shelved) or bibliographic error and local issues (reshelving, binding, missing issues, articles in use) simply compounded the problem.

Sathe et al. (2002) studied the impact of print versus electronic journals on research processes at the Vanderbilt University Medical Center. Do researchers use print and electronic formats for the same purposes? They found that faculty tended to prefer print over electronic formats: possibly an age-related phenomenon, possibly later adopters of the new technology. Some of the differences in the ways that print and electronic journals are used are significant. This was true in the case of print being favoured over electronic sources for browsing and for reading tables of contents. In contrast electronic sources were favoured over print for checking references and for printing or photocopying.

What value do researchers extract from journals? Tenopir, King and Bush (2004) surveyed medical faculty at the University of Tennessee regarding their use of journals and the values they attach to these readings. The most widely endorsed values of medical journals were that they provide a resource for primary research (30 per cent), enhance current awareness of subject matter (22 per cent), and support teaching (17 per cent) and writing (12 per cent).

According to Brennan et al. (2002), access to electronic journals is changing research habits since as well as being more convenient, electronic access allows for greater opportunities to follow up on relevant cited articles, thus facilitating a more comprehensive treatment of the literature. A fundamental shift in attitudes to the body of knowledge may be taking place. One respondent observed that he does not 'need to retain knowledge as long as access is maintained' and that his attitudes are now changing to reflect the fact that 'the aggregation of knowledge is now paramount' (Brennan et al., 2002: 523). Another respondent mentioned the explosion of meta-analyses in the last couple of years: a research form that was previously so cumbersome as to be impractical.

Finally, a really important question: can we translate the convenience offered by electronic information services into a financial value? Kurtz et al. (2000) in a study of the NASA Astrophysics Data Service (ADS), an abstracts service with links to full-text documents, offered one of the very few attempts to place a value on the impact of an information platform on a whole discipline. Use of ADS was clearly very intensive: in a typical month (March 1999), each scientist made, on average,

29 searches and read 20 abstracts and 5.5 articles. What difference does this make? One outcome was that finding searched-for or needed material could be achieved more quickly and conveniently through this type of electronic information service. The significance of this finding is not simply that there could be a time-saving here but also that a financial value can be attached to this outcome that might have important future policy and business ramifications.

Ageing and obsolescence studies

There are some interesting and important questions to be asked about ageing and obsolescence processes in digital libraries. Does use follow the same patterns of temporal decline that we see in the citations universe? What implications would flow from a better understanding of obsolescence as seen through the eyes of readers as opposed to authors?

In an early, print-only study using 835 medical journals as a test-bed, Tsay (2003) began with the working hypothesis that there is no difference between the age distributions of use (as measured by reshelving statistics) and citation. Tsay's findings showed that use decayed exponentially, with maximum use in year one. Citation showed a sharp initial rise from a low base to years 3 or 4, then an exponential decay. Finally, a comparison of the two curves showed that there was a very dramatic difference in year 1, the two curves intersect between years 2 and 3, and after that the citation curve exceeds the one for usage, though both curves fall off exponentially beyond this point. Tsay's results showed that the ageing profiles of use and citation were indeed significantly different, at least for print titles in medicine.

As we move into an increasingly electronic environment, what impact, if any, will ease of access have on the age profile of use? Boyce et al. (2004) suggested little change in reading patterns as a function of the age of the material and the profiles of use before and after the introduction of electronic access. Data spanning the 1960s through to the post-2000 period revealed similar profiles of readership of articles among scholars. There were no significant changes in the extent to which scholars read articles that were no more than one year old, or articles that were between two and five years old, or articles that were six or more years old in 1960 (pre-electronic era) and in 2000–2 (digital/Google era).

However, Liu (2003) conjectured that since older papers now have a much lower visibility in the digital age, both reading and citation habits may change to accommodate the ease of accessibility of digital materials, a point also made by (Houghton et al., 2004). A further point is what will happen to readings for articles that pre-date the digital archive, given the drastic fall-off in print readings noted earlier?

A systematic study of the NASA Astronomy Data Service (ADS) by Kurtz et al. (2000) found that

- articles 4–22 years old accounted for 2.5 reads per month;
- articles less than four years old accounted for 5 reads per month;
- very old articles (back to 1849) accounted for 0.025 reads per month.

Supporting Google Generation users

Studies of Internet usage by younger generations are indicators of future information-seeking behaviour and provide insights into the mental models scholars of the future acquire at an early age. Williams (1999) studied the behaviour in 10–11 year olds and noted that children tended to disregard written text, preferring audio and visual material because many sites are inappropriate for the age group concerned. In a study of Yahooligans, a search engine designed for 7–12 year olds, Bilal (2002) noted that children search according to their cognitive developmental ability and without understanding how the search engine works. Bilal acknowledged the inadequacies of Yahooligans' search mechanisms, but concluded that children needed to be exposed to effective web training. Prior knowledge and Internet experience were significant factors in successful searching and evidence suggested that children do not possess the necessary domain knowledge or experience and understanding of search engine functionality to use them effectively (Bilal, 2002; Madden et al., 2006; Slone, 2003).

Many reports on Internet use, particularly those published by bodies such as EDUCAUSE, identify trends which cannot be ignored by the academic community, such as the imminent influx of Internet-savvy students, to whom resources like Google and Wikipedia and instant messaging and social networking environments such as Facebook and MySpace are second nature, into an environment populated by aging faculty (Oblinger, 2003). Members of the born-digital Google Generation apparently bring with them a confidence in using the Internet for information retrieval purposes which belies their skills in critical evaluation and devising search strategies (Lorenzo and Dziuban, 2006; Rogers and Swan, 2004).

The ubiquitous use of search engines defines a conceptual model for information retrieval at an early age. The translation of this model into those of traditional IR systems such as library catalogues and bibliographic databases and federated search tools such as MetaLib which provide controlled access to organised information may be problematic and has implications for future user awareness and training programmes (Brophy and Bawden, 2005; Chen, 2006). Murumatsu and Praft (2001) reported that users have difficulty in understanding how search engines transform queries by using a variety of default search mechanisms, such as automatic Boolean operators, stop words, truncation and term order sensitivity. Thus cognitive models of the Internet, domain knowledge and understanding of the terminology, spelling, grammar and sentence structure contribute to the inability, particularly among younger (children under 13 years) and older (46–64) users to construct effective searches and evaluate the results (Slone, 2003).

Access to, and familiarity with, the Internet may also impact on the Google Generation's information-seeking skills and their educational aspirations. Factors such as policies and rules, technological and filtering controls and time constraints on teachers' ability to support the development of information literacy within the curriculum restrict access to the Internet in schools and prevent students from maximising the potential of the Internet in educational activities (Selwyn, 2006; Madden et al., 2006; Pew Project, 2002; Williams and Wavell, 2006).

The findings of these studies raise questions about the ability of schools and colleges to develop the search capabilities of the Google Generation to a level appropriate to the demands of higher education and research. Barriers to the use of electronic information resources have always existed and the TAPin project (Reid, 2007), an e-Lib initiative, demonstrated that one-to-one in-office support by librarians effectively increased the use of networked information by academic staff and boosted the departmental profile of library staff. Other perceived barriers to use of library resources include authenticated access to databases, searching and navigating library websites and lack of customer focus (OCLC, 2002).

Recent reports have identified generational differences as obstacles to information-seeking behaviour (Lorenzo, Oblinger and Dziuban, 2006; Lorenzo and Dziuban, 2006; Jones, 2002; Levin and Arafeh, 2002) and forecast challenges for information provision in higher education. The need for targeted instructional activities which recognise disciplinary differences in information-seeking behaviour and the specific needs of remote, off-campus users has been identified by Whitmire (2001). Gardner and Eng (2005) considered the implications for academic libraries of differences in the learning styles of Net Generation students, who had high expectations of IT infrastructures and round-the-clock access. Group work, peer learning, electronic learning environments such as WebCT, BlackBoard and Moodle and remote access to information resources for distance learning contribute to a need to support:

- demand for quality academic facilities and high academic achievement;
- the need for customisation of technology and research;
- the need for integration of technology into learning;
- the usage of new communication modes.

Initiatives designed to support users outside the physical library, for example the 'Roving Librarian' project at Harvard which, in spring 2003, placed librarians equipped with wireless-enabled laptops in spaces such as the students union, are quoted in Gardner and Eng (2005). Other innovative tactics such as relentless promotion, instruction and customer service are recommended to overcome barriers and market the support that users seem to consider unnecessary.

Concluding remarks

Despite the many difficulties in trying to extract general meaning from particular studies, the summary conclusions which follow attempt to capture a range of key issues as reflected in the current literature. The fact that we are at such an interim stage in the full evolution of the digital library means that these will have to remain highly provisional findings but they suggest a number of fruitful lines for further research. Researchers appear to be reading more primary journal materials than ever before and from a wider range of sources. The availability of end-user search tools and changing working practices as researchers engage more in Mode II knowledge production appear to be the key drivers.

Specialist secondary services remain strong only in a few areas with strong Mode I characteristics: generic services like the Web of Knowledge are very much in the ascendant. Less time is being spent on reading, per article, and researchers 'see' an increasingly narrow view of their own discipline as a result of the growth in the literature.

Despite many problems with the current publishing system, there is little consensus on the best way forward: positions are entrenched both in terms of stakeholder tribe and adherence to economic, technological or behavioural determinist positions. Where implemented, electronic versions of journals have displaced print use dramatically and at a much faster rate than some have anticipated. The introduction of electronic journal services impacts very negatively on print-only titles, such is the convenience and consumer acceptance of the new medium, raising big issues for the continuing value of the print legacy. There is some evidence that suggests, however, that the introduction of e-platforms actually increases print use by raising the profile of journals as an information source, and this is worthy of further investigation.

Convenience and digital visibility are crucial in the new information landscape. There is a strong correlation between print and electronic journals in that the more popular titles tend to be used (relatively) more heavily in both formats. Hence it is important for journals to be prominent in respect of any and all media platforms on which they appear.

In the face of the technological changes that have been occurring in relation to information search, mediated library services are declining rapidly in favour of user self-service. Even so, in the higher education setting, it would be wrong to assume that everyone is moving at the same pace in the direction of digital learning. There are, for example, differences between disciplines in the pace at which this type of change has been occurring. Thus, in order to understand more about the impact of online learning in the context of scholarly activity, future research in the field should differentiate between subject areas when examining information search behaviour.

There are issues of literacy in relation to online information searching, even among those engaged in advanced levels of study. Despite the huge increase in the use of electronic reserves, print still features as an important aspect of the day-to-day life of the typical academic. Researchers are not invariably technically proficient at searching and employ a range of coping strategies to navigate digital libraries. Hence, it is important for those involved in the design of digital libraries to ensure that information can be accessed easily and conveniently. Many online users still turn to printed materials and print-based and electronic information sources are both used, although for different purposes and at different times in the information-seeking cycle.

Notes

1. A major limitation of this study is that the use statistics are very difficult to interpret: they pre-date COUNTER compliance standards and the author admits that the interpretation of publisher-supplied usage data is exceedingly difficult.
2. This is a broadly similar argument to that employed when VHS technologies were introduced: rather than 'killing' cinema, home viewing created a new experience and expanded the size and scope of the overall film distribution market.
3. It should be noted, however, that use of print/online journals declined at a slightly faster rate than that for print-only journals.
4. Bohlin (2004) maintains that the establishment of priority derives from the archiving function and is thus at a lower level in the hierarchy.
5. Brown (2001 and 2003) provides some interesting and useful analysis of the usage and citation characteristics of the physics arXiv and chemical preprint servers.
6. Electronic separates may become even more popular due to the emergence of preprint servers and institutional repositories.

6

The emergence of digital scholarship

We have already seen that the emergence of online tools to engage with digitised information, especially since the mid-1990s, has opened up unprecedented information access routes on wide-ranging subjects for members of the public. More pertinently, these developments have created new opportunities for information search and use within formal learning contexts such as those found in higher education. The aim of this book is to examine the proposition that there is a Google Generation. This is not a new idea. Other authors have already identified this phenomenon and applied different labels to it, such as the Net Generation (Tapscott, 2009). Tapscott has claimed that the Internet and other computerised, electronic technologies – fixed and mobile – do not simply represent new channels through which standard hard-copy information can be obtained. Instead these technologies have changed the way young people engage with the world around them, including the way they socialise, spend their leisure time, obtain entertainment and learn. Our focus is placed on information seeking and usage in the context of learning.

Do young people – and students in particular – display new kinds of information-searching and information-using behaviours? Do they have different expectations about the way information as knowledge should be packaged and presented from older generations? If so, what do these changes mean for the way learning materials in educational contexts are packaged? If, as Tapscott (2009) claims, young people of his 'Net Generation' seek to become more involved in the creation of knowledge content, what does this mean for the roles played by academic tutors and employers in the future? If they expect to be able to access knowledge content, regardless of subject matter, instantly, what does this mean for the roles played by content repositories such as libraries in the future? These are important questions and this book does not pretend to have all the answers. Its aim is to explore available evidence about the use of online tools to find out whether information-related practices are changing and, if so, what their implications are for the future for all those involved in the production, storage and dissemination of knowledge content.

As we have seen already, there are a number of signs of change. In the wider social environment, ever-growing numbers of people are linked to online technologies such as the Internet across nearly all age groups (Madden, 2005; Horrigan, 2006). Young people, however, seem to be more richly linked in a broader diversity of ways than are older people. While most people up to the age of 65 now report use of e-mail, the under 40s remain ahead of older Internet users in the adoption of second-generation web tools (Dutton and Helsper, 2007; Madden and Fox, 2006).

Within more formal learning settings, as we saw in the previous chapter, evidence has emerged about the way e-books and e-journals are used and about different modes of adoption of online search facilities. It is not a simple case of 'off with the old' and 'on with the new', however. There are early adopters who readily explore new information search facilities and develop new learning styles. There are in addition those who still adhere to many conventional learning sources and strategies. The last observation can be true of online information-searching behaviours across age groups.

This chapter examines the literature from a wide range of sources – including academic research papers, articles from professional magazines and opinion pieces from library bulletins – to elicit information on the information behaviour of young people. A specific aim was to establish whether there has been a change in the way that teenagers (and young undergraduates) approach information, libraries and research, occasioned by advances in technology and, as importantly, in the *availability* of technology. Of major interest is the exploitation of Internet search engines – particularly Google – and use of portable ICT devices that can be used for information retrieval.

In order to test whether there is any evidence to suggest that today's young people are different from earlier generations, evidence from several different source-types were examined. These include:

- contemporaneous comparisons between teenagers and older users (Bilal and Kirby, 2002) or between a wide age-range of young people (Shenton and Dixon, 2003a, 2003b, 2003c, 2004);

- accounts of current activities of teenagers in which changing behaviour may be assumed because the subjects use technology not available in the past (e.g. Agosto, 2002; Agosto and Hughes-Hassell, 2005; Borgman et al., 1995);

- historic (1990s) studies of teenage information behaviour (e.g. Pivec, 1998; Soloman, 1993) which may be compared to later papers examining this topic (such as those by Agosto and Hughes-Hassell (2005) or Corradini (2006)), although it is difficult to compare studies as they are seldom replications of earlier work;

- commentary/opinion articles, such as by journalists (e.g. Knight and Manson, 2006), librarians (e.g. Pavey, 2006) or students themselves (e.g. Windham, 2005), often based on personal experience;

- miscellaneous material, such as from market research (e.g. Synovate, 2007), and reports of as yet unpublished work (e.g. Rodgers, 2007).

Not including market research or other miscellaneous material, 86 papers were reviewed and analysed for this purpose. Of these, 49 involved original research 'in the field' (e.g. Borgman et al., 1995; Cooper, 2002); seven reviewed past literature on the subject (e.g. Hsieh-Yee, 2001) and 24 were commentary/opinion articles. There were also six 'false drops' – articles retrieved which dealt too peripherally with the topic being investigated here to be of interest. In addition, data were re-examined from research conducted by the contributors that investigated the use of electronic and print information sources for scholarly information applications.

This review begins with an examination of young people's use of and ability with information and communications technology in their information behaviour, and their exploitation of other sources. Following this, we consider a variety of sources of opinion and commentary on the subject of the 'Google Generation'. Rather than simply outlining these, specific claims are taken from these articles and examined in the light of the research evidence to see the extent to which they can be validated. It is hoped that by taking this 'twin-track' approach of looking first at academic research and then at anecdote and opinion – and holding this up to the light of research findings – a detailed and authentic picture of the characteristics of the Google Generation and how they differ from previous cohorts may be established.

Overview of studies reviewed

Virtually half (24/49) of the research studies reviewed had sample sizes of 50 or below. Indeed, of the 15 studies with 100 plus subjects, five represent what is almost certainly the same sample of 188 children aged

4 to 18 years from various schools in the Whitley Bay area of the UK reported on by Shenton and Dixon (2002, 2003a, 2003b, 2003c, 2004). Another study in this category (Soloman, 1993) did not state the exact sample size, saying only that '902 OPAC transactions performed by about 500 students were observed ... A few children from each grade were observed' (p. 248), although whether an exact number is required in such an observational study is open to debate. Other studies with more than 200 participants were all survey based, including one (Livingstone et al., 2005) where a questionnaire was delivered face to face.

The qualitative work generally uses modest sized samples that are not generally selected so as to be representative of wider populations. Thus it is important to be cautious about generalising from such small-scale studies (such as those by Fidel et al., 1999, Agosto, 2002, or Hirsh, 1999, who worked with 8, 11 and 10 subjects respectively). The significance of this type of research lies with the insights it can provide into the way people think about questions and reflect in much richer ways on their behaviour than would be permitted by larger-scale surveys that use pre-structured questioning thats limit the ranges of responses permitted.

A point of interest here is the large number of studies that took place in an educational setting. This is not surprising with regard to children up to the age of 16 or 18, although, in fact, papers by Agosto (2005, 2006)[1] and Holloway and Valentine (2001) did not study this age group in a school context. However, all (10) of the studies which looked at young adults were university-based. As Large (2005) has pointed out:

> In comparisons between young people and adults, ... [research] ... has focused very heavily on university students, who may not be the most interesting group to compare with children and teens. It would be revealing to see how children compare with less well-educated adult populations whose language manipulation skills, for example, may be different from those in the university community. (p. 359)

Methods used

While a significant proportion of the studies reviewed here (38 out of 80) used a qualitative methodology, 11 studies used quantitative methodologies, most usually surveys. Much of this research, however, employed more than one data-gathering method, including observation (Soloman, 1993), video observation (Large et al., 1998), scrutiny of work resulting from the Internet or other research (Large et al., 1998) and open questionnaires (Corradini, 2006). Indeed, only nine of the forty research papers reviewed (e.g. Peter and Valkenburg, 2006; Gardner and Eng, 2005; Pivek, 1998; Costello et al., 2004) report findings from studies not incorporating at least one qualitative method.

The academic research evidence

Most academic studies have examined the behaviour of a current (or contemporary) cohort of young people (e.g. Agosto, 2002, 2005; Borgman et al., 1995) without comparing results with those accrued historically. There is, perhaps surprisingly, a relative absence of literature comparing age groups, and those studies that have done this (e.g. Shenton and Dixon, 2003a, 2003b, 2003c, 2004) tended to focus on age groups within the range of general education, rather than comparing teenagers with people in their late twenties or thirties and so on. Nevertheless, of particular importance for the current discussion is an outline of how young people behave. Whether similar patterns are reflected in the practices of their elders is of secondary importance.

Use of information technology

We have already examined patterns of change in the information and communication technology environment in wider social contexts and how these have varied across age groups. It is worth revisiting some of the evidence again here, though, in setting the scene of how such technology has impacted upon scholarly information-related activities. As seen in Chapter 2, studies of how young people use information technology – generally in the form of the Internet – in their everyday lives began appearing in the late 1990s. In one early study, Pivek (1998) found that the main use of the Internet was looking for and choosing friends. Holloway and Valentine (2001) also found this a major feature in the use of a computer at home. D'Esposito and Gardner (1999) added, in research carried out in 1997, that, in addition to communicating with and locating friends and relatives, downloading music was a popular Internet pastime – a practice that is still popular. According to market researchers Synovate (2007), the computer had become the most popular device for listening to music (81 per cent), although only one in four of its young respondents (25 per cent) listened online. The amount of downloads (41 per cent) had overtaken music purchased in shops (33 per cent) in people's collections.

In sum, it appears that from the beginning of its appearance in the home, the Internet has been used for recreational purposes and as a communication medium as well as to find information. As online technology has moved on, the range of online applications available to users has expanded along with the skills of users to utilise them. The Web 2.0 era has witnessed the growth of more advanced communication networks in the online world and greater involvement of users in the creation of content. In addition, the Internet is now available on an ever-widening array of platforms and devices, such as 'PDA, the Tablet PC, and the Ipod' (Shih and Allen, 2006: 90). This means that users can retain online access even when on the move. It is perhaps, therefore, not surprising that the Internet is now used more than television (Synovate, 2007; Los Angeles Times/Bloomberg, 2007a).

One further interesting observation by Windham (2005) was that the 'Net Generation' are more likely these days to log on to a news website for the latest information than to turn on a TV station such as CNN. Of course, the difference here is one of medium rather than the source itself. The CNN website may well be one consulted in preference to its TV partner – not, therefore, representing much of a radical change. It is relevant here to know whether young people's use of blogs or other personal web space sites is, in any way, driven by preferred news sources. It is apparent that the distinction between TV viewing and Internet activity is becoming blurred by the presence of TV channels broadcasting entirely or selectively over the Internet (one can now watch BBC News 24 on the Web, for example, raising the spectre of one being in the quantum 'super-position' of both watching and not watching TV at the same time). It has also been observed that in a news context, the reputation of brands drives loyalty to them and that similar principles may eventually come to apply to blogs (Gunter et al., 2008).

Interestingly, social networking, heralded as the innovation set to 'rapidly chang[e] the face of education' (Baird and Fisher, 2005) 'may not be enjoying the rampant success that has been assumed in the media (e.g. Walters, 2007). A study by the market research company Synovate found that 'only a quarter of respondents have ever used social networking sites like MySpace and blogging is still very niche (only

15 per cent ever do it)' (Synovate, 2007: unpaginated). However, a Los Angeles Times/Bloomberg entertainment poll (Los Angeles Times/Bloomberg 2007a) found that half of young adults visit social networking sites, but use drops away by those over 21. Clearly, as with other aspects of the take-up of new technology, more research is needed to establish a clearer picture.

Searching expertise

Much has been said recently about the apparent expertise of children using electronic resources. Indeed, the prestigious Pew Internet and American Life Project's 'Digital Disconnect' (Levin and Arafeh, 2002) was already writing about 'the widening gap between Internet-savvy students and their schools' five years ago, claiming from interviews with young people that they use the Internet for 'dozens of different education-related uses' (p. ii), including as a 'virtual tutor ... textbook and reference library ... guidance counsellor ... [and] study group' (p. iii), while their schools 'have not yet responded to the new ways in which students [use] the Internet' (p. iii).

On the same theme, Hay (2006: unpaginated) opines that 'Net Generation kids tend to be far more comfortable with and more proficient using information technologies than are their parents or teachers'. More specifically, Baird and Fisher (2005: 12) claim that young people are 'technologically savvy' and 'especially adept at quickly scanning a web page and deciding which links hold the promise of producing a "mother load" of information or valuable content'.

A major theme of this book is to look at the extent to which young people are, indeed, experts in ICT use, and to elicit from literature of the 1990s and 2000s whether the levels of expertise among children of a given age range has risen with ever more exposure to the technology. This appears to have been the assumption of many commentators, including those cited above and others (e.g. Kipnis and Childs, 2005; Windham, 2005).

Expertise in formulating search expressions and generally interrogating information systems (predominantly, of course, these days, the Internet) has been a preoccupation of researchers for a long time. There is little evidence in the literature generated for claims that young people are expert searchers, or even that the search prowess of young people has improved with time. Studies pre-date not only the Internet but other electronic systems. Soloman (1993), for example, describes a study by Joyce and Joyce (1970) in which researchers 'implemented a prototype data bank and observed children using its index scheme to find answers 'that would be sufficient to teach a classmate about a chosen topic' (p. 247). In a later study, which approximated an electronic environment a little more, Moore and St George (1991) investigated the information retrieval process used by grade six children (11 year olds) in New Zealand in an assignment about birds. Much difficulty was reported in selecting search terms with which to find appropriate material from a card catalogue, and participants did not try alternative terms if their original efforts proved unsuccessful.

In the electronic media, Soloman (1993) also found that children had difficulties formulating appropriate terms, due to their 'use of natural language questions (how to build bird's nests) and multiple concepts (horses poetry)' (p. 259). Spavold (1990) found children were 'less confident' in 'problem-solving' database queries when compiling and interrogating a database of family records, and that their grasp of commands was 'confused and easily forgotten' (p. 619). With adequate support and training, however, participants in both of these early studies did acquire a certain level of competence.

Later, Hirsh (1999) found that students considered only the presence or absence of words exactly describing their search topic/matching their search terms in deciding relevance. By focusing so narrowly on this aspect of material retrieved, they missed many other relevant documents. He also found that students did not use advanced search facilities or navigation aids.

Chen (2003) also noted difficulties in formulating search queries, claiming that 'children and youth' have trouble generating alternative search terms/synonyms (when the original terms prove fruitless) and often repeat the same search several times. Not surprisingly, they also found difficulty narrowing a search. Also unsurprisingly, research consistently suggests that students do not plan searches in advance (Bilal, 2001; Large et al., 1999; Shenton and Dixon, 2004).

One manifestation of the lack of query formulation is the prevalence of full phrase searching by young people (as noted above by Solomon, 1993). A review by Schacter et al. (1998: 847), for example, of the search logs associated with children's (given) search tasks indicated that 20 of the 32 children used 'full sentence requests, such as, "What are the three most common crimes in California?" and "How to reduce crime in California?"' in their query formulation. Other researchers (e.g. Chen, 2003; Bilal,

2000) have also noted full phrase searching in young people's query formulation.

It would be tempting to attribute this activity to the rise in the accessibility of the Internet. The Web, of course, may be searched with impunity using natural language (Searchenginewatch.com, 2005). This is taken to its logical conclusion in 'Ask.com' (previously 'Ask Jeeves') which encourages users to enter full phrases as search terms (an example in its help file is 'the following search example should successfully lead you to the desired information: "where can I find cheap airfare to New York?"' (Ask.com, 2007: unpaginated). However, a scrutiny of the literature shows that the practice of formulating queries in this way pre-dates the web. Marchionini (1989) is one researcher who noted such queries on a CD-Rom encyclopaedia. Younger subjects ['3rd and 4th graders', or 8 and 9 year olds] were more likely to use actual sentences to query the system' (p. 61) although many older participants (10–11 year olds) also adopted this practice. From her review of the literature, Valenza (2006) observed that students often assume search engines understand sentences and questions.

With regard to young people's understanding of the way information is organised, the way results are returned and differences between search interfaces, Valenza (2006) concluded from earlier literature that understanding of these features tended to be limited, citing Fidel et al. (1999), Bilal and Kirby (2002) and Chen (2003). In conclusion, it may be that the general lack of increase in expertise in information retrieval may be due – ironically – to the perceived ease with which digital systems (as exemplified by the Web) can be searched. This is because there appears to have been a consequent lack of support by teachers and other carers. A common theme of several studies (e.g. Bilal and Kirby, 2002; Hirsh, 1999; Fidel et al., 1999; Oblinger and Hawkins, 2006) is that more training is needed to enable effective use of digital technologies.

Evaluating electronic resources

One area of current interest, and, indeed, concern, is the way young people evaluate information from electronic sources. There is little evidence that this aspect of information has changed over the last ten or fifteen years. Two main criteria dominate the literature: relevance and quality/authority. With regard to the first of these, Chen (1993) was suggesting nearly fifteen years ago that teenagers did not review information retrieved (in this case from an online database) and, consequently, undertook unnecessary supplementary searches.

Later Schacter et al. (1998) found that the speed of young people's web searching also indicated that little time was spent in evaluating information (a result also found by Chen, 2003). In another study from the late 1990s, Williams (1999) observed information-seeking stopping at the point where articles were found and printed, especially with regard to younger users. Little regard was made to the text itself – a word in the title or an appropriate accompanying image was enough to confirm relevance. Maintaining this trend into the 2000s, Merchant and Hepworth (2002) studied the research habits of 40 pupils from 10 to 16 years, and found that teachers complained that when their charges found articles using difficult language, 'they just print off or copy down and hand in' (p. 84). Hsieh-Yee (2001), reviewing literature on Internet use generally, also concluded, from a résumé of papers on children's usage behaviour, that they had difficulty judging the quality of web pages.

Researchers have similarly found a lack of attention young people give to the issue of authority. Hirsh (1999), for example, found that students did not consider at all issues of authority of source when evaluating websites. Grimes and Boening (2001) found in a case study of 50 'freshmen' students in the USA that participants evaluated web resources in terms of quality of information 'only superficially, if at all' (p. 19). In fact, they were 'ill-equipped and unwilling to evaluate resources' (p. 20). Lorenzen (2001) found in his interviews with 15–17 year olds that many thought that if a site was indexed by Yahoo! it had to be authoritative, and so the question of evaluating websites did not arise. A later study, by Shenton and Dixon (2003c), found that there was no attempt by anyone (in any of the age groups studied which ranged from 4 to 16) to verify information in fact, and evaluative skills were lacking. Merchant and Hepworth (2002) suggested that it was 'difficult for students to understand that the first solution they find may not be the only answer' (p. 85).

D'Esposito and Gardner (1999), however, claim that in their qualitative study of 14 mainly undergraduates (admittedly older than the school-aged children studied by Shenton and Dixon), participants used many criteria for evaluating the quality of websites and the reliability of the information: 'authorship or page ownership, links to other sites, and the possibility of validation from other sources' (D'Esposito and Gardner, 1999: 458). However, in this study, participants were asked what steps they undertook to evaluate material. Studies such as that by

Shenton and Dixon (2003c), in which participants were observed rather than prompted, or those such as by Schacter et al. (1998), where participants are asked simply to rate information, consistently find that evaluative skills are barely in evidence.

Use of library and information services

Regarding use, understanding and awareness of library services, previous literature indicates that even in the mid-2000s, large numbers of young people are unaware that libraries offer Internet access. One study by Corradini (2006), for example, found that only 42 per cent of youngsters knew this, despite being library users. Indeed, the image of the library was still 'almost completely bound to its traditional printed materials' (p. 490). The international OCLC (Online Computer Library Center) (2002) found that although 70 per cent of university students used their library websites for some assignment-related information, only 20 per cent did so for most assignments. Full-text articles are used the most often (67 per cent), with electronic books (21 per cent) and online reference (6 per cent) being used the least often. However, a full 90 per cent of students also use their library's print resources, again reinforcing the view that the library is still seen as predominantly print-based. A contrasting survey in the UK by Myhill (2007), which found that the library OPAC and university web pages were well-used – especially by students in their final year – may have been due to the study design, which consisted of an online questionnaire hosted on the library website.

Findings indicating a lack of appreciation of the electronic services of libraries reflect those of earlier studies, and appear to indicate little change in terms of young people's perception of libraries. For example, in D'Esposito and Gardner's (1999) study of undergraduates' perception of the Internet, although participants acknowledged that the Internet was available in the library and that library web pages were accessible on the Internet, 'the general perception was that the library and the Internet were two separate and unrelated entities' (p. 58).

Early studies also corroborate later work with regard to the perceptions of 'libraries' and 'the Internet'. Fidel et al. (1999) found that for his small sample of 11th and 12th grade students (17 and 18 year olds) a visit to the school library was time-consuming and labour-intensive. Study participants all preferred to research information independently on the Internet. This attitude appears to have continued. Pavey (2006) claimed from personal experience that children often arrive at higher education level never having used a library. Even where the library is acknowledged to have a variety of electronic resources, these may not be well exploited. In an opinion piece, Lippincott (2005) claimed that students often found 'library-sponsored' sources of information difficult to negotiate, and so preferred to use the more simplistic Google.

Opinion, assumption and anecdotal evidence

Apparent differences in the information behaviour of current and earlier teenagers is often claimed by authors writing opinion pieces, much of it based on personal experience or opinions, often lacking in empirical evidence (e.g. Kipnis and Childs, 2005; Geck, 2006) or inferring differences from data which might not necessarily support them (Gardner and Eng, 2005). The following analysis tests these views against the body of empirical evidence accrued from the research literature. Meanwhile, it is worth noting some general assumptions made by opinion and commentary pieces. First, the cohort of youngsters discussed is generally considered as a homogenous body – indeed, hence a group name 'Google Generation'. Second, everyone seems to be equipped with the latest gadgetry – iPod, laptop, mobile phone connected to the Internet, etc., and will have been brought up on a diet of ICT. None of the literature reviewed discusses young people who do not wish to be surrounded by technology or do not have the resources to be so. Third, there is an assumption that the students are overwhelmingly dedicated to studying (see, for example, Gardner and Eng, 2005) and are happy to invest time exploring information sources for the most appropriate in order to carry out their assignments. As described below, there is much evidence to refute some of these assumptions.

The claims

Google Generation show a preference for visual information over text (e.g. Kipnis and Childs, 2005).

There is certainly a strong liking for the visual in picture form, but text still carries a lot of influence in conveying information (the popularity of texting – even over voice messages – testifies to this fact). Text still rules. But there are also new forms of grammar emerging. A new form of shorthand text communication has emerged online together with the use of visual symbols to convey emotion. This is a form of substitution for the lower form of 'social presence' (Short et al., 1976) offered by online texting compared to face-to-face communication. The growing popularity of video cameras and live video links via the Internet demonstrates that as people of all ages become more confident with ICTs, technologies improve and costs reduce, video links may come to replace text links in the social networking context. This may be significant in higher education as well for certain types of communication between tutor and student, where face-to-face links are more reassuring than text links. It is worth noting, as Sullivan (2005) does, that audio and visual forms of information presentation are hardly new: 'Audio and visual methods of storytelling and learning have served a vast population for many … millennia' (Sullivan, 2005: 58).

There is also an issue within this topic about reading. There is an underlying theme in the commentary and opinion pieces written on the topic of young people and information technology, that reading is eschewed these days in favour of computers, video games, digital music players, video cams, cell phones 'and all the other toys and tools of the digital age' (Prensky, 2001: unpaginated). Prensky cites unreferenced figures that 'today's average college grads have spent less than 5,000 hours of their lives reading, but over 10,000 hours playing video games (not to mention 20,000 hours watching TV)'. Similarly, Kipnis and Childs (2005) opine that, because of this use of and familiarity with digital media, 'providing documentation that is text heavy is a disservice to the students' (p. 27).

In fact, there is evidence that young people are reading more than previously, despite the additional attractions vying for their attention these days. The BBC (Rodgers, 2007: unpaginated) cites (as yet unpublished) research from the University of Manchester's Dale Southerton that 'people in the UK are reading more than they did a quarter of a century ago … while Britons spent just three minutes a day on average reading a book in 1975, by 2000 this rose to seven minutes. And when magazines and newspapers were taken into account, Britons were reading five minutes more every day in 2000, compared to their 1970s counterparts.' The article adds that 'The new findings fly in the face of many people's assumptions about modern Britain.' The market research company Synovate also found in a survey on how young people spend their lesisure time that books are read regularly by 49 per cent of respondents, and 41 per cent read magazines regularly (Synovate, 2007).

The news that young people are reading is not surprising when one considers the 'Harry Potter' phenomenon. Both the latest (and last) in the series *Harry Potter and the Deathly Hallows* (Rowling, 2007) and the earlier *Harry Potter and the Half-Blood Prince* (Rowling, 2006) contain no fewer than 608 pages, and *Harry Potter and the Order of the Phoenix* (Rowling, 2003) is even longer, being 768 pages and 255,000 words (BBC, 2003) long. Despite this, sales have been enormous, with more than two million copies of *The Half-Blood Prince* being sold in the first 24 hours in the UK (BBC, 2005).

Clarke and Foster (2005) undertook a survey of over 8,000 primary and secondary pupils in England to explore why some pupils chose to read and others did not. They found that 'half the sample of pupils said they enjoy reading either very much or quite a lot and rated themselves as proficient readers. The majority of pupils read every day or once/twice a week ... Pupils generally held positive attitudes towards reading – agreeing with statements that reading is important and disagreeing with statements that reading is boring, hard, or for girls rather than boys' (2005: 2).

Even when electronic media are considered, there is some evidence that text was not eschewed by young users, simply because information was presented in other ways. Apart from studies by Fidel et al. (1999) and Large et al. (1998) which showed children opting for textual information in order to complete assignments more effectively, Loh and Williams (2002) show that text may be as interesting to children as other media even when there is no pressure to complete school work. They looked at children's perceptions of web design elements and features they considered 'cool'. The researchers concluded that 'content was more important for children than presentation; the novelty, colour, sound, and animation may initially draw children to a Web site, but after the novelty effect faded, it was interesting content that motivated children to return to the site' (quoted in Large, 1998: 364).

Even if it were the case that young people prefer visual information, it could be argued that, rather than be a disservice to them by continuing to provide information in this way, as suggested by Kipnis and Childs (2005), the disservice would be to accede to such wishes. According to the US National Institute for Literacy (NIFL, 2007):

> The ability to read and understand complicated information is important to success in college and, increasingly, in the workplace.

An analysis of the National Assessment of Educational Progress [US Department of Education project] long-term trend reading assessments reveals that only half of all White 17 year olds, less than one-quarter of Latino 17 year olds, and less than one-fifth of African American 17 year olds can read at this level. By age 17, only about 1 in seventeen 17 year olds can read and gain information from specialized text, for example the science section in the local newspaper. (Haycock and Huang, 2001)

Clearly, therefore, it is the still the duty of educators to promote literacy – in its narrow sense of reading text – to young people.

> *Google Generation want a variety of learning experiences,* and are used to being entertained (Kipnis and Childs, 2005; Hay, 2000).

Information media must be interesting or they will fail to be used to their full potential, which is simply to restate the above in a slightly different way and to expose it as a tautology. Some library commentators argue that games technologies, for example, should be used to engage users in new and exciting ways (e.g. Squire and Steinkuehler, 2005). However, great care is needed here. There are analogies with work conducted on broadcast TV news 20–30 years ago. News-makers increasingly used entertainment show production techniques to the detriment of news content (Postman, 1985). These techniques enhanced 'interest' but impeded learning.

The research literature on young people's use of information technology in their learning suggests that in the case of assignment completion at least, what was more important than entertainment or interest was to finish by expending the least amount of effort. Large et al. (1998), for example, in an admittedly older study, found that young people seldom used the multimedia resources when searching to solve school-based tasks as it was harder to extract the exact information required. Fidel et al. (1999) found this also. The children he observed 'kept exploration to a minimum, and … ignored entertaining diversions on the screen, such as moving images' (p. 28) in order to complete tasks. This behaviour was even more marked in the study by Large et al. (1998), mentioned above, where moving and still images were almost ignored in the quest to find text that could be printed out and used to answer a set task. However, there was evidence in both papers that when students were not under any obligation to find specific information, they 'often relied on information that was displayed in a graphic form [using graphics] as if they were abstracts or even indexes to Web sites. They inferred from graphics what the sites were about and whether or not they were likely to be useful' (Fidel et al. 1999: 35).

There is some indirect evidence to refute the claim that today's young people do not like being passive recipients of information (Kipnis and Childs, 2005) or that they want to learn through exploration (Windham, 2005). In fact, as noted above, many examples may be found in research studies that showed a distinct disinclination to explore. Those already mentioned relate to the Internet/CD-Rom and electronic resources generally. This appears to be a manifestation of a general inclination to take the easiest route possible in undertaking tasks. Shenton and Dixon (2003b, 2004), for example, found that in researching for school assignments, pupils used the same sources (e.g. the same website) over a number of searches. Unsurprisingly, these were often the most convenient or accessible sources used (e.g. a reference book at home). In fact, there were several ways in which seekers attempted to simplify the search process in order to expend the minimal effort (e.g. the first sources found were frequently the only ones used; only one search term used; quality of information rarely assessed or corroborated). Similarly, Fidel et al. (1999) found that students kept exploration to a minimum, even ignoring multimedia in an effort to complete tasks with the least effort possible.

Away from academic study, an interesting poll by Los Angeles Times/Bloomberg into TV watching habits is worth quoting at length. It found that:

> About a third of teenagers [aged 12–17] said they didn't have TiVo or any other recording devices, but of those who did, a third are still watching the *same* number of TV shows at their scheduled times, while another 13 per cent said they are watching *more* shows at their respective times. However, a fifth said they are recording shows and watching them on their own schedule. Nearly half of the young adults [aged 18–24] said they don't have any recording devices, but 23 per cent are watching the *same* number of shows at their scheduled times, while 12 per cent are watching *more*, while about a fifth are recording shows and watching them at their convenience. (Los Angeles Times/Bloomberg, 2007b: unpaginated)

In other words, only 20 per cent of teenagers and young adults are 'time-shifting' their TV viewing.

> *Google Generation have shifted decisively to digital forms of communication*, preferring typing to handwriting (e.g. Frand, 2000), messaging to talking on the phone (e.g. Windham, 2005).

It is almost certainly true that many children are acquiring advanced key skills, both for using mobile phones and computer keyboards, but the popularity of messaging is probably determined largely by its low cost relative to voice, so it is difficult to see this as a fundamental trend. Windham's (2005) assertion that today's students eschew the telephone may also only be partially true. She claims that 'it's not that we can't use the telephone … it's just that doing either is so much more difficult. Using e-mail to set up meetings, ask simple questions, or send in excuses for absences has become so commonplace that few students turn to anything else' (p. 56). Although not explicitly saying so, it seems clear that the communication here is between student and university staff. By contrast, Agosto and Hughes-Hassell (2005) found that many of their sample of (younger) respondents (aged 14–17) expressed only 'limited interest in communicating via computers (Internet, e-mail), [feeling that (cellular)] telephones were more convenient and afforded increased personal contact' (p. 154), albeit the study looked at general information-seeking, and did not focus on communication with superiors/staff etc.

We are not aware of any research that really digs deep into these issues. Anecdotally, it seems likely that many children would prefer to type an assignment rather than use handwriting, but the deeper question raised above cannot be answered at the moment – we think it is still wide open.

> *Google Generation 'multi-task'* (e.g. Windham, 2005) and are good at this (e.g. Long, 2005).

There is some evidence for the former, according to a Los Angeles Times/Bloomburg poll (2007b): 'About three in five teens and young adults said they prefer to multitask rather than focusing on doing one thing at a time. Multitasking relieves boredom, according to more than half of those who said they prefer to have several things going at once.' However, there is no hard evidence (indeed, this appears to have been a neglected area of academic research) into whether young people 'multi-task' more than other age groups or whether they are adept at handling a number of simultaneous information streams together. Further, there is little evidence to support the extent of multi-tasking claimed by some commentators. The idea that 'many young people today are accustomed to watching TV, talking on the phone, doing homework, eating, and interacting with their parents all at the same time' (Frand, 2000: 18) is, frankly, faintly ridiculous – although such claims are common. To give another example, Long (2005: 187) claims that while doing homework 'the iPod is in the ear listening to music. Instant messaging is going on with a variety of other kids via some sort of handheld device. The phone is cradled between head and shoulder for conversation ... and the PC is cranked up to the Internet.' It is no surprise that with such extravagant and persistent claims, there is a general assumption that young people can multi-task with ease.

> *Google Generation are impatient and have zero tolerance for delay –* information and entertainment needs must be fulfilled immediately (e.g. Johnson, 2006; Shih and Allen, 2006).

This statement is often presented as a truism of the age in which we live though it is not simply the preserve of the younger generation. Studies of online user behaviour have revealed that the need for rapid response crosses all generational boundaries in the digital environment. The speed of new media has cultivated a lowered tolerance for delay. Furthermore, the 'anthropomorphization' of technology (Luczak et al., 2003) means that users respond to computerised devices in the way they do to people (see also Reeves and Nass, 1996). Users assign personalities to technologies, especially interactive technologies, and expect them to respond in the same way. There is no evidence that we aware of to suggest that young people are more impatient in this regard than older people. All we can do is to repeat the obvious: that older age groups have memories that pre-date digital media experiences; the younger constituency does not.

> *Google Generation find their peers more credible as a source of information than authority figures,* hence their intense interest in social networking and the effectiveness of viral marketing (e.g. Manuel, 2002).

On balance, we think this is a myth. It depends of course on the specific context: the popularity of social networking does not provide evidence per se that immediate peers are valued over authoritative content, merely that technology is being used to cement existing social and collaborative networks, extending them where necessary.

Research in the specific context of the information resources that children prefer and value in a secondary school setting (Madden et al., 2007) shows that teachers, relatives and textbooks are consistently valued above the Internet for helping to complete homework assignments. We feel that this claim is not incisive: it seems to have more to do with the social networking subculture and teenagers' naturally rebellious tendencies. Its specific application to the world of education and libraries is pretty questionable.

> *Google Generation need to feel constantly connected to the Web* and their social and family networks (Frand, 2005).

This may be true of some but not all users. The significance and nature of these connections will vary as a function of the user's personality and background and some will develop a stronger dependence on social networks than others. And older people are catching up fast in terms of their use of online networks: 'Lots of people think that older people are not plugged into the digital world. This is clearly wrong,' according to an Age Concern spokesman quoted in a report published by the UK *Daily Telegraph*. 'Many are extremely engaged with the Internet and use it regularly to keep in touch with family, to shop and take part in communities' (*Daily Telegraph*, 23 August 2007). The concept of the web-savvy older generation was reinforced by data published by the UK communications regulator. Ofcom (2007e) reported that the over 65s spent four hours a week *longer* online than 18–24s. This evidence clearly runs counter to the notion that there is a specific age-defined 'Google Generation'.

> *Google Generation learn by doing rather than knowing* – while their elders are still reading the manual, Google Generation teenagers are cracking the problem by trial and error rather than by scientific method (e.g. Lippencott, 2005; Long, 2005).

Even though older generations may use the Internet, use per se may not be sufficient to define what it means to be a fully paid-up member of the 'Google Generation'. The latter is defined instead by the nature of a user's online behaviour. In particular, this means that those of the Google

Generation are more sophisticated users and acquire their skills through trial and error. Once again, research evidence provided by Ofcom (2006) provides mixed support for this idea. It certainly appeared that teenagers and young adults were more likely than adults aged 55 and over to learn about digital services by online trial and error. Younger online users were no more likely to do this, however, than those aged 35–54, among whom we can probably count a significant proportion of parents of under 20s (see Figure 6.1). These findings therefore present less than clear-cut evidence from which to confer the Google Generation with any special status.

Figure 6.1 Learning about online services

Preferred ways to learn about digital services and products

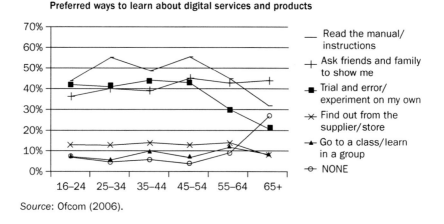

Source: Ofcom (2006).

> *Google Generation prefer quick information in the form of easily digested short chunks rather than full text.*

There is overwhelming evidence from primary deep log studies conducted by the authors of a distinctive form of online information behaviour associated with students (see Huntington and Nicholas, 2008). In a series of analyses, the use made of e-journals and e-books by university students and academics was examined using three online databases.[2] Compared with faculty, students conducted many more search sessions but viewed relatively few pages. Students more often relied on simple thematic (rather than author) searches and were actually less likely than academic staff to view abstracts rather than full text. However, both students and academics shared a general tendency to shallow, horizontal, 'flicking' behaviour in digital libraries. Browsing and rapid viewing were the norm for all: more leisurely reading appears to be only occasionally undertaken online, and more often occurs offline or not at all. However, where more detailed online reading did take place, this was more likely to be found among students than among academics. In the strict sense of a specific Google Generation trait, we think that the claim that the quick presentation of information is a younger generation phenomenon is not fully supported. All online users increasingly exhibit this characteristic.

There is considerable evidence to support the view that many students do not explore information in any deep or reflective manner. The lack of any evaluative efforts on the part of information users has been documented above. According to Levin and Arafeh (2002) most students stop searching once they reach a point that is judged to be good enough to get by rather than putting themselves out to find the very best sources for their assignments. The Internet has come to be viewed as a way to complete schoolwork as quickly and painlessly as possible, with minimal effort and minimal engagement. For some, this includes viewing the Internet as a mechanism to plagiarise material or otherwise cheat, a practice described by Valenza (2006) as 'slacker culture'.

> *Google Generation have a poor understanding and lack of respect for intellectual property,* as exemplified by illegal music downloads and rampant plagiarism (Shih and Allen, 2006; Frand, 2005).

This seems to be only partly true. Both adults (83 per cent) and children aged 12–15 (76 per cent) self-report that they are aware that there are illegal as well as legal ways to access films, music and computer software on the Internet (Ofcom, 2006). On this evidence therefore we cannot posit 'poor understanding' on the younger generation. There are telling age differences when asked whether illegal accessing of online content should really be illegal. In this context, people aged 16–24 years (50 per cent) are more likely than those aged over 54 years (20 per cent) to say that accessing of copyrighted online content should be classified as legal. The over 54s (67 per cent) are much more likely than the 16–24s (40 per cent) to regard such activity as illegal (Ofcom, 2006).

It is worth noting that the issue of illegal copying has not just arisen with the advance of the home computer and the rise of facilitating soft/hardware. Concern about music copying, for example, goes back to the early 1980s (if not earlier) when the British Phonographic Industry (BPI) ran a 'Home Taping Is Killing Music' campaign, putting that slogan on record sleeves and in the music press (Dixon, 2005). With regard to software copying, an anti-copyright infringement advertising campaign run by the Software Publishers Association (SPA) 'Don't Copy That Floppy' began in 1992 (Wiseman, 2007).

> *Google Generation are format agnostic* and have little interest in the containers (reports, book chapters, encyclopaedia entries) that provide the context and wrapping for information 'nuggets'.

This statement may be true of some young users but certainly not all. We have not found any studies that address this important issue even obliquely, so we feel this one is still wide open. It is a hugely important issue for libraries and publishers, which makes its neglect in the research literature surprising. In the future, presentation will still be important in the online environment. There is an expectation that when online, the world becomes more interesting because the technology offers potentially more diverse and interesting styles of content presentation.

Future educational applications will need to recognise this fact and react accordingly. The idea, often referred to in the online news context as shovelware, of migrating offline content online in a form as close as possible to its original offline design will not generally work. The online world promises more and must deliver to be successful. But we certainly know at present, from e-book research, that offline printed books are preferred for cover-to-cover reading, while reference books that are dipped into here and there transfer best to the online environment (Gunter, 2005).

> *For the Google Generation, virtual reality may be as real as the real experience* (e.g. Frand, 2005).

This is probably a myth, since we cannot believe that younger people have a different understanding and experience of reality than their parents or grandparents. It is, however, generally salient to the project in the more limited sense that some libraries are experimenting with virtual reality environments in an attempt to better integrate their physical library with their digital resources and services.

Any blurring of what is real and what is virtual could though eventually become an issue in virtual worlds of the massive multiplayer variety such as Second Life. Here there are real business transactions taking place involving virtual money that can be converted into real money. Although it is clear that you are in a fantasy computer animated world, nevertheless there are real people underlying the avatars and some transactions are 'real' in the sense that they can cost you or make you real money. In a learning context, the virtual becomes 'real' if genuine learning transactions are taking place that determine the award of qualifications that have real-world recognition. So this is a complex issue and the impact of such virtual worlds on their participants could be very real in some circumstances.

Concluding remarks

In the next and final chapter, the lessons learned from this and earlier chapters will be pulled together with other relevant evidence to present a view of what the future might hold. As we have seen so far, the idea of a 'Google Generation' that is qualitatively different in terms of its information search procedures and habits from other generations is only partly supported by relevant evidence. Clearly, the existence of the Internet and the plethora of online tools it has generated have enhanced the ways people can search for information. Moreover, in an education context, the Internet and the World Wide Web have given rise to new tools for teaching and learning. Students turn to online sources for course-related information and as channels through which to engage dynamically with course materials, tutors and other students. New approaches to the construction of courses and to the publication of course-related texts have also emerged along with the Internet. All these changes carry potentially important implications for the roles of libraries, publishers and higher education institutions in the future. Will these changes be demanded by and will they serve a distinctive age-defined generation? Or will they be expected by anyone who has become Internet savvy?

Notes

1. Agosto's (2002) paper does use a school setting, however.
2. These databases were: Synergy, a digital journal database produced by Blackwell (2003) and covering more than 700 journals; OhioLINK, the database of a consortium in Ohio offering more than 6,000 journals (2004–7); and Oxford Scholarship Online (2007), a collection of e-monographs.

7

What next?

The review of evidence so far has indicated that information and communications technologies have exhibited dramatic growth in penetration post-1994. In addition, the nature of online technologies has evolved in a number of significant ways that may have implications for the future delivery of higher education. Digital technology has become firmly established and the Internet has been widely adopted, bringing with it a wide range of applications that have relevance to information searching and storage and knowledge acquisition and learning.

Recent predictions for the telecommunications and media worlds by one major consultancy have pointed out that while technology infrastructures have been established to ensure that most people in developed countries potentially can gain access to basic applications, connectivity per se does not remove all digital divides (Deloitte, 2007a, 2007b). In the case of the Internet, for example, there are varying degrees of connectivity. To take full advantage of advanced applications in the online world, broadband connectivity is essential. Yet this technology has not reached or been adopted by everyone. Even where governments have taken steps to facilitate broadband penetration, a plateau can be reached quite quickly with significant proportions of the population remaining without connectivity. In the United States, broadband penetration reached 60 per cent in 2002, but by 2006 it had only grown to 70 per cent. In the United Kingdom, nearly one in ten Internet users surveyed were lapsed users. Meanwhile, among non-users, a clear majority indicated that they had no intention of acquiring an Internet connection in the next year.

Despite the promise held by new technologies to bring fresh educational benefits to young people, even in developed countries like the UK significant numbers of children and their families do not have ready access to a computer (Livingstone, 2008). Thus, even though large proportions of children state that they find the Internet a valuable resource in getting information for their homework, this position does not apply to all children.

One of the key problems holding back universal or near-universal penetration could be the centrality of the personal computer to accessing the Internet. The PC alone, however, does not make the Internet relevant for everyone. For some applications, such as video-conferencing, additional equipment must be obtained to enhance the functionality of the basic PC. The most popular online activities comprise e-mail, search, surfing, shopping, booking travel, messaging, listening to and downloading music, and playing games. Some of these activities are best handled by the PC with its full keyboard. Others could be effectively handled by other devices. E-mail and messaging, for example, could be appropriately handled by mobile devices (Deloitte, 2007b).

Convergence of technology, application and consumption

One of the most significant developments to characterise rapidly evolving information and communication technologies has been the convergence of applications and facilities across technology platforms that has, in turn, been reflected in the way information consumers utilise technology devices. The association of discrete functions with specific technologies has been superseded by the emergence of multi-faceted technologies. Content is now produced and packaged for distribution across different technology platforms. Thus in the worlds of entertainment and news, producers now create content not for one medium but for multiple media applications, for example for television, for the Internet and for mobile phone consumption. Technologies once associated predominantly with one type of content now convey different types of content. Hence mobile phones are used not simply for voice communications but also as channels through which to convey text and pictures.

These changes have been reflected in turn in new business partnerships between service suppliers that were once associated with distinct sectors of provisions with their own non-overlapping markets of operation. Thus BSkyB, a broadcaster, and Google, a search engine, have teamed up to provide web-based search, advertising and video services to broadband Internet subscribers. Vodafone, a telecommunications operator, and Google have jointly produced a portfolio of Internet-based services available via mobile phones. The BBC and YouTube, a social network provider, have teamed up to supply BBC-branded entertainment channels to the social network's subscriber base. BT, a telecommunications operator, has joined with Sony (Japan), a computer and electronics manufacturer, to add wireless broadband Internet functionality to computer games consoles allowing such devices to be used for voice calls, video and text messaging as well as game playing (see Ofcom, 2007e).

The significance of these developments for information searching and educational applications derives from the implications they have for seamlessly switching between technologies for a range of different applications provided in different modalities. Such developments could cultivate a different mindset on the part of future generations in respect of the application expectations of specific technologies and will increase the choices available to information consumers in terms of opportunities to obtain, use and create content and in the tools that will become available to communicate that content with others.

New functions of specific communications technologies are taken up very quickly. The pace of innovation adoption is increasing all the time. The increasingly varied use of mobile phones is perhaps the best example of these developments. These are no longer purely voice messaging devices. Mobile phones are today widely used for sending text messages, creating and storing picture files, accessing the Internet and the reception of music, speech broadcasts and television programmes (Ofcom, 2007e).

The social web

Looking further at the expansion of Internet applications, key developments include the use of content generation tools by Internet users and the dramatic penetration among online populations of social networking. The latter application emerged as perhaps the biggest success within the Web 2.0 context during the first decade of the twenty-first century. The 'social web' has been coined as a term designed to represent these developments.

The Internet has opened up opportunities for ordinary people to become content creators or, if you like, 'citizen publishers'. Vast new information sources have become established in online repositories that have been the result of spontaneous cooperation and collaboration on the part of international virtual communities. Wikipedia has emerged as probably the biggest and best known repository of this type. Although English has been the dominant language in which information content has been generated within this forum, by 2007 content was actually held in over 250 different languages (Ofcom, 2007e). Other major social networks have emerged in which individuals produce and post content about themselves creating vast social contact networks. These networks have social functions in that they represent environments in which individuals can maintain contact with people they already know as well as making new social (and business) contacts. Such networks can also serve as information exchanges where online social contacts can provide advice, opinions, recommendations and critiques on a wide range of issues.

Online social networks have been widely adopted, especially by young people in the 15–30 age bracket (Deloitte, 2007a). Providers of these services must consider how to construct effective and profitable business models. One currency that they could trade in this very public environment is privacy. Premium fees could be charged to users who seek to go 'public' in a limited fashion and restrict access to their details to approved individuals. Deloitte's view on this is that such charging might actually encourage a broadening of the demographic profiles of online social networks with older users – who may be more likely to value such privacy – becoming more prevalent, while younger users may find such conditions less appealing.

The other major development identified with Web 2.0 is user-generated content. Here, Deloitte envisaged continuing expansion of the market, particularly in the context of video sharing on sites such as YouTube. However, the suggestion that YouTube posed a serious threat to established broadcasters might be both premature and overemphasised. While YouTube enjoys 100 million downloads every day and boasts 70 million unique users each month, the average video in the system is around three minutes long. The amount of time spent viewing YouTube videos globally therefore is around a tenth of the amount of time BBC TV programmes are watched in the UK alone.

Blogging is another rapid-growth user-generated content phenomenon. The impact of blogs, however, is limited given that an overwhelming majority receive few visitors (Deloitte, 2007a). In general, there is a lot of user-generated content – whether in video or text form – that is mediocre and of little interest to anyone other than family and friends of the content producers. Nonetheless, the user-generated content phenomenon is widely established and although many participants may have limited production skills the use of these technologies – especially among the Google Generation – has become normative.

Finding the tipping point

One key variable in deciding whether an ICT or ICT application is likely to be an important determinant of the future architecture or processes underpinning learning is the extent to which it has already become established. This decision rests on whether an ICT or its application has reached a tipping point or a critical mass of adoption beyond which it is likely to be adopted by a majority of potential users. Historical analyses of adoption of innovations have indicated that this point is usually reached at between 10 and 25 per cent penetration of the potential user population.

On this basis, it is clear that the Internet will play an important part in the provision of education at all levels in the future. The tipping point in terms of Internet adoption was reached across most age groups by 2000 in the UK and also in the USA. Other countries in the developed world have also displayed similar levels of penetration and adoption. Only the over-65s lag behind in general Internet adoption.

Another important driver has been adoption of broadband Internet. This has represented a later online development and one that has critical importance to educational applications of digital technologies because it allows for the flow of much larger quantities of information much more rapidly than the earlier narrowband Internet. By 2006, four in ten people in the UK (39 per cent) reportedly had a broadband Internet connection (Ofcom, 2006). The level of broadband adoption was widespread among all age groups up to 65, but was most widely adopted among those aged 15–24 years (81 per cent of Internet users in that age group).

Adoption of ICTs represents an initial step. Ultimately, though, it is the way that ICTs are used and the extent of adoption of specific applications that are of critical importance in the context of education delivery. The Web 2.0 developments that have occurred primarily since 2000 have been trumpeted as a significant new stage in the development of the Internet. These developments reflect the increasingly widespread use of the Internet for content creation and social networking. These applications have so far been used mostly for personal and social reasons, but they also provide tools that could have value in learning contexts. It is in the realm of Web 2.0 that the Google Generation comes into its own. Even Generations Y and X, however, have been adopters of these technologies and such trends could have important implications for the use of these tools in the context of lifelong learning. So far, though, tipping points have been reached only for some of these applications and only among particular online user groups.

In the UK, content creation in the form of online users building their own web diaries or weblogs – one Web 2.0 tool that has been identified as having potential value in educational contexts in the future – has been a minority pastime. Just one in six Internet users in general (16 per cent) claimed to have contributed to a blog, although this claim was much more prevalent among those aged 16–24 years (37 per cent) (Ofcom, 2006). In another survey conducted only with Internet users aged 16–24 years, only around one in ten (11 per cent) said they had ever blogged (Synovate, 2007).

In the US, 9 per cent of Internet users said they had ever created a blog (Lenhart, 2005). Given that two-thirds of Americans were online at this time this represents 6 per cent of the general population. Blog creation was more than twice as widespread among 12–17s (19 per cent) and 18–28s (20 per cent). As 87 per cent and 84 per cent of these two age groups reportedly went online at this time, this meant that in 2005 17 per cent of all (offline and online) individuals across these age groups had created a blog. Blog creation was also more widespread among Internet users with broadband connections (11 per cent) than dial-up connections (4 per cent).

Blog use remains on the cusp of the tipping point zone in the UK, while blog creation has not reached that zone yet. In the US, blog creation has reached the tipping point zone among those aged under 29 but not yet among older people.

Another online information source to which users can contribute as content providers is Wikipedia. American research among Internet users found that significant minorities reported using this source, but usage gradually declines with age (Rainie and Tancer, 2007). The biggest users were those aged 18–29 (44 per cent), followed by those aged 30–49 (38 per cent). College graduates were also more likely than others to be users (50 per cent). In this case, however, two kinds of use as a reference source or as a contributor were not distinguished. In an e-learning context, both types of utility are anticipated for wiki technology. Nonetheless, these findings indicate that wikis are being widely used by young people and a tipping point has been passed among many age groups.

Social networking sites have been identified as another Web 2.0 leisure activity that could have more valuable applications in a formal learning context. In research conducted across Europe with Internet users, nearly one in four (23 per cent) said they used an online social network at least once a month, a figure that grew to nearly one in three (32 per cent) among 16–24 year olds (European Interactive Advertising Association, 2007). In the US, while only a minority of the general population (16 per cent) said they used online social networking sites, this figure grew dramatically to over half (55 per cent) of 12–17 year olds (Lenhart, 2006; Lenhart et al., 2005). Since by 2000, most teenagers in the US admitted to using e-mail and instant messaging with friends in the context of school assignments, the latest social networking phenomenon may enable them to widen the net of social contacts who might also be used as an education support group.

In considering what might happen in the future, therefore, the ICT adoption patterns of the Google Generation indicate that they are already becoming accustomed to normative use of Web 2.0 technologies across a range of information-gathering and educational contexts. Such technologies may be conditioning a different mindset in relation to learning in which students are willing to engage in remote online contact with tutors, engage in interactive learning settings and seek immediate access to the information they need in digital environments in which they can adapt that content to their own requirements. They will also willingly engage in partnership with tutors and other students in the establishment of a more personalised educational development plan tailored to their individual needs.

Google Generation: e-learning and higher education

The Google Generation is defined by being born at a time when not only information and communications technologies were prevalent, which was true to some degree for the pre-Google era, but also when a diverse range of applications had entered common usage. Quite literally, the 'Google' generation might be defined in terms of being born during an era when applications such as search engines were readily available. Young people in developed countries today enter a world in which access to wired and wireless communications networks is the norm. Large quantities of information flows through these networks and users can gain access to vast amounts of content for information and entertainment purposes. ICTs do not suddenly appear. Most have evolved gradually over time, passing through a number of iterations to reach their current point of development. Online networks existed during the pre-Google generation stage in the 1980s, for example, though they were not as sophisticated as present-day networks and lacked the latter's capacity. Telephone communication existed during that period as well, but mobile communications that can be carried anywhere did not.

In the education context, the learning environment for students of all ages has changed in many fundamental ways during the Google era as compared with earlier eras. The evolution of ICTs has driven these changes and government and transnational policies have created development frameworks within which new forms of teaching and learning have emerged. Research from around the world has indicated the growing importance of online resources to students and scholars working in higher education. This trend has been given momentum by the roll-out of broadband networks that can carry larger quantities of content more quickly and by the development of increasingly sophisticated information search tools that have facilitated the ease with which content can be located within a massively rich networked information environment (Edwards and Bruce, 2002; Tillman, 2003).

Research in schools has indicated that pre-teenage and teenage children are able to describe in detail a wide range of technologies that they use on a regular basis in all aspects of their lives. They are readily able to provide informed opinions about these technologies and their efficacy in the context of different applications. Young people use technologies to search for and retrieve information content for different purposes. They use technology devices to replay content at their convenience. They use technologies for social interaction purposes. In many respects teenagers use digital technologies to manage many aspects of their daily lives. More specifically, technologies and digital resources are valued in educational contexts. It does seem, however, that specific technology applications were often judged to have greater relevance to some subject areas than to others (Davies, 2008).

With the evolution of online networked technologies, scholars and students have turned increasingly to information sources beyond their university libraries. Some studies have indicated overwhelming majorities of students, for instance, conduct such searches and the Internet has emerged as a primary information source (Chang and Perng, 2001; Dong, 2003). Internet services that have been found to have special value in relation to academic research include online journals, e-mail for networking with other researchers and access to websites that provide research-relevant content (Asemi, 2005). While the Internet may be rated highly for providing a lot of useful and relevant information and represents a convenient one stop-shop for information searching, however, searches are not always easy or successful and it has not yet reached the point where it has replaced printed content (Asemi, 2005).

In Europe, the rapid spread of ICTs during the 1990s led the European Union to formulate objectives for their effective utilisation in educational institutions. In particular, there was great interest in exploring the potential of e-learning. This line of development embraced considerations about infrastructure, training and competencies, services and contents, and applications. Multimedia technologies were conceived to have the capability to improve the quality of learning by facilitating access to a wider range of richer educational resources. The Internet was regarded as having a central part to play in this context. The roll-out of new online learning applications called for a fresh perspective or orientation in education requiring a different sets of skills – sometimes referred to as 'digital literacy' (European Commission, 2001a).

E-learning was regarded as having a particularly important role to play in the delivery of higher education. The European Union took the view at the turn of the millennium that e-learning (incorporating distance learning) would become the mainstream within a few years. In fact, e-learning would be embraced by corporate and educational institutions in relation to training and tuition. Initial principles were formalised in 1999 within the Bologna Declaration (*http://www.bologna-berlin2003 .de/pdf/bologna_declaration.pdf*). This agreement was designed to encourage countries across Europe not only to examine ways in which e-learning applications could be developed, but also to seek to harmonise such developments so that a pan-European body of knowledge of the field could be established. This sharing of information and experiences was encouraged particularly among universities in Europe.

A subsequent action plan was published for the establishment of an e-Europe in which all citizens, homes and businesses would be brought into the digital age, 'creating a digitally literate Europe' that was both socially cohesive and inclusive (European Commission, 2001b). It was seen as essential that all citizens become actively involved in the Information Society. To do so, though, they would need to acquire the competencies and skills necessary to take advantage of the Internet and other digital technologies and applications. Educational systems would have an important part to play in achieving this objective by utilising ICTs in ways that would establish them as normative information resources and by imparting the skills needed to utilise them fully.

At the time of this new thinking, it was recognised that higher educational institutions had for some time used computer applications, but at a fairly elementary level in relation to skills development and to impart knowledge. Word processing, spreadsheets, electronic databases and electronic mail all emerged during the late 1980s and 1990s as standard practices. The expansion in use of global networks and the emergence of communications infrastructures and software that enable online users to download significant quantities of content and to become online content creators and publishers, however, have dramatically changed the online landscape and diversity of applications that can be utilised by students.

What then does the future hold? What kind of standard learning scenario will emerge for the Google Generation over the next ten years? To answer this question, we need to consider the kinds of technology developments that will have an impact on higher education over the next ten years. This needs to be done, however, in a wider social context that considers patterns of online technology adoption and application on the part of the Google Generation outside formal educational settings. One monitoring exercise concerned with tracking the impact of new technologies on learning and teaching in the United States has adopted this wider perspective and identified several important areas for consideration (New Media Consortium, 2007).

First, the future of higher education will be affected by a changing academic environment driven by rising costs and falling revenues and the need to adopt new models for the delivery of education. In particular, one forecast was that there will be a growth in demand for distance learning provision as the steadily rising costs of higher education render full-time study in residence less popular. In addition, the emergence of government policies promoting lifelong learning – a feature of European as well as North American educational policy – will also encourage more people to consider learning and training as processes that can occur at any life stage and that need to be slotted in around other professional and personal commitments.

Second, increasing globalisation is changing the way people work and spend their leisure time. It has produced dramatic growth in the availability of information on almost every conceivable topic and for students provides them with more diverse perspectives and wider opportunities in relation to learning.

Third, there is a presumption that the Google Generation is information and communications literate when this is not invariably the case. The growth in phenomena such as online social networking and user-generated content signal that new skills are being acquired by participants and are required by all who wish to join in these activities. In fact, information literacy levels can still vary significantly within as well as across generations and not all Web 2.0 participants are engaged in such activities at the high skill end of the user spectrum.

Fourth, the emergence of new online technologies has generated new forms of publishing. Electronic publishing provides an alternative information source and is also an alternative platform on which to produce scholarly outputs. At present, such outputs are still regarded as academically inferior to traditional modes of academic publishing in terms of their scholarly standing, although much depends here on the establishment of traditional methods for quality control of published outputs in the online world that mirror those in the offline world in terms of the ways they are implemented. Web 2.0 technologies have nonetheless opened up new for areas for academic debate and additional (and often speedier) opportunities for academic publishing.

Fifth, there is another development that is associated with the emergence of online technologies. Electronic outlets have opened up wider access to publishing opportunities. User-generated content facilities have not only triggered the phenomenon of the so-called 'citizen journalist', but also the amateur scholar. Sites such as Wikipedia invite anyone to contribute 'knowledge' to online content repositories that have come to command some degree of authority as information sources. In these cases, there are questions of information authority and credibility that must be addressed, but proponents of such Web 2.0 applications would argue that quality control is built in and that mistakes are 'outed' by users and corrected as an ongoing process.

Sixth, the successful implementation of new technologies in higher education in the future will be affected by how much dissonance arises between the views of institutions and students of what constitutes technology and in terms of the way technologies are adapted to formal learning processes. For the Google Generation – or more precisely for individuals borne after 1993 – electronic (wired and wireless) communications technologies are a normal part of everyday life. They are understood in terms of their dominant applications rather that purely in terms of their technological distinctiveness. Technologies are tools to be used and preferential usage patterns naturally emerge. If ICTs are to play a successful and effective part in higher education they must engage students in ways that are seen as relevant and appropriate. Any institutionally driven concept of new online technologies as representing alternative platforms on which to disseminate educational content in traditional learning formats could be doomed to failure if they attempt to engage students of the Google Generation in ways that are regarded as inappropriate or non-normative (New Media Consortium, 2007).

The New Media Consortium identified six areas where Web 2.0 technologies will impact upon higher education:

- user-generated content;
- social networking;
- mobile phones;
- virtual worlds;
- new forms of scholarly publishing;
- massively multiplayer educational gaming.

User-generated content

One of the principal outcomes of the emergence of online technologies since the mid-1990s has been the development and adoption of facilities for users of online communications media to generate their own content. Internet users, for instance, can upload images, video or audio clips or textual content to established sites such as Flickr, YouTube and Google Video. This content is then available to large user groups in which participants are audiences and producers. Self-publishing can also take place online in the form of websites, web diaries or blogs and wikis. These tools facilitate the creation of shared collections of information resources. They are also being adopted within educational contexts and are already changing the way scholars are thinking about course development and delivery. These online tools are not limited by classroom boundaries. Content can readily be constructed in a variety of forms – textual, audio, static or moving images or multi-modal. Online content building tools can also connect people and encourage collaborative course building which, in the higher education context, can involve both tutors and students as creative learning partners. Content can be constructed or tagged from other online sources. Substantial online repositories or reference libraries can be established using readily available tools with low cost barriers.

Social networking

This is the biggest and fastest growing online phenomenon that has become especially popular and widely used among young people of the Google Generation. Two of the best known sites dominated by young users are Facebook and MySpace. Through these sites, users can establish an online profile or identity, connect to other people and share information. These networks, for most users, have a primarily social function. However, the fact that online social networking has become the norm for many students has encouraged the exploration of its potential as an educational tool. In addition to the established networks, the tools for the construction of online social networks are readily available off the shelf and cost barriers are low. Some initiatives have already taken off in the United States. Tools such as CollegeRuled (*http://www .collegeruled.com*) in which students can create and share class schedules and Elgg (*http://www.elgg.com*), an open source system that allows users to set up a blog and web profile and provides an RSS reader and file repository with podcasting capability, have already become widely established. Online social networks could be built around special-interest topics or to discuss the works of well known writers or scholars with links to multi-modal reference sources that users could further contribute towards.

As competition between social networking sites grows, their providers will need to become innovative in the kinds of tools and services they make available to their users in order to create and maintain 'brand' distinctiveness. New ways of engaging users over and above standard user-generated content facilities will be essential to enable social network sites to retain market share. New tools will both engage users in more advanced and creative forms of online interactivity and will also combine virtual experiences with real-world activities. One of the most popular social networks among 15–24 year olds, Bebo, has joined forces with OpenSocial, a social network alliance led by Google, to provide a wider array of advanced tools for content creation and modification. It has introduced another scheme called The Gap Year in which six Bebo users will be chosen to travel the world completing challenges while reporting back to social networkers about their experiences.

In a further initiative Bebo has launched interactive online video dramas (*Kate Modern* and *Sofia's Diary*) which not only offer a source of ongoing entertainment, with events unfolding daily, but to which social network users can contribute story ideas as well as engage directly with the characters via the latter's own social network postings on Bebo. These real-time interactive dramas will roll out on other major social networks such as MySpace and YouTube bringing them within reach of potential audiences of tens of millions (Carter, 2007). Such developments may have been conceived initially with social and entertainment objectives as their primary aims, but they will cultivate new forms of online interactivity that could spread to and create fresh expectations for online learning applications.

Mobile phones

These devices have become a worldwide technological phenomenon. In recent years, however, their functionality has expanded dramatically as they have become increasingly computerised. Mobile phones have become storehouses of content and access channels to remote content repositories. Many of the interactive functions of computer-mediated communication have migrated from the wired to the wireless world. Content – whether in text, audio or video form – can be uploaded from and downloaded to mobile devices almost as readily as fixed computer stations. The small size of mobile phones can render their keyboard functionality less usable than normal computer keyboards. In the future, however, mobile phones will have integrated projection systems that can project full size keyboards made of light. This will facilitate content generation via these devices. The ability to receive, store and send content in real time while working in remote locations will have great value for some disciplines. Tutors will be able to transmit course content, particularly via audio and video clips, to remote students who may need to fit in their studies around employment. As the storage capacity of mobile devices grows, larger volumes of content will be transported that can not only be accessed while users are on the move but also plugged into fixed workstations in different locations.

Among mobile phone users in the UK, for example, two-thirds (68 per cent) use these devices to take photos, nearly half (48 per cent) use them to store photos, and nearly one in four (23 per cent) record video clips on their mobile phones. In Japan, by 2007, these applications had been adopted respectively by 82 per cent, 71 per cent and 9 per cent of mobile phone users. More than one in three Internet users in the UK (35 per cent) reportedly used their mobile phones to gain wireless access to the Internet. This figure was lower in the USA (22 per cent) but much higher in Japan (63 per cent) (Ofcom, 2007e).

Virtual worlds

These are immersive 3D environments in which users can move around, usually in the form of avatars. Popular systems that have emerged in recent years include *Second Life*, *Active Worlds* and *There*. These virtual worlds go beyond massive multiplayer online games in that they embrace not only a large number of active participants but also a wide range of activities. In *Second Life*, for instance, participants may establish themselves as landowners where they can construct their own virtual homes or businesses.

Many aspects of real life can be represented in virtual form in this electronic parallel world. These worlds have already been used to disseminate information among their members. A number of major news providers have created news services within *Second Life*. Sky News has built a virtual replica of its newsroom and Channel 4 has established its 4 Radio service in *Second Life*. Sky will give away virtual TV sets to *Second Life* residents so that they can receive its news service in their virtual homes. The 4 Radio service will provide podcasts of a variety of speech and music programmes in *Second Life*. To grow its virtual audience, *Second Life* residents who visit the 4 Radio site will be given branded watches through which they will be able to tune into its broadcasts wherever they are in *Second Life* (Bulkley, 2007).

Virtual worlds can also be used as educational spaces. Even virtual libraries have been established in these environments. Virtual worlds provide platforms for information and experience sharing, for role-playing and for acting out scenarios, including teaching and learning situations.

New forms of scholarly publishing

Online technology has opened up a range of new forms of producing, evaluating and disseminating scholarly work. Examples of these developments that already exist include online dissemination of pre-publication works, online discussions of topics or the works of specific authors and online publishing of finished works. Books and journals are already being widely published in electronic forms, though their availability may be restricted to approved users or dependent upon payments. Web 2.0 tools, as already seen above, have provided new opportunities for the creation of content. The social networking aspect of many of these tools also means that they encourage collaborative work between writers. Ideas can be shared quickly among large numbers of other users. Some tools, such as wikis, can create collaborative content, producing and editing scenarios in which large teams of content users also play an active part in the construction of information resources. This approach has already been used in relation to online textbooks, encyclopaedias and dictionaries, academic course materials and papers. New forms of scholarly publishing online are likely to grow in prevalence over the next five to ten years. Some will operate as closed networks available only to accredited contributor-users, while others will be open source with contributions also deriving from outside higher education circles.

Reports have surfaced, usually online in the form of blogs, of academics who have turned to online publishing in preference to traditional modes. One such report told of academic authors in the United States who had published books online and invited readers to comment on their contents, in one case by writing comments in spaces alongside each paragraph (Young, 2006). In this case, there is an opportunity to observe a book under development. The author in question subsequently reacted to some readers' observations by revising the text. Digital publishing could therefore produce repositories that contain not only a single text version of a book, but potentially multiple versions together with the comments of various other 'contributors' or 'critics'. Such scenarios might, of course, generate questions about intellectual property rights and royalty entitlements but could become commonplace in the future. Books in the future could become the outcomes of online 'conversations' between authors and readers.

Elsewhere, it has been recognised that there is still much to be learned about the use of 'e-books' or 'digital books'. While these works are being rolled out in public libraries across the United Kingdom, this is being done cautiously and in the context of a series of exploratory field projects designed to examine different usage models (Garrod and Weller, 2005). For some forecasters, digital books have a future but their perceived usefulness is restricted to particular domains. Prime targets for digitisation among academic works are the more widely used textbooks and reference collections to which many users often need flexible access and only wish to look at selected extracts (see Beam, 2006).

E-books can only be used if someone has the right equipment. Research in the UK survey found that most e-book readers (91 per cent) used a personal computer to read these books, while only small proportions (less than 10 per cent) used portable devices (Gunter, 2005). New technologies, such as the Kindle produced by Amazon, could promote e-book consumption in the future by providing readers with a portable device that is similar in size to the average paperback and has the capacity to hold up to 200 books. The use of electronic ink gives the text an appearance not unlike the printed page of a paperback. The same device can provide access to online sites such as wikis and blogs that provide further content (Bone, 2007).

Massively multiplayer educational gaming

Massively multiplayer games have become popular and widespread. Initially conceived as sources of entertainment, they have also become a a significant online social networking phenomenon. These games can be either competitive or collaborative in nature. The principles of online game playing have also been repurposed to achieve educational goals. In one American project, the Synthetic Worlds Initiative at Indian University, a 3D world based on MMO principles has been created in which students are transported virtually back to Shakespearian times where they can learn about the customs, language and events of that period. Thus students can be fully immersed in a learning situation where they engage in interactive ventures that are played out on screen and over which they have some control in terms of their own movements in that environment. They can acquire information, exchange views with other participants, and learn not just by being told things but also by actively engaging in virtual situations.

Formality of learning

Discussions about the applications of Web 2.0 tools in educational contexts have led theorists and researchers to think about what is meant by 'learning'. Proponents of Web 2.0 have presumed not only that it represents a new tool kit that can have great value in learning contexts, but also that its effective application requires a rethink about the nature of 'learning' itself. A distinction has been made between 'formal' and 'informal' learning. The Web embraces informality and this perspective on learning is therefore deemed to be forward looking. Some writers, however, have argued that this simplistic dichotomy is not helpful (Crook, 2008). More than that, it may not even be based upon an accurate conception of learning. There is a need to embrace both approaches to learning. The formal versus informal distinction does not actually take the form of a categorical divide whereby learning is either one thing or the other. It might be more useful and more accurate to consider these two terms as representing opposite ends of a learning style continuum. Hence, learning experiences can vary in terms of their degree of 'formality'.

Formality in the learning process becomes crystallised when a deliberate act of teaching is accompanied by a deliberate act of learning. This 'contract' between teacher and learner is defined by both taking up agreed but different roles in the learning interaction. It is perhaps most clearly manifest as a phenomenon in the classroom. Teaching takes on a structured format with the teacher being the sole creator and deliverer of the content. The learner's role is to watch and listen and absorb that content. When these conditions are broken down into a less structured format then learning loses some of its formality.

In a Web 2.0 setting, teachers and learners are invited to behave differently from the traditional formal learning arrangement and to adopt different roles at different times. Both may be content creators and content deliverers as well as content receivers. In this setting also learning can assume a more 'social' nature with teacher and learner engaging with each other differently and more often on equal terms. In that respect, online learning adopts some of the character of other predominant and voluntary online behaviours in which students engage, such as social networking. Within a Web 2.0 learning set-up therefore learning may be both at once formal and informal and teachers and learners become more of a partnership in which they share a common learning experience. Learning can still retain elements of formality, but not all the time. Traditional teaching methods may still have relevance, but not all the time. This more flexible, mixed modal style of learning will require some adjustment and also, initially, some experimentation and piloting to ensure that it works effectively.

Uptake of digital media and higher education

The uptake of new online technologies in the future could have a significant impact upon higher education practices and, in turn, on the position of traditional forms of publishing in this world and also on the role of libraries. Predicting the future is never easy. Such predictions are based on lessons learned from analysis of historical innovation adoption trends and on an assumption that recent technology adoption trends will continue at a specified pace, possibly reflecting the growth curves observed from established technologies at the time when they were classified as 'new'.

Future projections can be guided to some extent by observations about generic media and communications trends. It is also important to examine trends of a more specialised kind in relation to developments in publishing and e-learning. It is developments in these last two areas that might have particularly acute implications for higher education and the role of libraries.

A recent review of universities and colleges in the United States by Ithaca Strategic Services has discussed the impact of online digital technology on scholarly publishing (Brown et al., 2007). This review of academic publishing circumstances was positioned in the broader context of general Internet-related developments. Interviews were carried out with a sample of senior university administrators, academic press directors and librarians from higher education institutions across the United States.

The Internet was generally endorsed as universal in terms of its availability in the US academy. This observation would be equally true of the UK academy. Research reviewed earlier in this book has confirmed that the Internet is a highly and extensively valued information resource and this point has become particularly pertinent in formal education settings.

In the academy, a distinction was made between formal and informal scholarly publishing. Both activities have been prevalent and important features of academic work since long before the digital era. Formal scholarly publishing comprises a set of activities traditionally linked to the production of printed academic outputs such as books and journals. Informal scholarly 'publications' include lecture notes, presentation slides, supporting hand-outs, module and course outlines, working papers, exchanges of correspondence between researchers and a variety of other printed forms of information exchange. Such outputs are characterised by having a limited circulation. In the digital era these outputs can be made more widely available when placed in electronic formats and posted to websites that may be accessible by anyone with the appropriate technology. Furthermore, these outputs have been further enhanced by new forms of online publication in the form of blogs, wikis, social network postings and other devices associated with Web 2.0. These informal types of publishing are being increasingly used and regarded as bone fide academic outputs. As such they pose a challenge to traditional academic forms of publishing and the role of academic presses in this process (Brown et al., 2007).

Many scholars in the US were observed to be turning to electronic resources. Formal scholarly publishing has been affected by this trend and has had to contemplate new production, distribution and economic models. The Ithaca researchers forecast that print will remain in use in the future. It may even continue as the preferred type of format for certain forms of usage such as cover-to-cover reading and for display purposes. The progressive and relentless adoption of online learning resources, however, has created an imperative for publishers to produce new outputs electronically as well as in print and to digitise old publications. The use of digital technologies might introduce new models of production such as print-on-demand, thus creating economies in print-runs. The emergence of online learning resources has also been accompanied by preferences for new styles of presentation. The Internet is a dynamic environment and users expect online content producers to utilise new formats that reflect the capabilities of the medium. Pictures are as important as words to many online users. Furthermore, dynamism is reflected in terms of effective use of multi-modal formats and regularly updated content.

The digital era is transforming the way universities and scholars disseminate knowledge content and the way that students engage with that content and learn from it. Hence in the future, all content may need to be available in electronic form, even though some or even much of it is also still available in hard copy. Scholars will engage normatively with electronic research and publishing environments. Journals have led the way in migrating online and books are following on. E-books were seen in the Ithaca analysis as being an important part of the future. Leading scholarly publishers such as Elsevier and Springer have been driving this market forward and have experimented with new business models that determine how revenue yields will be derived from electronic modes of content distribution. Distributors such as Amazon and Google's Mobipocket have also tested online e-book retail models.

The principle of parallel publishing of books and other scholarly resources in electronic as well as hard copy modes, however, is not the only development that takes advantage of the capabilities of digital technology. Perhaps even more significant, given earlier observations about Web 2.0, is the use of the distinctive dynamic formats that are available for information presentation and dissemination in that environment. Multi-modal formats are increasingly preferred by the Google Generation (see Livingstone and Bovill, 2001a).

In the scholarly context, outputs that form part of the learning environment for students, the information exchange environment for researchers and possibly also performance criteria for scholars include not just published books and journal articles, but also raw primary data (such as raw data sets), preliminary and non-peer reviewed discussion of working papers, conference or workshop proceedings and reports, and dynamic information repositories in wiki settings that enable teams of scholars (and students) to build reference sources of draft papers, lectures and other dynamic learning resources. Even books may become dynamic and ever changing. This does not mean simply more rapid updating and production of new editions online, but a continual and dynamic interactive process in which a book is published online in draft form that allows readers to contribute comments and suggestions about its content as virtual marginalia. This concept has already been trialled in respect of a book called *Gamer Theory*, authored by a cultural studies scholar, McKenzie Wark. Online critiques and commentaries contributed to this online publication have been utilised by the author to inform regular amendments and revisions to the original text. Thus a scholarly book published in digital form becomes a dynamic, interactive and ongoing conversation between the author and readers.

The growing significance of Web 2.0 technologies has redefined the Web. It is no longer simply a huge repository of content. It is now the site of dynamic interplay between online users who engage in conversations about information and information sources. Such online communities have spread rapidly in number and memberships. One concern is whether they have spread so quickly that there has been insufficient time to establish business models that render them viable operations. Will there be echoes of the dotcom bubble that burst at the turn of the millennium? While significant market capital values were attached to the bigger networks such as MySpace, YouTube and Facebook within a few years of their launch, none had acquired huge revenues. Nonetheless, social networks have been recognised as having vast potential as marketing tools through which consumers can be cultivated. Furthermore, advances in online advertising techniques and business models have created new opportunities to generate promising and secure revenues from online communities.

Evidence that supports their potential longevity has emerged from the retail sector where leading retail organisations have shown increased interest in utilising online social networks to promote customer loyalty and capture new customers. Three routes have been followed whereby retailers buy a presence with an existing social network, buy out an existing network or create their own (Siwicki, 2006).

Purchasing a ready-made online social network can prove to be a major boon to a retailer provided there is a good match between the product line and the interests and needs of the online community. Interesting pioneering developments have already taken place in the United States. Alibris Inc., a major retailer of books, DVDs and CDs, launched a space on MySpace to promote textbooks to high school and college students who were known to be major users of this network. A different approach was adopted by Abebooks, a distributor of rare, old and new books. It purchased the specialist social network LibraryThing with 66,000 members who were not just big consumers of this print medium but also enjoyed interacting with others to discuss books. This online community will not just expand the potential customer base of Abebooks but will provide a valuable marketing research tool through which the search terms used and online sites visited can be tracked. Such information was expected to enhance the online merchandising techniques of this book retailer.

These commercial applications of Web 2.0 could have interesting lessons for higher education institutions and libraries in the future. If these online communities can be utilised to promote the business goals of retailers, why should similar principles not apply also to education? Web 2.0 developments have served to empower people both as consumers and as citizens. Different social networks may serve common basic purposes for their members, but may be established in the first place for distinctive reasons. While some networks are designed to promote a general web presence with distinctly social motivations, others may be established to cater to the needs of groups of people who share a special interest. Often, people belong to more than one social network. This opens up the possibility of linkages between networks. The promotional opportunities here for commodity and service providers are clearly apparent.

As there is emerging evidence that people are going online for educational purposes and that Internet-based conversations about service suppliers can be evaluative, it is important that those suppliers are at least aware of what their customers are saying about them in the virtual world. For retailers the importance of this type of online presence stems not least from the knowledge that consumers often regard other consumers as the most credible and trustworthy sources of feedback about brands, products and services. It may be important that libraries and education service suppliers (e.g. universities) take this point on board as well.

So what does the future hold? Is there a distinctive 'Google Generation' of young people for whom the preferred learning scenarios will depart radically from the more traditional ones that have become ingrained in the scholarly environment over many past generations? Will higher education institutions need to revise their practices in order to satisfy the evolving learning expectations and match the information-seeking styles of their students? What does all this mean for the nature of knowledge resources and repositories? In the context of the current analysis, one primary objective has been to map out what the position might be in 2017 – a point at which many of the Google Generation (those born after 1993) will be in higher education. Here are some forecasts and observations.

Digital technologies have transformed communication and information searching activities for everyone and will continue to evolve over the next ten years. The Internet has been at the centre of this development and has become ubiquitous in the higher education environment and widespread in developed societies in many other settings.

This phenomenon is not restricted to the 'Google Generation'. While there is an age-related profile whereby digital technologies have been adopted earlier by young people than the middle-aged and older generations, in countries such as the UK and USA (and many others) older generations have caught up with younger generations and overwhelming majorities of all age groups, except the eldest (over 65s), have Internet experience and use online information services.

Digital technology penetration in its broadest sense has therefore become normative. This means that most people across most age groups have used the Internet and other forms of digital technology (interactive digital television, digital radio and mobile phones with content sending and receiving capabilities) at some time. Digital divides still persist and these are linked to socio-economic conditions more than age. These divides will be broken down over the next ten years.

Within the education context, access to online technologies is available to all, but the extent to which they will transform learning styles and procedures will depend upon the way they are used both by educators and students. Web 2.0 applications have caused the way the Internet in general is used to evolve rapidly in the past five years. These developments are expected to continue and to evolve still further in the next ten years. This means that online repositories will be expected not simply to provide quick and easy access to sought-after knowledge content but also to utilise dynamic, interactive and personalised online tools in the process.

The pace at which changes will occur will depend upon how soon tipping points are reached in respect of specific online information-related applications. A tipping point is reached when between 10 and 25 per cent of potential users have become actual users. Thus it is not a single identifiable point that is the same for all innovations. It represents a critical mass of adoption beyond which wider adoption accelerates very quickly. Social networking has passed the tipping point among young people aged less than 30 years, while user content creation activities such as blogs and wikis are widely used though not necessarily in a creative interactive fashion. On current evidence, however, it is probably safe to predict that tipping points for these applications in an education context will be reached within the next ten years.

The use of online scholarly content that has been both formally and informally published has been steadily growing since 2000. This trend will continue as the leading academic publishers that dominate the market continue to expand their e-book and e-journal portfolios. This trend will be supplemented by further significant growth in the production of informally published scholarly content as universities utilise such devices to cater for the needs of growing and increasingly remotely located student numbers, as pre-formal publication outputs become a more accepted part of the scholarly knowledge generation process and as academic teamworking online becomes established practice in the development of new research projects and outputs from those projects.

The success of online knowledge content provision cannot be presumed simply on the basis of its increased availability and accessibility. It must adopt the kinds of presentation formats that have greatest appeal to users. The empirical evidence to date has indicated that the current generation of young learners prefer dynamic, multi-modal forms of online content presentation. Of course, it is essential that online knowledge content has authority and credibility, but it must also engage the interest of potential users.

With the projected and highly significant growth of informal scholarly publishing, more 'home-grown' content creation will occur. This will derive from a combination of the efforts of individual scholars and the efforts of research or teaching teams working together to build knowledge repositories online. With the provision of in-house training, digital technology literacy will expand among content providers and users (who will often reside in the same online community and adopt either role at different times). As these developments take place, the distinction between informal and formal published works in terms of quality of presentation formats will be eroded which could have significant implications for the roles played by established scholarly publishing companies and for academic libraries.

With more knowledge content available and with less visible or obvious surface feature credibility distinctions between content from formal as opposed to informal publications, the brand or reputation of the content supplier will become paramount for setting it apart from the multitude of other suppliers. Thus content suppliers that are clearly identifiable and have a reputation for producing high-quality content that is accurate and trustworthy will capture learner-consumers' attention and loyalty.

Further, if informal content publishers such as scholars provide rich home-grown, knowledge content repositories supported by hyperlinks to other recommended knowledge resources, the need for traditional libraries could be circumvented. What kind of roles will exist for libraries in this rapidly changing digital scholarly world?

The answer to this question has multiple parts.

- First, where a major library already holds a significant repository then its holdings must be digitised so that they become available online, in some instances via open access and in others via restricted access.

- Second, online interfaces must not only be user-friendly but also adopt the preferred presentation formats of newly emerging young Internet users. This means that interfaces must be dynamic and multi-modal to engage interest.

- Third, Web 2.0 features should be incorporated into the architecture of online repositories enabling more dynamic, interactive engagement with knowledge content. This could take the form of supplementary content creation opportunities linked to specific knowledge themes or to the works of specific authors via online synchronous and asynchronous interaction tools in text, audio or video formats.

- Fourth, in extending the last recommendation, the growth in popularity of virtual worlds – which has already been identified in this book and by others as facilitating important new educational applications – could be incorporated into future library services. An important aspect of engaging online users is to create personalised services that in some ways mirror the type of personal service expected in the real world. Thus virtual library environments could be established in which librarian hosts are represented in a virtual space as avatars who escort visitors around a virtual library to the section where the sought reference materials can then be digitally accessed.

- Fifth, a library offering a service to the scholarly community should tap into informally published scholarly knowledge holdings and networks to provide a priority hyperlinked support resource that is integrated within the architecture of those sites. These informal academic publishing repositories will become normative and accepted practice.

References

Abdullah, N. and Gibb, F. (2006) *A Survey of e-Book Awareness and Usage amongst Students in an Academic Library*, in Proceedings of International Conference of Multidisciplinary Information Sciences and Technologies, Merida, Spain, 25–28 October. Online at: *http://eprints.cdlr.strath.ac.uk/2280/01/FGibb_survey_ebook.pdf* (accessed 16 July 2007).

Abrams, S. and Luther, J. (2004) 'Born with the chip', *Library Journal*, 129(8): 34–7.

Adams, J. and Bonk, S.C. (1995) 'Electronic information technologies and resources: use by university faculty and faculty preferences for related services', *College and Research Libraries*, 56(2): 119–31.

Agosto, D. (2002) 'A model of young people's decision-making in using the Web', *Library and Information Science Research*, 24: 311–41.

Agosto, D. (2006) 'Toward a model of the everyday life information needs of urban teenagers, Part 1: Theoretical model', *Journal of the American Society for Information Science and Technology*, 57(10): 1394–403.

Agosto, D. and Hughes-Hassell, S. (2005) 'People, places, and questions: an investigation of the everyday life information-seeking behaviors of urban young adults', *Library and Information Science Research*, 27: 141–63.

Alexander, B. (2006) 'Web 2.0: a new wave of innovation for teaching and learning', *EDUCAUSE Review*, March–April, pp. 37–44.

American Library Association (2001) '21st century literacy', *ALA Action*, 1. Online at: *http://www.ala.org/ala/prfotools/21centurylit/21stcenturyliteracy.htm* (accessed 20 June 2007).

Anderson, B. (2004) *Information Society Technologies: Social Capital and Quality of Life*, E-Living Project Report. Colchester: Chimera, University of Essex.

Anderson, B. and Yttri, B. (2004) *Telework and Quality of Life*, The e-Living: Life in a Digital Europe Conference, Essen.

Anderson, B., Brynin, M., Raban, Y. and Gershuny, J. (2006) *Information and Communication Technologies in Society*. London: Routledge.

Anuradha, K.T. and Usha, H.S. (2006) 'Use of e-books in an academic and research environment: a case study from the Indian Institute of Science', *Program: Electronic Library and Information Systems*, 40(1): 48–62.

AOL (2000) *American Online/Roper Cyberstudy 2000*, Roper CNT375, cited by R.E. Rice and C. Haythornwaite (2006) 'Perspectives on internet use: access, involvement and interaction', in L.E. Leivrouw and S. Livingstone (eds), *The Handbook of New Media* (updated student edition). London: Sage, pp. 92–113.

Asemi, A. (2005) 'Information searching habits of Internet users: a case study on the Medical Sciences University of Isfahan, Iran', *Webology*, 2(1): Article 10. Online at: *http://www.webology.ir/2005/v2n1/a10* (accessed 4 August 2007).

Ask.com (2007) 'Ask.com Search Tips', Ask.com website. Online at: *http://sp.uk.ask.com/en/docs/about/tipsforsearching.shtml* (accessed 18 July 2007).

Atkin, D. and LaRose, R. (1994) 'An analysis of the information services adoption literature', in J. Hanson (ed.), *Advances in Telematics*, Vol. 2. New York: Ablex, pp. 91–110.

Atkinson, R.C. and Wilson, H.A. (1968) 'Computer-assisted instruction', *Science*, 162: 73–7.

Avery, V., Chamberlain, E., Summerfield, C. and Zealey, L. (eds) (2007) *Office for National Statistics: Focus on Digital Age*. Basingstoke: Palgrave Macmillan.

Baird, D. and Fisher, M. (2005) 'Neomillenial user experience design strategies: utilizing social networking media to support "Always on" learning styles', *Journal of Educational Technology Systems*, 34(1): 5–32.

Bakker, P. and Sadaba, C. (2008) 'The impact of the internet on users', in L. Kung, R.G. Picard and R. Towse (eds), *The Internet and the Mass Media*. London: Sage, pp. 86–101.

Bar-Ilan, J., Peritz, B.C. and Wolman, Y.A. (2003) 'Survey on the use of electronic databases and electronic journals accessed through the web by the academic staff of Israeli universities', *Journal of Academic Librarianship*, 29(6): 346–61.

BBC Online (2003) 'Potter book five: on sale on 21 June', CBBC News website. Online at: *http://news.bbc.co.uk/cbbcnews/hi/uk/newsid_2661000/2661257.stm* (accessed 18 July 2007).

BBC Online (2005) 'Worksheet: Half-Blood Prince sets UK record', CBBC News website. Online at: *http://news.bbc.co.uk/cbbcnews/hi/newsid_4700000/newsid_4701400/4701409.stm* (accessed 18 July 2007).

Beam, A. (2006) 'The brave new book', Boston.com News, June. Online at: *http://www.boston.com/news/globe/living/articles/2006/06/07* (accessed 3 August 2007).

Beenjtes, J.W.J., Koolstra, C.M., Marseille, N. and van der Voort, T.H.A. (2001) 'Children's use of different media: for how long and why?', in S. Livingstone and M. Bovill (eds), *Children and Their Changing Media Environment: A European Comparative Study*. Mahwah, NJ: Lawrence Erlbaum Associates, pp. 85–112.

Belefant-Miller, H. and King, D.W. (2003) 'A profile of faculty reading and information-use behaviors on the cusp of the electronic age', *Journal of the American Society for Information Science and Technology*, 54(2): 179–81.

Bell, D. (1979) 'The social framework of the information society', in M.L. Dertouzos and J. Moses (eds), *The Computer Age: A Twenty-Year View*. Cambridge, MA: MIT Press, pp. 163–211.

Bennett, L. and Landoni, M. (2005) 'E-books in academic libraries', *Electronic Library*, 3(1): 9–16

Bijker, W.E. and Law, J. (eds) (1992) *Shaping Technology/Building Society: Studies in Socio-technical Change*. Cambridge, MA: MIT Press.

Bilal, D. (2000) 'Children's use of the Yahooligans! web search engine: I. Cognitive, physical, and affective behaviors on fact-based search tasks', *Journal of the American Society for Information Science and Technology*, 51(7): 646–65.

Bilal, D. (2001) 'Children's use of the Yahooligans! web search engine: II. Cognitive and physical behaviors on research', *Journal of the American Society for Information Science and Technology*, 52(2): 118–36.

Bilal, D. (2002) 'Perspectives on children's navigation of the World Wide Web: does the type of search task make a difference?', *Online Information Review*, 26(2): 108–17.

Bilal, D. and Kirby, J. (2002) 'Differences and similarities in information seeking: children and adults as Web users', *Information Processing and Management*, 38: 649–70.

Bjørk, B.C. (2004) 'Open access to scientific publications: an analysis of the barriers to change?', *Information Research*, 9. Online at: *http://informationr.net/ir/9-2/paper170.html* (accessed 18 September 2006).

Blough, K. (2003) 'E-books sales lead off 2003', press release, Association of American Publishers, 18 March. Online at: *http://www.publishers.org/press/releases.cfm?PressreleaseArticleID=138* (accessed 6 May 2005).

Bohlin, I. (2004) 'Communication regimes in competition: the current transition in scholarly communication seen through the lens of the sociology of technology', *Social Studies of Science*, 34: 365–91.

Bone, J. (2007) 'The digital reader that will provide 200 books at the touch of a button', *The Times*, 20 November, p. 8.

Bontrhon, K., Urquhart, C., Thomas, R., Armstrong, C., Ellis, D., Everitt, J., Fenton, R., Lonsdale, R., McDermott, E., Morris, H., Phillips, R., Spink, S. and Yeoman, A. (2003) 'Trends in use of electronic journals in higher education in the UK: views of academic staff and students', *D-Lib Magazine*, 9. Online at: *http://www.dlib.org/dlib/june03/urquhart/06urquhart.html* (accessed 18 September 2006).

Borghuis, M.G.M (1997) 'User feedback from electronic subscriptions: the possibilities of logfile analysis', *Library Acquisitions: Practice and Theory*, 21(3): 373–80.

Borgman, C., Hirsh, S., Walter, V. and Gallagher, A. (1995) 'Children's searching behavior on browsing and keyword online catalogs: the Science Library Catalog Project', *Journal of the American Society for Information Science*, 46(9): 663–84.

Borgman, C.L. (2000) 'Digital libraries and the continuum of scholarly communication', *Journal of Documentation*, 56: 412–30.

Boyce, P., King, D.W., Montgomery, C. and Tenopir, C. (2004) 'How electronic journals are changing patterns of use', *Serials Librarian*, 46: 121–41.

Boyd, D. (2004) *Revenge of the User*. Online at: *http://www.zephoria.org/*.

Brennan, M.J., Hurd, J.M., Blecic, D.D. and Weller, A.C. (2002) 'A snapshot of early adopters of e-journals: challenges to the library', *College and Research Libraries*, 63: 515–26.

Brooks, R. (2008) 'Top authors to go digital with ebooks', *Sunday Times*, 17 February, p. 5.

Brophy, J. and Bawden, D. (2005) 'Is Google enough? Comparison of an internet search engine with academic library resources', *Aslib Proceedings*, 57(6): 498–512.

Brown, C. (2001) 'The e-volution of preprints in the scholarly communication of physicists and astronomers', *Journal of the American Society for Information Science and Technology*, 52: 187–200.

Brown, C. (2003) 'The role of electronic preprints in chemical communication: analysis of citation, usage, and acceptance in the journal literature', *Journal of the American Society for Information Science and Technology*, 54: 362–71.

Brown, L., Griffiths, L. and Rascoff, M. (2007) *University Publishing in a Digital Age*, Ithaka Report, 23 July. Online at: *http://www.ithaka.org* (accessed 4 August 2007).

Bryant, L. (2007) 'Emerging trends in social software for education', in *Emerging Technologies for Learning, Vol. 2*. Coventry: British Educational Communications and Technology Agency. Online at: *http:www.becta.org.uk* (accessed 3 July 2007).

Brynin, M. and Lichtwardt, B. (2004) *Work, Home and Work at Home: Implications for the New Economy and New Forms of Work, Final Report*, E-Living Project Report. Colchester: ISER, University of Essex.

Brynin, M., Rabar, Y. and Soffer, T. (2004) *The New ICTs: Age, Gender and the Family*, E-Living Project Report. Colchester: ISER, University of Essex. Online at: *http://www.eurescom.de/e-living* (accessed 18 February 2008).

Buchman, D. and Funk, J. (1996) 'Video and computer games in the '90s: children's time commitment and game preference', *Children Today*, 24: 12–15.

Buckingham, D. (2006) 'Is there a digital generation?', in D. Buckingham and R. Willett (eds), *Digital Generations: Children, Young People, and New Media*. Hillsdale, NJ: Lawrence Erlbaum Associates, pp. 1–13.

Budd, J.M and Connaway, L.S. (1997) 'University faculty and networked information: results of a survey', *Journal of the American Society for Information Science*, 48(9): 843–52.

Bulkley, K. (2007) 'News on the virtual second', *The Guardian*, MediaGuardian, 21 May, p. 6.

Calvert, S.L. (1999) *Children's Journeys through the Information Age*. Boston: McGraw-Hill.

Calvert, S.L. (2005) 'Cognitive effects of video games', in J. Raessens and J. Goildstein (eds), *Handbook of Computer Game Studies*. Cambridge, MA: MIT Press, pp. 125–31.

Calvert, S.L. and Tan, S. (1994) 'Impact of visual reality on young adults' physiological arousal and aggressive thoughts: interaction versus observation', *Journal of Applied Developmental Psychology*, 15: 125–39.

Carter, M. (2007) 'Online drama proves a lucrative hit', *The Guardian*, MediaGuardian, 12 November, p. 7.

Castells, M. (1996–8) *The Information Age*, 3 vols: Vol. 1: *The Rise of the Network Society* (1996); Vol. 2: *The Power of Identity* (1997); Vol. 3: *End of Millennium* (1998). Oxford: Blackwell.

Chang, N.C. and Perng, J.H. (2001) 'Information search habits of graduate students at Tatung University', *International Information and Library Review*, 33(4): 341–6.

Chen, H.G. and Crowston, K. (1997) 'Comparative diffusion of the telephone and World Wide Web: an analysis of rates of adoption'. Online at: *http://www.crowston.syr.edu/papers/webnet97.*

Chen, S. (1993) 'A study of high school students' online catalog searching behavior', *School Library Media Quarterly*, Fall, pp. 33–40.

Chen, S. (2003) 'Searching the online catalog and web', *Journal of Educational Media and Library Sciences*, 41(1): 29–43.

Chen, X. (2006) 'MetaLib, WebFeat, and Google: the strengths and weaknesses of federated search engines compared with Google', *Online Information Review*, 30(4): 413–27.

Church, J. (ed.) (1995) *Social Trends 25*. London: HMSO.

Church, J. (ed.) (1996) *Social Trends 26*. London: HMSO.

Clarke, A. and Foster, A. (2005) *Children's and Young People's Reading Habits and Preferences: The Who, What, Why, Where and When.* London: National Literacy Trust.

Coats, R. (2001) 'Power users: a profile of online newspaper consumers'. Online at: *http://www.digitaledge.org/specialreports.html.*

Cole, J.I., Suman, M., Schramm, P., Lunn, R. and Aquino, J.S. (2004) *Ten Years, Ten Trends: The Digital Future Report – Surveying the Digital Future, Year 4.* Los Angeles: USC Annenberg School, Center for the Digital Future.

Connaway, L.S. and Snyder, C. (2005) 'Transaction log analyses of electronic book (eBook) usage', *Against the Grain*, 17(1). Online at: *http://www.oclc.org/research/publications/archive/2005/connaway-snyder-atg.pdf.*

Cooper, L. (2002) 'A case study of information-seeking behavior in 7-year-old children in a semistructured situation', *Journal of the American Society for Information Science and Technology*, 53(11): 904–22.

Corradini, E. (2006) 'Teenagers analyse their public library', *New Library World*, 107 (1230/1231): 481–98.

Costello, B., Lenholt, R. and Stryker, J. (2004) 'Using Blackboard in library instruction: addressing the learning styles of Generations X and Y', *Journal of Academic Librarianship*, 30(6): 452–60.

Creasey, G.L. and Myers, B.J. (1986) 'Video games and children: effects in leisure activities, schoolwork and peer involvement', *Merrill-Palmer Quarterly*, 32: 251–62.

Cronin, B. (1995) 'E-journals and tenure', *Journal of the American Society for Information Science*, 46 (9): 700–3.

Crook, C. (2008) 'Theories of formal and informal learning in the world of web 2.0', in *Theorising the Benefits of New Technology for Youth:*

Controversies of Learning and Development, Report of an ESRC Seminar Series, 'The Educational and Social Impact of New Technologies on Young People in Britain', University of Oxford and London School of Economics and Political Science, pp. 30–4.

Currah, A. (2009) *What's Happening to Our News*. Oxford: University of Oxford, Reuters Institute for the Study of Journalism.

D'Esposito, J. and Gardner, R. (1999) 'University students' perceptions of the Internet: an exploratory study', *Journal of Academic Librarianship*, 25(6): 456–61.

Davidson, P. (2005) 'Gadgets rule on college campuses', *USA Today*, 28 March. Online at: *http://www.usatoday.com/tech/news/2005-03-28-college-tech-usat_x.htm* (accessed 18 July 2007).

Davies, C. (2008) 'Views of young people', in *Theorising the Benefits of New Technology for Youth: Controversies of Learning and Development*, Report of an ESRC Seminar Series, 'The Educational and Social Impact of New Technologies on Young People in Britain', University of Oxford and London School of Economics and Political Science, pp. 9–10.

Davis, P.M. (2002) 'For electronic journals, total downloads can predict number of users', *Portal*, 4: 379–92.

Davis, P.M. (2003) 'Information-seeking behavior of chemists: a transaction log analysis of referral URLs', *Journal of the American Society for Information Science and Technology*, 55: 326–32.

Davis, P.M. (2004a) 'Patterns in electronic journal usage: challenging the composition of geographic consortia', *College and Research Libraries*, 63: 484–97.

Davis, P.M. (2004b) 'Tragedy of the commons revisited: librarians, publishers, faculty and the demise of a public resource', *Portal*, 3: 547–62.

de Groote, S.L. and Dorsch, J.L. (2001) 'Online journals: impact on print journal usage', *Bulletin of the Medical Library Association*, 89: 372–8.

de Groote, S.L. and Dorsch, J.L. (2003) 'Measuring use patterns of online journals and databases', *Journal of the Medical Library Association*, 91: 231–40.

Deloitte (2007a) *Media Predictions: TMT Trends 2007*. Online at: *http://www.deloitte.com/dtt/cda/doc/content/dtt_mediaPredictions011107* (accessed 3 August 2007).

Deloitte (2007b) *Telecommunications Predictions: TMT Trends 2007*. Online at: *http://www.usiia.org/news/dtt_TelecomPredictions* (accessed 3 August 2007).

Dimmick, J., Chen, Y. and Li, Z. (2004) 'Competition between the internet and traditional news media: the gratification-opportunities niche dimension', *Journal of Media Economics*, 17(1): 19–33.

Dixon, A. (2006) 'Track Back', *Guardian Unlimited Online*. Online at: *http://blogs.guardian.co.uk/culturevulture/* (accessed 6 September 2007).

Dominick, J.R. (1984) 'Video games, television violence and aggression in teenagers', *Journal of Communication*, 34: 136–47.

Dong, X. (2003) 'Searching information and evaluation of the Internet: a Chinese academic user survey', *International Information and Library Review*, 35(2–4): 163–87.

Dorval, M. and Pepin, M. (1986) 'Effect of playing a video game on a measure of spatial visualization', *Perceptual and Motor Skills*, 62: 159–62.

Dutton, W. and Helsper, E.J. (2007) *The Internet in Britain – 2007*. Oxford: Oxford Internet Institute. Online at: *http://www.oii.ox.ac.uk/microsites/oxis* (accessed 25 August 2007).

Dutton, W.H., Rogers, E.M. and Jun, S.H. (1987) 'The diffusion and impacts of information technology in households', in *Oxford Surveys in Information Technology*, Vol. 4. New York: Oxford University Press, pp. 133–93.

Eason, K., Richardson, S. and Yu, L. (2000) 'Patterns of use of electronic journals', *Journal of Documentation*, 56(5): 477–504.

Eason, K., Yu, L.Z. and Harker, S. (2000) 'The use and usefulness of functions in electronic journals: the experience of the SuperJournal Project', *Program*, 34: 1–28.

Edmunds, J. and Turner, B. (2003) *Generations, Culture and Society*. Buckingham: Open University Press.

Edwards, S.L. and Bruce, C.S. (2002) 'Reflective internet searching: an action research model', *The Learning Organization: An International Journal*, 9(4): 180–8.

European Commission (2000) *Eurobarometer 53*. Online at: *http://www.europa.eu.int/comm/public_opinion/archives/eb/ebs_158_en.pdf*.

European Commission (2001a) *e-Learning: Better e-Learning for Europe*. Brussels: Directorate-General for Education and Culture.

European Commission (2001b) *Spot: ICT in European Universities: Trends and Perspectives*. Brussels: SOCRATES-MINERVA Programme, Directorate-General for Education and Culture of the European Commission.

European Commission (2002) *Eurobarometer 57*. Online at: *http://www.europa.eu.int/comm/public_opinion/archives/eb/eb57/eb57_en.htm*.

European Commission (2003) *Eurobarometer 58*. Online at: *http://www*
.europa.eu.int/comm/public_opinion/archives/eb/eb58/eb58_en.htm.

European Interactive Advertising Association (2007) 'Social networking
to drive next wave of internet usage'. Online at: *http://www.eiaa.net/*
news/eiaa-articles-details.asp?id=1068 (accessed 3 July 2007).

Fearn, H. (2008) 'Grappling with the digital divide', *Times Higher*
Education, 14 August, pp. 37–9.

Ferguson, D. and Perse, E. (2000) 'The World Wide Web as a functional
alternative to television', *Journal of Broadcasting and Electronic*
Media, 44(2): 155–74.

Fidel, R., Davies, R., Douglass, M., Holder, J., Hopkins, C., Kushner, E.,
Miyagishima, B. and Toney, C. (1999) 'A visit to the information mall:
web searching behavior of high school students', *Journal of the*
American Society for Information Science, 50(1): 24–37.

Findahl, O. (2001) 'Swedes and the Internet – Year 2000'. Online at: *http://*
www.worldinternetinstitute.com/filer.Swedes_and_the_internet_2000.pdf.

Flaxbart, D. (2001) 'Conversations with chemists: information-seeking
behavior of chemistry faculty in the electronic age', *Science and*
Technology Libraries, 21: 5–26.

Flichy, P. (2006) 'New media history', in S. Livingstone and M. Bovill
(eds), *Children and Their Changing Media Environment: A European*
Comparative Study. Mahwah, NJ: Lawrence Erlbaum Associates,
pp. 186–204.

Forsyth, A.S. and Lancy, D.F. (1987) 'Simulated travel and place
location: learning in a computer adventure game', *Journal of*
Educational Computing Research, 3: 377–94.

Fox, S. (2005) 'Digital divisions', Pew Internet and American Life
Project. Online at: *http://www.pewinternet.org*.

Fox, S. (2006) 'Are "wired seniors" sitting ducks?', Data Memo, Pew
Internet and American Life Project.

Frand, J.L. (2000) 'Information-age mindset: changes in students and
implications for higher education', *EDUCAUSE Review*, 35(5):
15–24. Online at: *http://educause.edu/apps/er/erm00/articles005/*
erm0051.pdf (accessed 12 May 2006).

Franklin, B. and Plum, T. (2004) 'Library usage patterns in the electronic
information environment', *Information Research*, 9. Online at: *http://*
informationr.net/ir/9-4/paper187.html (accessed 18 September 2006).

Frederickson, J., Warren, B., Gillott, H. and Weaver, P. (1982) 'The name
of the game is literacy', *Classroom Computer News*, May/June,
pp. 23–7.

Friedlander, A. (2002) *Dimensions and Use of the Scholarly Information Environment*. Washington, DC: Digital Library Federation and Council on Library and Information Resources. Online at: *http://www .clir.org/PUBS/reports/pub110/contents.html* (accessed 11 July 2007).

Friedman, T. (1995) 'Making sense of software: computer games and interactive textuality', in S. G. Jones (ed.), *CyberSociety: Computer-Mediated Communication and Community*. Thousand Oaks, CA: Sage, pp. 73–89.

Fry, J. and Talja, S. (2004) 'The cultural shaping of scholarly communication: explaining e-journal use within and across academic fields', in ASIST, *Proceedings of the 67th ASIST Annual Meeting*, 41. Medford, NJ: Information Today.

Funk, J.B. (1993) 'Video games', *Adolescent Medicine: State of the Art Reviews*, 4: 589–98.

Funk, J., Germann, J. and Buchmann, D. (1997) 'Rating electronic games in the United States', *Trends in Communication*, 2: 111–26.

Fyffe, R. (2002) 'Technological change and the scholarly communications reform movement: reflections on Castells and Giddens', *Library Resources and Technical Services*, 46: 50–61.

Gallup, G. (1982) 'The typical American teenager', *Seattle Times*, 19 May, p. 17.

Gardner, S. and Eng, S. (2005) 'What students want: Generation Y and the changing function of the academic library', *Libraries and the Academy*, 5(3): 405–20.

Garrod, P. and Weller, J. (2005) *Ebooks in UK Public Libraries: Where We Are Now and the Way Ahead*. Issue paper from the Networked Services Policy Task Group. Online at: *http://www.ukoln.ac.uk/public/ nstg/e-books*.

Geck, C. (2006) 'The generation Z connection: teaching information literacy to the newest net generation', *Teacher Librarian*, 33(3): 19–23.

Gibbins, P. (1994) *The New Production of Knowledge*. London: Sage.

Gladwell, M. (2000) *The Tipping Point: How Little Things Can Make a Big Difference*. London: Little, Brown.

Graham, P. and Goodrum, A.A. (2007) 'New media literacies: at the intersection of technical, cultural, and discursive knowledges', in R. Mansell, C. Avgerou, D. Quah and R. Silverstone (eds), *The Oxford Handbook of Information and Communication Technologies*. Oxford: Oxford University Press, pp. 473–93.

Greenfield, P.M. (1994) 'Video games as cultural artefacts', *Journal of Applied Developmental Psychology*, 15(1): 3–12.

Greenfield, P.M., Brannon, G. and Lohr, D. (1994) Two-dimensional representation of movement through three-dimensional space: the role of video game expertise', *Journal of Applied Developmental Psychology*, 1(1): 87–103.

Greenfield, P.M., de Winstanley, P., Kilpatrick, H. and Kaye, D. (1994) 'Action video games and informal education: effects on strategies for dividing visual attention', *Journal of Applied Developmental Psychology*, 15(1): 105–23.

Greenfield, P.M., Camaioni, P., Ercoloni, L., Weiss, B., Laubder, A. and Stevenson, H. (1994) 'Cognitive socialization by computer games in two cultures: inductive discovery or mastery of an iconic code', *Journal of Applied Developmental Psychology*, 15(1): 59–85.

Griffin, T. (ed.) (1998) *Social Trends 28*. London: HMSO.

Griffiths, M.D. (1991) 'Amusement machine playing in childhood and adolescence: a comparative analysis of video games and fruit machines', *Journal of Adelescence*, 14: 53–73.

Griffiths, M.D. (1995) *Adolescnt Gambling*. London: Routledge.

Griffiths, M.D. (2005) 'The therapeutic value of video games', in J. Raessens and J. Goldstein (eds), *Handbook of Computer Game Studies*. Cambridge, MA: MIT Press, pp. 161–71.

Grimes, D. and Boening, C. (2001) 'Worries with the Web: a look at student use of web resources', *College and Research Libraries*, January, pp. 11–22.

Gunter, B. (2005) 'The promise of e-books', *Library and Information Update*, 4(10): 25.

Gunter, B. and McLaughlin, C. (1992) *Television: The Public's View*. London: Independent Television Commission and John Libbey.

Gunter, B., Sancho-Aldridge, J. and Winstone, P. (1994) *Television: The Public's View – 1993*. London: Independent Television Commission and John Libbey.

Gunter, B., Campbell, V., Touri, M. and Gibson, R. (2009) 'Blogs, news and credibility', *Aslib Proceedings: New Information Perspectives*, Special Issue: *Blogging and the Erosion of Public and Private Life Spheres*, 61(2): 185–204.

Gunter, B., Russell, C., Withey, R. and Nicholas, D. (2004) 'Broadband in Britain: how does it compare with narrowband?', *Aslib Proceedings: New Information Perspectives*, 56(2): 89–98.

Hay, L. (2000) 'Educating the Net Generation', *The School Administrator*. Online at: *http://www.aasa.org/publications/saarticledetail.cfm?mnitemnumber=...* (accessed 15 May 2007).

Haycock, K. and Huang, S. (2001) 'Are today's high school graduates ready?', *Thinking K–16*, 5(1): 3–17.

Hayes, B., Lancy, D.F. and Evans, B. (1985) 'Computer adventure games and the development of information-processing skills', in G.H. McNick (ed.), *Comprehension, Computers and Communication*. Athens, GA: University of Georgia Press, pp. 60–6.

Heinstrom, J. (2003) 'Fast surfers, broad scanners and deep divers as users of information technology – relating information preferences to personality traits', *Proceedings of the 66th Annual Meeting of the American Society for Information Science and Technology*. Arizona: Information Today, pp. 247–54.

Heinstrom, J. (2006) 'Fast surfing for availability or deepdiving into quality – motivation and information seeking among middle and high school students', *Information Research*, 11(4). Online at: *http://informationr.net/ir/11-4/paper265.html* (accessed 31 August 2007).

Herman, E. (2001) 'End users in academia: meeting the information needs of university researchers in an electronic age. Part 2', *Aslib Proceedings*, 533(10): 431–57.

Hernon, P., Hopper, R., Leach, M.R., Saunders, L.L. and Zhang, J. (2007) 'E-book use by students: undergraduates in economics, literature, and nursing', *Journal of Academic Librarianship*, 33(1): 3–13.

Hirsh, S.G. (1999) 'Children's relevance criteria and information seeking on electronic resources', *Journal of the American Society for Information Science*, 50(14): 1265–83.

Hitlin, P. and Rainie, L. (2005) 'Teens, technology and school', data memo, Pew Internet and American Life Project, Washington, DC. Online at: *http://www.pewinternet.org*.

Holloway, S. and Valentine, G. (2001) 'Children at home in the wired world', *Urban Geography*, 22(6): 562–83.

Horrigan, J.B. (2001) 'Pew Internet Project', data memo, Pew Internet and American Life Project, Washington, DC. Online at: *http://www.pewinternet.org*.

Horrigan, J.B. (2006a) 'The internet as a resource for news and information about science', Pew Internet and American Life Project, Washington, DC. Online at: *http://www.pewinternet.org*.

Horrigan, J.B. (2006b) 'Home broadband adoption 2006', Pew Internet and American Life Project, Washington, DC. Online at: *http://www.pewinternet.org*.

Horrigan, J.B. (2007) 'A typology of information and communication technology users', Pew Internet and American Life Project, Washington, DC. Online at: *http://www.pewinternet.org*.

Horrigan, J.B. and Rainie, L. (2002) 'The broadband diffusion', Pew Internet and American Life Project, Washington, DC. Online at: *http:// www.pewinternet.org*.

Houghton, J.W., Steele, C. and Henty, M. (2003) *Changing Research Practices in the Digital Information and Communication Environment.* Canberra: Australian Department of Education, Science and Training.

Houghton, J.W., Steele, C. and Henty, M. (2004) 'Research practices and scholarly communication in the digital environment', *Learned Publishing*, 17: 231–49.

Hsieh-Yee, I. (2001) 'Research on Web search behaviour', *Library and Information Science Research*, 23: 167–85.

Huebner, J. (2005) 'A possible declining trend for worldwide innovation', *Technological Forecasting and Social Change*, 72: 970–86.

Hunter, K. (ed.) (1996) *The Tulip Final Report.* New York: Elsevier Science. Online at: *http://www.elsevier.com/wps/find/librariansinfo .librarians/tulipfr* (accessed 20 July 2007).

Huntington, P. and Nicholas, D. (2008) *Student Information Seeking Behaviour in Context. Work Package 4, Information Behaviour of the Researcher of the Future*, British Library/JISC Study. London: University College London, Department of Information Studies.

Institute for the Future (2002) *Final Synthesis Report of the e-Journal User Study.* Menlo Park, Palo Alto, CA.

iProspect (2007) *Social Networking User Behaviour Study.* Available at: *http://www.iprospect.com/about/researchstudy_2007_socialnetworkin gbehavior* (accessed 3 July 2007).

ITC (1998) *Television: The Public's View – 1997.* London: Independent Television Commission.

Jacobs, N. (2001) 'Information technology and interests in scholarly communication: a discourse analysis', *Journal of the American Society for Information Science and Technology*, 52: 1122–33.

Jacoby, J. and Laskowski, M.S. (2004) 'Measurement and analysis of electronic reserve usage: toward a new path in online library service assessment', *Portal*, 4: 219–32.

Jamali, H.R., Nicholas, D. and Huntington, P. (2005) 'The use and users of scholarly e-journals: a review of log analysis studies', *Aslib Proceedings*, 57(6): 554–71.

James, M., Wotring, C. and Forrest, E. (1995) 'An exploratory study of the perceived benefits of electronic bulletin board use and their impact on other communication activities', *Journal of Broadcasting and Electronic Media*, 39: 30–50.

Jansen, M.B.J. and Spink, A. (2006) 'How are we searching the World Wide Web? A comparison of nine search engine transaction logs', *Information Processing and Management*, 42(1): 248–63.

Jarvis, J. (2007) 'Friendship on the web will thrive and make a fortune', *The Guardian*, Media Guardian, 3 December, p. 6.

Jeffries, L. and Atkin, D. (1996) 'Predicting use of technologies for communication and consumer needs', *Journal of Broadcasting and Electronic Media*, 40: 318–30.

Johnson, L. (2006) 'The sea change before us', *EDUCAUSE Review*, March/April, pp. 72–3.

Johnsson-Smaragdi, U. (2001) 'Media use styles among the young', in S. Livingstone and M. Bovill (eds), *Children and Their Changing Media Environment: A European Comparative Study*. Mahwah, NJ: Lawrence Erlbaum Associates, pp. 113–40.

Jones, M.B. (1984) 'Videos games as psychological tests', *Simulation and Games*, 15: 131–57.

Jones, S. (2002) 'The Internet goes to college', Pew Internet and American Life Project. Washington, DC. Online at: *http://www.pewinternet.org/pdfs/PIP_College_Report.pdf* (accessed 19 July 2007).

Jones, T., Hanney, S., Buxton, M. and Burns, T. (2004) 'What British psychiatrists read: questionnaire survey of journal usage among clinicians', *British Journal of Psychiatry*, 185: 251–7.

Joyce, B.R. and Joyce, E.A. (1970) 'The creation of information systems for children', *Interchange*, 1: 1–12.

Judge, E. and Sabbagh, D. (2007) 'How Facebook has become a very British way to stay in touch', *The Times*, 12 December, p. 8.

Kafai, Y. and Bates, M.J. (1997) 'Internet Web-searching instruction in the elementary classroom: building a foundation for information literacy', *School Library Media Quarterly*, 25: 103–11.

Kawashima, T. et al. (1991) 'Development of skill of children in the performance of the family computer game "Super Mario Brothers"', *Journal of Human Ergology*, 20(2): 199–215.

Kayany, J. and Yelsma, P. (2000) 'Displacement effects of online media in the socio-technical contexts of households', *Journal of Broadcasting and Electronic Media*, 44(2): 215–29.

Ke, H.R., Kwakkelaar, R., Tai, Y.M. and Chen, L.C. (2002) 'Exploring behavior of E-journal users in science and technology: transaction log analysis of Elsevier's ScienceDirect OnSite in Taiwan', *Library and Information Science Research*, 24: 265–91.

Kidd, T. (2002) 'Electronic journal usage statistics in practice', *Serials*, 15(1): 11–17.

Kiesler, S., Sproull, L. and Eccles, J.S. (1983) 'Second class citizens', *Psychology Today*, 17(3): 41–8.

King, D.W. and Montgomery, C.H. (2002) 'After migration to an electronic journal collection: impact on faculty and doctoral students', *D-Lib Magazine*, 8(12).

King, D.W. and Tenopir, C. (2001) 'Using and reading scholarly literature', *Annual Review of Information Science and Technology*, 34: 423–77.

King, D.W., Tenopir, C., Montgomery, C.H. and Aerni, S.E. (2003) 'Patterns of journal use by faculty at three diverse universities', *D-Lib Magazine*, 9. Online at: *http://www.dlib.org/dlib/october03/king/10king.html* (accessed 18 September 2006).

Kipnis, D. and Childs, G. (2005) *Educating Generation X and Generation Y: Teaching Tips for Librarians*, AISR Staff Papers and Presentations. Academic and Instructional Support and Resources, pp. 25–33.

Kling, R. and Callahan, E. (2003) 'Electronic journals, the internet and scholarly communication', *Annual Review of Information Science and Technology*, 37: 127–77.

Kling, R. and McKim, G. (2000) 'Not just a matter of time: field differences and the shaping of electronic media in supporting scientific communication', *Journal of the American Society for Information Science*, 51(14): 1306–20.

Kling, R., McKim, G. and King, A. (2003) 'A bit more to it: scholarly communication forums as socio-technical interaction networks', *Journal of the American Society for Information Science and Technology*, 54: 47–67.

Knight, J. and Manson, K. (2006) 'Secret lives of Generation Y', @ *Sunday Times Online*, 12 February. Online at: *http://technology.timesonline.co.uk/tol/news/tech_and_web/article72* (no longer available).

Koenig, M.E.D. (2001) 'Lessons from the study of scholarly communication for the new information era', *Scientometrics*, 51: 511–23.

Kortelainen, T. (2004) 'An analysis of the use of electronic journals and commercial journal article collections through the FinELib portal', *Information Research*, 9. Online at: *http://informationr.net/ir/9-2/paper168.html* (accessed 18 September 2006).

Kress, G. (2003) *Literacy in the New Media Age*. London: Routledge.

Kress, G. and van Leeuwen, T. (1996) *Reading Images: The Grammar of Visual Design*. London: Routledge.

Kubey, R. and Larson, R. (1990) 'The use of experience of the new video media among children and adolescents', *Communication Research*, 17: 107–30.

Kurtz, M.J., Eichhorn, G., Accomazzi, A., Grant, C.S., Murray, S.S. and Watson, J.M. (2000) 'The NASA Astrophysics Data System: overview', *Astronomy and Astrophysics* (Supplement Series), 143: 41–59.

Lancaster, F.W. and Sandore, B. (1997) *Technology and Management in Library and Information Services*. London: Library Association.

Lancy, D.F. and Hayes, B.L. (1988) 'Interactive fiction and the reluctant reader', *English Journal*, 77: 42–6.

Large, A. (2005) 'Children, teenagers, and the Web', *Annual Review of Information Science and Technology*, 39: 347–92.

Large, A., Beheshti, J. and Breuleux, A. (1998) 'Information seeking in a multimedia environment by primary school students', *Library and Information Science Research*, 20(4): 343–76.

Lawrence, G.H. (1986) 'Using computers for the treatment of psychological problems', *Computers in Human Behaviour*, 2: 43–62.

Lazinger, S.S., Bar-Ilan, J. and Peritz, B.C. (1997) 'Internet use by faculty members in various disciplines: a comparative case study', *Journal of the American Society for Information Science*, 48(6): 508–18.

Leibscher, P., Abels, E.G. and Denman, D.W. (1997) 'Factors that influence the use of electronic networks by science and engineering faculty at small institutions. Part II: Preliminary use indicators', *Journal of the American Society for Information Science*, 48(6): 496–507.

Lenhart, A. (2005) 'Protecting teens online', Pew Internet and American Life Project, Washington, DC. Online at: *http://www.pewinternet.org* (accessed 20 July 2006).

Lenhart, A. (2007) 'Social networking websites and teens: an overview', Pew Internet and American Life Project, Washington, DC. Online at: *http://www.pewinternet.org*.

Lenhart, A. and Fox, S. (2006) 'Bloggers: a portrait of the Internet's new storytellers', Pew Internet and American Life Project, Washington, DC, 19 July.

Lenhart, A., Madden, M. and Hitlin, P. (2005) 'Teens and technology', Pew Internet and American Life Project, Washington, DC. Online at: *http://www.pewinternet.org*.

Lenhart, A., Maya, S. and Graziano, M. (2001) 'The Internet and education', Pew Internet and American Life Project, Washington, DC. Online at: *http://www.pewinternet.org*.

Lenhart, A., Simon, M. and Graziano, M. (2001) *The Internet and Education: Findings of the Pew Internet and American Life Project*. Online at: *http://www.pewinternet.org/pdfs/PIP_Schools_Report.pdf*.

Levin, D. and Arafeh, S. (2002) 'The digital disconnect: the widening gap between internet-savvy students and their schools', Pew Internet and

American Life Project, Washington, DC. Online at: *http://www .pewinternet.org.*

Levin, D., Arafeh, S., Lenhart, A. and Rainie, L. (2002) 'The digital disconnect: the widening gap between Internet savvy students and their schools', Pew Internet and American Life Project, Washington, DC. Online at: *http://www.pewinternet.org/pdfs/PIP_Schools_Internet_ Report.pdf.*

Liebenau, J. (2007) *Innovation Trends: Prioritising Emerging Technologies Shaping the UK to 2017*, DTI Occasional Paper No. 8. London: Department of Trade and Industry.

Liebscher, P. and Marchionini, G. (1988) 'Browse and analytical search strategies in a full-text CD-ROM encyclopedia', *School Library Media Quarterly*, 16 (Summer): 223–33.

Lin, C.A. (1994) 'Exploring potential factors for home videotext adoption', in J. Hanson (ed.), *Advances in Telematics*, Vol. 2. New York: Ablex, pp. 111–21.

Lin, C.A. (1998) 'Exploring the personal computer adoption dynamics', *Journal of Broadcasting and Electronic Media*, 41(1): 95–112.

Ling, R. (2004) *Social Capital and ISTs*, E-Living Project Report. Colchester: Telenor, University of Essex. Online at: *http://www .eurescom.de./e-living* (accessed 18 February 2008).

Linn, M.C. and Peterson, A.C. (1985) 'Emergence and characterization of sex differences in spatial ability: a meta-analysis', *Child Development*, 56: 1479–98.

Lippincott, J. (2005) 'Net generation students and libraries', *EDUCAUSE Review*, March/April, pp. 56–66.

Littleton, K., Light, P., Joiner, R. and Messer, D. (1992) 'Pairing and gender effects on children's computer-based learning', *European Journal of Psychology of Education*, 4: 311–24.

Liu, Z.M. (2003) 'Trends in transforming scholarly communication and their implications', *Information Processing and Management*, 39: 889–98.

Liu, Z. (2006) 'Print vs. electronic resources: a study of user perceptions, preferences, and use', *Information Processing and Management*, 42(2): 583–92.

Livingstone, S. (2008) 'Introduction', in *Theorising the Benefits of New Technology for Youth: Controversies of Learning and Development*, Report of an ESRC Seminar Series, 'The Educational and Social Impact of New Technologies on Young People in Britain'. University of Oxford and London School of Economics and Political Science, pp. 6–8.

Livingstone, S. and Bober, M. (2005) *UK Children Go Online: Final Report of the Key Project Findings*. Swindon: Economic and Social Research Council.

Livingstone, S. and Bovill, M. (2001a) *Families, Schools and the Internet*. Online at: *http://www.media@lse* (accessed 2 August 2007).

Livingstone, S. and Bovill, M. (eds) (2001b) *Children and Their Changing Media Environment: A European Comparative Study*. Mahwah, NJ: Lawrence Erlbaum Associates.

Livingstone, S., Bober, M. and Helsper, E. (2005) 'Active participation or just more information?', *Information, Communication and Society*, 8(3): 287–314.

Loftus, G.A. and Loftus, E.P. (1983) *Mind at Play: The Psychology of Video Games*. New York: Basic Books.

Loh, C.S. and Williams, M.D. (2002) 'What's in a Web site? Student perceptions', *Journal of Research on Technology in Education*, 34(3): 351–63.

Long, S. (2005) 'Digital natives: if you aren't one, get to know one', *New Library World*, 106 (1210/11): 187–9.

Lorenzen, M. (2001) 'The land of confusion? High school students and their use of the World Wide Web for research', *Research Strategies*, 18: 151–63.

Lorenzo, G. and Dziuban, C. (2006) *Ensuring the Net Generation Is Net Savvy*, ELI Paper 2, ed. D. Oblinger. EDUCAUSE Learning Initiative. Online at: *http://www.educause.edu/ir/library/pdf/ELI3006.pdf* (accessed 23 July 2007).

Lorenzo, G., Oblinger, D. and Dziuban, C. (2006) *How Choice, Co-creation, and Culture Are Changing: What It Means to Be Net Savvy*, ELI Paper 4. EDUCAUSE Learning Initiative. Online at: *http://www.educause.edu/ir/library/pdf/ELI3008.pdf* (accessed 23 July 2007).

Los Angeles Times/Bloomberg (2007a) 'Los Angeles Times/Bloomberg Survey of Pop Culture and Entertainment in the United States: Computers, Cell Phones and Multitasking'. Online at: *http://www.latimes.com/news/custom/timespoll/*.

Los Angeles Times/Bloomberg (2007b) 'Los Angeles Times/Bloomberg Survey of Pop Culture and Entertainment in the United States: Jon Stewart? No Way. Teens Stay Caught Up By Watching Local News'. Online at: *http://www.latimes.com/news/custom/timespoll/*.

Luczak, H., Roetting, M. and Schmidt, L. (2003) 'Let's talk: anthropomorphization as means to cope with stress of interacting with technical devices', *Ergonomics*, 46(13–14): 1361–74.

Mabe, M.A. (2001) 'Digital dilemmas: electronic challenges for the scientific journal publisher', *Aslib Proceedings*, 53: 85–92.

Mabe, M.A. and Amin, M. (2002) 'Dr Jekyll and Dr Hyde: author-reader asymmetries in scholarly and publishing', *Aslib Proceedings*, 54: 149–57.

McDonald, J.D. (2007) 'Understanding journal usage: a statistical analysis of citation and use', *Journal of the American Society for Information Science and Technology*, 58(1): 39–50.

McGrath, M. (2002) 'Assumptions versus reality: user behaviour in sourcing scholarly information', *Interlending and Document Supply*, 30: 120–5.

Mackay, H. and Gillespie, G. (1992) 'Extending the social shaping of technology approach: ideology and appropriation', *Social Studies of Science*, 22: 685–716.

MacKenzie, D. and Wajcman, J. (eds) (1999) *The Social Shaping of Technology*, 2nd edn. Philadelphia, PA and London: Open University Press and Taylor & Francis.

McKnight, C. (1997) *Electronic Journals: What Do Users Think of Them?* Proceedings of the International Symposium on Research, Development and Practice in Digital Libraries ISDL'97, Tsukuba, Ibaraki, Japan, 18–21 November. Online at: *http://www.dl.slis.tsukuba.ac.jp/ISDL97/proceedings/mcknight.html* (accessed 19 July 2007).

McKnight, C. and Price, S. (1999) 'A survey of author attitudes and skills in relation to article publishing in paper and electronic journals', *Journal of Documentation*, 55: 556–76.

Madden, M. (2005) 'Generations online', Pew Internet and American Life Project, Washington, DC. Online at: *http://www.pewinternet.org*.

Madden, M. and Fox, S. (2006) 'Riding the waves of "Web 2.0"', Pew Internet and American Life Project, Washington, DC. Online at: *http://www.pewinternet.org* (accessed 28 June 2007).

Madden, A.D., Ford, N.J., Miller, D. and Levy, P. (2006) 'Children's use of the internet for information seeking', *Journal of Documentation*, 62(6): 744–61.

Madden, A.D., Eaglestone, B., Ford, N.J. and Whittle, M. (2007) 'Search engines: a first step to finding information: preliminary findings from a study of observed searches', *Information Research*, 12(2). Online at: *http://informationr.net/ir/12-2/paper294.html* (accessed 19 July 2007).

Mahé, A. (2004) 'Beyond usage: understanding the use of electronic journals on the basis of information activity analysis', *Information Research*, 9. Online at: *http://informationr.net/ir/9-4/paper186.html* (accessed 18 September 2006).

Manuel, K. (2002) 'Teaching information literacy to Generation Y', *Journal of Library Administration*, 36: 195–217.

Manville, G. and Schiel, G. (2008) 'Generation Y is wired up and ready for action so what's the problem?', *Times Higher Education*, 14 August, pp. 24–5.

Marchionini, G. (1989) 'Information-seeking strategies of novices using full-text electronic encyclopedia', *Journal of the American Society for Information Science*, 40: 54–66.

Martzoukou, K. (2005) 'A review of Web information seeking research: considerations of method and foci of interest', *Information Research*, 10(2).

Matheson, J. and Pullinger, J. (eds) (1999) *Social Trends 29*. London: The Stationery Office.

Mayfield, K. (2001) 'E-book forecast: cloudy', *Wired News*, 11 January. Online at: *http://www.wired.com/news/culture/0,12844,00* (accessed 6 May 2005).

Mehta, U. and Young, V.E. (1995) 'Use of electronic information resources: a survey of science and engineering faculty', *Science and Technology Libraries*, 15(3): 76–85.

Merchant, L. and Hepworth, M. (2002) 'Information literacy of teachers and pupils in secondary schools', *Journal of Librarianship and Information Science*, 34(2): 81–9.

Miller, C.T. and Harris, J.C. (2004) 'Scholarly journal publication: conflicting agendas for scholars, publishers, and institutions', *Journal of Scholarly Publishing*, 35: 73–91.

Miller, S. (2002) *Information-seeking Behaviour of Academic Scientists in the Electronic Age*. Ottawa: Canadian National Site License Project Evaluation Task Group.

Milne, P. (1999) 'Electronic access to information and its impact on scholarly communication', *Proceedings of the Conference on Information Online and On Disc 99*, 19–21 January. Sydney, Australia. Online at: *http://www.csu.edu.au/special/online99/proceedings99/305b.htm* (accessed 9 July 2007).

Monopoli, M., Nicholas, D., Giorgiou, P. and Korfiati, M. (2002) 'A user oriented evaluation of digital libraries: case study of the electronic journals service of the Library and Information Service of the University of Patras, Greece', *Aslib Proceedings*, 54(2): 103–17.

Moore, P. and St George, A. (1991) 'Children as information seekers: the cognitive demands of books and library systems', *School Library Media Quarterly*, 19(3): 161–8.

MSNBC (2001) 'Internet growing as news medium, at times exceeding traditional media usage'. Online at: *http://www.thefreelibrary.com/ Internet+Growing+as+News+Medium+at+Times+Exceeding+Traditional+ Media*.

Murdock, G., Hartmann, P. and Gray, P. (1992) 'Contextualising home computing: resources and practice', in R. Silverstone and E. Hirsch (eds), *Consuming Technologies: Media and Information in Domestic Spaces*. London: Routledge, pp. 146–60.

Murumatsu, J. and Pratt, W. (2001) *Transparent Queries: Investigating Users' Mental Models of Search Engines*. Paper presented at the 24th Annual International Conference of SIGIR (Special Interest Group on Information Retrieval), New Orleans, 9–13 September, pp. 217–24.

Myhill, M. (2007) 'Canute rules the waves? Hope for e-library tools facing the challenge of the "Google generation"', *Program: Electronic Library and Information Systems*, 41(1): 5–19.

Nawrocki, L.H. and Winner, J.L. (1983) 'Video games: instructional potential and classification', *Journal of Computer-based Instruction*, 10: 80–2.

New Media Consortium (2007) *The Horizon Report 2007*. Stanford, CA: New Media Consortium with EDUCAUSE Learning Initiative.

Nicholas, D. and Huntington, P. (2003) 'Micro-mining and segmented log file analysis: a method for enriching the data yield from Internet log files', *Journal of Information Science*, 29: 391–404.

Nicholas, D., Huntington, P. and Watkinson, A. (2003) 'Digital journals, Big Deals and online searching behaviour: a pilot study', *Aslib Proceedings*, 55(1/2): 84–109.

Nicholas, D., Huntington, P. and Watkinson, A. (2005) 'Scholarly journal usage: the results of deep log analysis', *Journal of Documentation*, 61(2): 248–80.

Nicholas, D., Huntington, P., Jamali, H.R. and Watkinson, A. (in press) 'The users of digital scholarly journals and their information seeking behaviour', *Journal of the American Society for Information Science and Technology*.

Nicholas, D., Huntington, P., Williams, P. and Dobrowolski, T. (2004) 'Re-appraising information seeking behaviour in a digital environment: bouncers, checkers, returnees and the like', *Journal of Documentation*, 60: 24–43.

Nicholas, D., Dobrowolski, T., Withey, R., Russell, C., Huntington, P. and Williams, P. (2003) 'Digital information consumers, players and purchasers: information seeking behaviour in the new digital interactive environment', *Aslib Proceedings*, 55: 23–31.

NIFL (National Institute for Literacy) (2007) National Assessment of Educational Progress. Online at: *http://www.nifl.gov/nifl/facts/NAEP.html* (accessed 12 July 2007).

Noble, R.L and Coughlin, C. (1997) 'Information-seeking practices of Canadian academic chemists: a study of information needs and use of resources in chemistry', *Canadian Journal of Communication*, 22(3). Online at: *http://www.cjc-online.ca/viewarticle.php?id=425andlayout= html* (accessed 19 July 2007).

Norris, P. (2001) *Digital Divide: Civic Engagement, Information Poverty and the Internet Worldwide.* Cambridge: Cambridge University Press.

NSBA (2007) *Creating and Connecting: Research and Guidelines on Online Social and Educational Networking.* National School Boards Association. Online at: *http://www.nsba.org/site/view.asp?CID= 63andDID=41430* (accessed 5 October 2007).

Oblinger, D. (2003) 'Boomers, Gen-Xers and Millenials: understanding the new students', *EDUCAUSE Review*, 38: 37–47.

Oblinger, D. and Hawkins, B. (2005) 'The myth about students: "we understand our students"', *EDUCAUSE Review*, 40(5): 12–13.

Obst, O. (2003) 'Patterns and costs of printed and online journal usage', *Health Information and Libraries Journal*, 20: 22–32.

OCLC (Online Computer Library Center) (2002) *How Academic Librarians Can Influence Students' Web-Based Information Choices*, White Paper on the Information Habits of College Students. Online at: *http://www.mnstate.edu/schwartz/informationhabits.pdf* (accessed 13 July 2007).

Odlyzko, A. (2002) 'The rapid evolution of scholarly communication', *Learned Publishing*, 15: 7–19.

Ofcom (2006) *The Consumer Experience.* London: Office for Communications.

Ofcom (2007a) *Public Service Broadcasting Annual Report.* London: Office for Communications.

Ofcom (2007b) *New News, Future News*, Ofcom Discussion Document. London: Office for Communications.

Ofcom (2007c) *Communications Market Report: Converging Communications Markets*, Research Document. London: Office for Communications.

Ofcom (2007d) *The Future of Children's Television Programming: Research Report.* London: Office for Communications.

Ofcom (2007e) *The International Communications Market 2007*, Research Document. London: Office for Communications.

Oyen, A.S. and Bebko, J.M. (1996) 'The effects of computer games and lesson contexts on children's mnemonic strategies', *Journal of Experimental Child Psychology*, 62(2): 173–89.

Palmer, J.P. and Sandler, M. (2003) 'What do faculty want?', *Netconnect*, January.

Papert, S. (1980) *Mindstorms*. New York: Basic Books.

Patsula, P. (1999) *Applying Learning Theories to Online Instructional Design*. Online at: *http://www.patsula.com/usefo/webbasedlearning/tutorial1/index2.htm*.

Pavey, S. (2006) 'School librarians and the Google generation', *ALISS Quarterly*, 2(1): 3–7.

Pellegrino, J.W., Hunt, E.B., Abate, R. and Farr, S. (1987) 'A computer-based test battery for the assessment of static and dynamic spatial reasoning abilities', *Behaviour Research Methods*, 19: 231–6.

Peter, J. and Valkenburg, P. (2006) 'Research Note: individual differences in perceptions of Internet communication', *European Journal of Communication*, 21(2): 213–26.

Pew Internet and American Life Project (2000–2005) Online at: *http://www.pewinternet.org*.

Pew Internet and American Life Project (2002) 'The digital disconnect: the widening gap between Internet-savvy students and their schools'. Online at: *http://www.pewinternet.org/PPF/r/67/report_display.asp*.

Pew Research Center for the People and the Press (1995). Online at: *http://www.people-press.org*.

Pilgrim, M. (2002) *Adding Titles to Links*. Online at: *http://diveintomark.org/archives/2002/06/* (accessed 18 July 2007).

Pivec, F. (1998) 'Surfing through the Internet – the new content of teenagers' spare time', *Aslib Proceedings*, 50(4): 88–92.

Postman, N. (1985) *Amusing Ourselves to Death: Public Discourse in the Age of Show Business*. New York: Penguin.

Prensky, M. (2001) 'Digital natives, digital immigrants'. Online at: *http://www.marcprensky.com/writing/Prensky%20-%20Digital%20Natives,%20Digital%20Immigrants%20-%20Part1.pdf* (accessed 19 July 2007).

Price, D. (1965) *Little Science, Big Science*. New York: Columbia University Press.

Pullinger, D. (1999) 'Academics and the new information environment: the impact of local factors on use of electronic journals', *Journal of Information Science*, 25(2): 164–72.

Rainie, L. (2005) 'Data memo: the state of blogging', Pew Internet and American Life Project, Washington, DC. Online at: *http://www.pewinternet.org* (accessed 10 February 2005).

Rainie, L. and Tancer, B. (2007) 'Data memo: 36% of online American adults consult Wikipedia', Pew Internet and American Life Project, Washington, DC. Online at: *http://www.pewinternet.org* (accessed 28 June 2007).

Rainie, L., Kalechoff, M. and Hess, D. (2002) 'College students and the web', Pew Internet and American Life Project, Washington, DC. Online at: *http://www.pewinternet.org* (accessed 28 June 2007).

Raltivarakan, B. (2007) 'School learning goes Web 2.0'. Online at: *http://www.rareplay.com/index* (accessed 30 June 2007).

Reeves, B. and Nass, C. (1996) *The Media Equation: How People Treat Computers, Television, and New Media Like Real People and Places.* New York: Cambridge University Press.

Reid, M. (2007) 'Online social networks, virtual communities, enterprises, and information professionals – part 1: past and present'. Online at: *http://www.infotoday.com/searcher/jul07/Reid_Grey.shtml* (accessed 5 October 2007).

Reitsma, R. (2003) 'Online newspapers don't stop the press yet', Forrester. Online at: *http://www.forrester.com/ER/Research/DataSnapshot/ Except/ 0,1317,16480,FF.html.*

Roberts, R.J. Jr and Ondrejko, M. (1995) 'Perception, action and skill: looking ahead to meet the present', in M.M. Haith, J.B. Roberts Jr and B.F. Pennington (eds), *The Development of Future-Oriented Processes.* Chicago: University of Chicago Press, pp. 138–52.

Rodgers, L. (2007) 'UK still loves a good page-turner', *BBC News Online*, 10 July 2007. Online at: *http://news.bbc.co.uk/1/hi/uk/6287344.stm.*

Roesnita, I. and Zainab, A.N. (2005) 'The pattern of e-book use amongst undergraduates in Malaysia: a case of to know is to use', *Malaysian Journal of Library and Information Science*, 10(2): 1–23.

Rogers, D. and Swan, K. (2004) 'Self regulated learning and the Internet', *Teachers College Record*, 106(9): 1804–24.

Rogers, E.M. (1986) *Communication Technology.* New York: Free Press.

Rogers, E.M. (1995) *Diffusion of Innovations*, 4th edn. New York: Free Press.

Rogers, E.M. and Shoemaker, F. (1971) *Diffusion of Innovations*, 2nd edn. New York: Free Press.

Rogers, S.A. (2001) 'Electronic journal usage at Ohio State Univerisity', *College and Research Libraries*, 62(1): 25–34.

Romano, F. (2001) 'The possible future of ebooks and print publishers'. Online at: *http://www.clir.org/pubs/reports/pu106/ebooks* (accessed 5 May 2005).

Rose, B. and Rosin, L. (2002) 'Internet 9: the media and entertainment world of online consumers'. Available at: *http://www.edisonresearch.com/I9_FinalPresentation_1%20per%20page.pdf*.

Rowland, F., Bell, I. and Falconer, C. (1997) 'Human and economic factors affecting the acceptance of electronic journals by readers', *Canadian Journal of Communication*, 22(3). Online at: *http://www.cjc-online.ca/viewarticle.php?id=426andlayout=html* (accessed 20 July 2007).

Rowlands, I., Nicholas, D. and Huntington, P. (2004) 'Scholarly communication in the digital environment: what do authors want?', *Learned Publishing*, 17: 261–73.

Rowling, J.K. (2003) *Harry Potter and the Order of the Phoenix*. London: Bloomsbury.

Rowling, J.K. (2006) *Harry Potter and the Half-Blood Prince* (children's edition), 2nd edn. London: Bloomsbury.

Rowling, J.K. (2007) *Harry Potter and the Deathly Hallows* (children's edition). London: Bloomsbury.

Rudner, L.M., Gellmann, J.S. and Miller-Whitehead, M. (2002) 'Who is reading on-line education journals? Why? And what are they reading?', *D-Lib Magazine*, 8(12). Online at: *http://www.dlib.org*.

Rusch-Feja, D. and Siebecky, U. (1999) 'Evaluation of usage and acceptance of electronic journals', *D-Lib Magazine*, 5(10). Online at: *http://www.dlib.org/dlib/october99/rusch-feja/10rusch-feja-summary.html* (accessed 19 July 2007).

Sandstrom, P.E. (2001) 'Scholarly communication as a socioecological system', *Scientometrics*, 51: 573–605.

Sathe, N.A., Grady, J.L. and Giuse, N.B. (2002) 'Print versus electronic journals: a preliminary investigation into the effect of journal format on research processes', *Journal of the Medical Library Association*, 90: 235–43.

Schacter, J., Chung, G. and Dorr, A. (1998) 'Children's internet searching on complex problems: performance and process analyses', *Journal of the American Society for Information Science*, 49: 840–50.

Searchenginewatch.com (2005) 'Hello natural language search, my old over-hyped search friend', Searchenginewatch.com. Online at: *http://blog.searchenginewatch.com/blog/061005-095006* (accessed 18 July 2007).

Selnow, G.W. (1984) 'Playing video games: the electronic friend', *Journal of Communication*, 34: 148–56.

Selwyn, N. (2006) 'Exploring the "digital disconnect" between net-savvy students and their schools', *Learning Media and Technology*, 31(1): 5–17.

Shaw-Kokot, J. and de la Varre, C. (2001) 'Using a journal availability study to improve access', *Bulletin of the Medical Library Association*, 89: 21–8.

Shenton, A. and Dixon, P. (2002) 'Youngsters' use of public libraries for information: results of a qualitative research project', *New Review of Children's Literature and Librarianship*, 8: 33–53.

Shenton, A. and Dixon, P. (2003a) 'A comparison of youngsters' use of CD-ROM and Internet as information resources', *Journal of the American Society for Information Science and Technology*, 54(11): 1029–49.

Shenton, A. and Dixon, P. (2003b) 'Sequential or selective access? Young people's strategies for finding information in non-fiction books', *New Review of Children's Literature and Librarianship*, 9(1): 57–69.

Shenton, A. and Dixon, P. (2003c) 'Models of young people's information seeking', *Journal of Librarianship and Information Science*, 35(1): 5–22.

Shenton, A. and Dixon, P. (2004) 'Issues arising from youngsters' information-seeking behaviour', *Library and Information Science Research*, 26: 177–200.

Shih, W. and Allen, M. (2006) 'Working with Generation-D: adopting and adapting to cultural learning and change', *Library Management*, 28(1/2): 89–100.

Shiu, E. and Lenhart, A. (2004) 'How Americans use instant messaging', Pew Internet and American Life Project, Washington, DC. Online at: *http://www.pewinternet.org*.

Shoham, S. (1998) 'Scholarly communication: a study of Israeli academic researchers', *Journal of Librarianship and Information Science*, 30(2): 113–21.

Siebenberg, T.R., Galbraith, B. and Brady, E.E. (2004) 'Print versus electronic journal use in three Sci/Tech disciplines: what's going on here?', *College and Research Libraries*, 65: 427–38.

Siwicki, B. (2006) 'Can social networking sway shoppers', *Internet Retailer*, September. Online at: *http://www.internretailer.com/internet/marketing-conference/44521* (accessed 5 October 2007).

Skilbeck, C. (1991) 'Microcomputer-based cognitive rehabilitation', in A. Ager (ed.), *Microcomputers and Clinical Psychology: Issues, Applications and Future Developments*. Chichester: Wiley, pp. 95–118.

Slone, D.J. (2003) 'Internet search approaches: the influence of age, search goals, and experience', *Library and Information Science Research*, 25(4): 403–18.

Smith, E.T. (2003) 'Changes in faculty reading behaviors: the impact of electronic journals on the University of Georgia', *Journal of Academic Librarianship*, 29: 162–8.

Solomon, P. (1993) 'Children's information retrieval behaviour: a case analysis of an OPAC', *Journal of the American Society for Information Science*, 44(5): 245–64.

Spavold, J. (1990) 'The child as naïve user: a study of database use with young children', *International Journal of Man–Machine Studies*, 32: 603–25.

Spink, A., Bateman, J. and Jansen, B.J. (1998a) 'Users' searching behavior on the Excite Web search engine', in M.E. Williams (ed.), *Nineteenth National Online Meeting Proceedings*. New York: Information Today, pp. 375–86.

Spink, A., Bateman, J. and Jansen, B.J. (1998b) 'Searching heterogeneous collections on the Web: behavior of Excite users', *Information Research*, 4. Online at: *http://www.shef.ac.uk/~is/publications/infres/paper53.html* (accessed 12 July 2007).

Spink, A., Bateman, J. and Jansen, B.J. (1999) 'Searching the Web: a survey of Excite users', *Internet Research, Electronic Networking Applications and Policy*, 9: 117–28.

Spink, A., Wolfram, D., Jansen, M.B.J. and Saracevic, T. (2001) 'Searching the web: the public and their queries', *Journal of the American Society for Information Science and Technology*, 52(3): 226–34.

Spiselman, D. (2001) 'The possible future of ebooks and print publishers'. Online at: *http://www.planetebook.com/mainpage.asp?webpageid=122* (accessed 27 May 2005).

Squire, K. and Steinkuehler, C. (2005) 'Meet the gamers', *Library Journal*. Online at: *http://www.libraryjournal.com/article/CA516033.html* (accessed 12 July 2007).

Star, L. (ed.) (1995) *The Cultures of Computing*. Oxford: Blackwell.

Subrahmanyan, K. and Greenfield, P.M. (1994) 'Effect of video game practice on spatial skills in girls and boys', *Journal of Applied Developmental Psychology*, 15(1): 13–22.

Suchman, L. (1996) 'Supporting articulation work', in R. Kling (ed.), *Computerization and Controversy: Value Conflicts and Social Choices*, 2nd edn. San Diego, CA: Academic Press, pp. 407–23.

Sullivan, K. (2005) 'Collection development for the "chip" generation and beyond', *Collection Building*, 24(2): 56–60.

Synovate (2007) 'Leisure time: clean living youth shun new technology'. Online at: *http://www.synovate.com/current/news/article/2007/02* (accessed 3 July 2007).

Talja, S. and Maula, H. (2003) 'Reasons for the use and non-use of electronic journals and databases: a domain analytic study in four scholarly disciplines', *Journal of Documentation*, 59: 673–91.

Tapscott, D. (1998) *Growing up Digital: The Rise of the Net Generation*. New York: McGraw-Hill.

Tapscott, D. (2009) *Grown Up Digital: How the Net Generation Is Changing Your World*. New York: McGraw-Hill.

Tenopir, C. (2003a) *Use and Users of Electronic Library Resources: An Overview and Analysis of Recent Research Studies*. Washington, DC: Council on Library and Information Resources. Online at: *http://www.clir.org/pubs/abstract/pub120abst.html* (accessed 14 August 2007).

Tenopir, C. (2003b) 'Information metrics and user studies', *Aslib Proceedings*, 55: 13–17.

Tenopir, C. and Ennis, L. (2002) 'A decade of digital reference: 1991–2001', *Reference and User Services Quarterly*, 41: 264–73.

Tenopir, C. and King, D.W. (2002) 'Reading behaviour and electronic journals', *Learned Publishing*, 15: 259–65.

Tenopir, C., King, D.W. and Bush, A. (2004) 'Medical faculty's use of print and electronic journals: changes over time and in comparison with scientists', *Journal of the Medical Library Association*, 92: 233–41.

Tenopir, C., King, D.W., Boyce, P., Grayson, M. and Zhang, Y. (2003) 'Patterns of journal use by scientists through three evolutionary phases', *D-Lib Magazine*, 9. Online at: *http://www.dlib.org/dlib/may03/king/05king.html* (accessed 18 September 2006).

Tierney, R.I.U., Kieffer, I., Stowell, L., Desai, E., Whalin, K. and Moses, A.G. (1992) *Computer Acquisition: A Longitudinal Study of the Influence of High Computer Access on Students' Thinking, Learning and Interaction*, Apple Classrooms of Tomorrow Research Report No. 16. Cupertino, CA: Apple Computer, Inc.

Tillman, H.N. (2003) 'Evaluating quality on the net'. Online at: *http://www.hopetillman.com/findqual* (accessed 4 August 2007).

Torma, S. and Vakkari, P. (2004) 'Discipline, availability of electronic resources and the use of Finnish National Electronic Library', *Information Research*, 10. Online at: *http://informationr.net/ir/10-1/paper204.html* (accessed 18 September 2006).

Trachtman, P.A. (1981) 'A generation meets computers – and they are friendly', *Smithsonian*, 12(6): 50–61.

Trelle, S. (2002) 'Information management and reading habits of German diabetologists: a questionnaire survey', *Diabetologia*, 45: 764–74.

Tsay, M.Y. (2003) 'Library journal use and citation age in medical science', *Journal of Documentation*, 55: 543–55.

UCLA (2000) *The UCLA Internet Report: Surveying the Digital Future*. UCLA Centre for Communication Policy. Online at: *http://www.ccp.ucla.edu*.

UCLA (2003) *The UCLA Internet Report: Surveying the Digital Future – Year Three*. UCLA Center for Communications Policy. Online at: *http://www.worldinternetproject.net*.

UNDP (1999) *Human Development Report 1999*. New York: UNDP/ Oxford University Press.

Valenza, J.K. (2006) 'They might be gurus', *Teacher Librarian*, 34(1): 18–26.

Vaughan, K.T.L. (2003) 'Changing use patterns of print journals in the digital age: impacts of electronic equivalents on print chemistry journal use', *Journal of the American Society for Information Science and Technology*, 54: 1149–52.

Walter, P.L. (1996) 'A journal use study: checkouts and in-house use', *Bulletin of the Medical Library Association*, 84: 461–7.

Walters, D. (2007) 'Hyper-connected generation rises', *BBC News online*, 9 May. Online at: *http://news.bbc.co.uk/1/hi/technology/6637865.stm* (accessed 5 September 2007).

Wang, P. (2001) 'Methodologies and methods for user behavioural research', *Annual Review of Information Science and Technology*, 34: 53–9.

Webster, F. (2002) *Theories of the Information Society*, 2nd edn. London: Routledge.

Webster, F. (2006) 'The information society revisited', in L.E. Lievrouw and S. Livingstone (eds), *The Handbook of New Media* (updated student edition). London: Sage, pp. 443–57.

Wellman, B. (1988) 'Structural analysis: from method and metaphor to theory and substance', in B. Wellman and S.D. Berkowitz (eds), *Social Structures: A Network Approach*. Cambridge: Cambridge University Press.

Whitmire, E. (2001) 'A longitudinal study of undergraduates' academic library experiences', *Journal of Academic Librarianship*, 27(5): 378–85.

Williams, D.A. and Wavell, C. (2006) *Information Literacy in the Classroom: Secondary School Teachers' Conceptions*, Aberdeen Business School Research Report 15. Aberdeen: Robert Gordon University.

Williams, P. (1999) 'Net Generation: the experiences, attitudes and behaviour of children using the Internet for their own purposes', *Aslib Proceedings*, 50(9): 315–22.

Williams, R. and Edge, D. (1996) 'The social shaping of technology', *Research Policy*, 25: 865–99.

Windham, C. (2005) 'Father Google and Mother IM: confessions of a Net Gen learner', *EDUCAUSE Review*, 40(5): 42–59.

Winner, L. (1986) 'Do artefacts have politics?', in *The Whale and the Reactor: A Search for Limits in an Age of High Technology*. Chicago: University of Chicago Press, pp. 19–39.

Wiseman, J. (2007) 'Anti-piracy: Don't Copy That Floppy'. Online at: *http://www.johnwiseman.ca/blogging/technology/anti-piracy-dont-copy-that-floppy/* (accessed 6 September 2007).

Worel, S.L. (2004) 'Journal-citation-seeking behavior at two health sciences libraries', *Journal of the Medical Library Association*, 92: 91–4.

Wright, J.C., Huston, A.C., Vandewater, E.A., Bickman, D., Scantlin, R., Kotler, J., Caplovitz, A., Lee, J., Hofferth, S. and Finkelstein, J. (2001) 'American children's use of electronic media in 1997: a national survey', *Journal of Applied Developmental Psychology*, 22: 11–47.

Writenews.com (2003) 'E-book sales expected to top $10 million in 2003', 17 October. Online at: *http://www.writenews.com/2003/101703_ebooks_10mill* (accessed 7 May 2005).

Wulff, J.L. and Nixon, N.D. (2004) 'Quality markers and use of electronic journals in an academic health sciences library', *Journal of the Medical Library Association*, 92: 315–22.

Young, J.R. (2006) 'Book 2.0: scholars turn monographs into digital conversations', *Chronicle of Higher Education*, 51: 41. Online at: *http://www.chronicle.com/free/v52/i47/47a02201* (accessed 3 August 2007).

Zhang, Y. (2001) 'Scholarly use of Internet-based electronic resources', *Journal of the American Society for Information Science*, 52(8): 628–54.

Index

Abebooks, 167
Active Worlds, 160
ADS – *see* NASA Astrophysics Data
    Service
Amazon Kindle, 85, 162
American Chemical Society, 95, 111
articles – *see* journal articles
arXiv, 106, 108, 122
Ask.com, 131
Australia, 95
average Joes, 73

Baby Boomers, 45, 54, 65
BBC, 128, 135, 149–50
Bebo, 159
Beilstein, 112
Belgium, 70
Betamax video tape, 22
BlackBoard, 120
Blackwell, 146
blogging, 15–16, 51, 53–4, 68–70,
    73, 86–7, 89, 128, 150, 152,
    158–9, 162, 165, 169
Bologna Declaration, 155
book reading, 30, 34–5, 135
Boom Echo generation, 65
British Phonographic Industry (BPI),
    144
British Telecom (BT), 149
broadband Internet, 10–11, 48–52, 60
BSkyB, 148

Bulgaria, 47
Bust generation, 65

California, 130
citizen publishers, 149
CNN, 128
cognitive skills, 74–5
CollegeRuled.com, 159
comics, 34–7, 44, 58
computer games:
    cognitive benefits of, 75–8
    use of, 38, 78–80
computer literacy, 74
connectors, 61–2
Copenhagen, 107
COUNTER project, 122
cybernauts, 73

Data for Internet Penetration, 32
Denmark, 107
diffusion of innovations theory,
    23–7, 99
diffusion of technology, 3–5
digital disconnect, 129
digital dissidents, 73
digital divides, 25
Digital Future Project, 46, 53
digital learning, 84–6
digital literacy, 155
digital media uptake, 164–71
digital transition, 96–106

digital visibility, 102, 121
disciplinary differences in use of e-resources, 106–9
Duke University, 101

e-books:
  awareness of, 103–4
  sales, 84–6, 166
  use of, 103–4, 142, 162
e-learning, 15, 68, 87–9, 153–8, 164
e-Lib programme, 97, 119
e-living project, 42, 47
Edinburgh University, 112
educational gaming, 162–3
EDUCAUSE, 118
electronic journals:
  acceptance, 97, 115
  and librarians, 111
  and publishers, 112–13
  evolution, 98–102
  impact on research, 116
  subject differences in use, 108–9
  use, 97, 114
  versus print journals, 102–3, 116, 121
  see also journal articles
electronic publishing, 157
Elgg.com, 159
Elsevier, 97, 101, 166
Encarta, 87
Evolution (computer game), 76

Facebook, 14, 55, 69–70, 86, 89, 118, 158, 167
FinELib, 108–9
Finland, 107
Finnish National Electronic Library – see FinELib
Flickr, 158
France, 22, 70

Gamer Theory, 167
gaming, 162–3
  see also computer games; video games
Generation X, 6, 25, 28, 30, 53, 56, 151
Generation Y, 6, 11, 13, 28, 30, 32, 53–4, 56
Germany, 47, 70, 100
globalisation, 156
Google Generation:
  and e-learning, 153–8
  and higher education, 153–8
  and intellectual property, 143–4
  and learning scenarios, 82–3
  and virtual reality, 144
  definition, 6–7
  evaluation of e-resources, 131–3
  format agnostic, 144
  information-seeking behaviour, 118–20, 129–31, 143
  learning experiences, 137–8
  multitasking, 139–40
  peers as information sources, 140–1
  preference for practice over knowing, 141–2
  preference for quick information, 142–3
  preference for visual information, 134–7
  reading behaviour, 134–7
  searching expertise, 129–31
  shift to digital communication, 139
  TV viewing, 137–8
  use of information services, 133–4
  use of Internet, 11
  use of IT, 127–9
  use of library, 133–4
  use of media, 33–8, 43–4

use of web, 141
zero tolerance for delay, 140
see also Net Generation

Hachette publishing, 85
Harry Potter, 136
Harvard, 120
higher education, 164–71
Hjørland, Birger, 107

ICT – *see* information and
communication technology
Indian Institute of Science, 103
Indian University, 163
information access, 27–8
information and communication
technology (ICT):
adoption, 4–5, 9, 23–6, 41–2,
46–9
and consumption, 148–9
development, 19–23
educational use, 153–8
history, 19–23
impact on life, 1–2, 41–2
impact on research practices, 94–6
pre-Internet era, 7–8
use by age, 37
information behaviour, 109–17
information literacy, 17, 156
information needs, 94–6
Information Society Index, 32
information society, 19–21
information technology (IT) – *see*
ICT
information use, disciplinary
differences, 106–9
information-seeking behaviour, 12,
110–11, 118–20
innovation adoption, 4–5, 90–2
see also ICT adoption
interactive technologies, 74–5

Internet:
adoption, 15–17
as information source, 12–13
educational use, 14–15, 83–4,
86–90
impact on communication, 2
use by age, 44–9, 52–9, 80–2
Internet era, 41–2
iPod, 85, 128, 134, 140
Israel, 47, 102
Italy, 47, 70
Ithaca Strategic Services, 164

Japan, 149, 160
Johns Hopkins University, 101
journal articles:
decay, 117–18
finding, 110–11
reading, 113–15
use, 115–17
writing, 109–10

Kate Modern, 159
King, Stephen, 84

lacklustre veterans, 61–2
Leading Boomers, 56
learning styles, 86–90
librarians and e-journals, 111
LibraryThing, 167
literacy, 71–4
Los Alamos National Laboratory,
106

magazine reading, 29, 31, 34–7, 44,
58, 60, 73, 135–6
media:
Google generation era, 30–3
Internet era, 8–9
pre-Google generation era, 28–30
pre-Internet era, 7–8

media literacy, 71–4
MetaLib, 119
Mobile Phones, 160
Moodle, 120
MSN, 69
MySpace, 14, 55, 69–70, 86, 89,
    118, 128, 159, 167

NASA Astrophysics Data Service, 99,
    116, 118
National Assessment of Educational
    Progress, 137
Net Generation, 93, 120, 123, 128–9
    see also Google Generation
net literacy, 90
New Zealand, 130
newspaper reading, 29–32, 34–5, 44,
    58, 60, 135
Nordic School, 107
Norris, Pippa, 25
Norway, 47

obsolescence – see journal article
    decay
Ofcom (Office of Communication),
    13, 43–4, 47–9, 57–9, 78,
    141–4, 149–52, 160
Office for National Statistics in
    Britain (ONS), 47–9
OhioLINK, 146
omnivores, 61–2
online learning, 83–4
OPAC, 126, 133
OpenSocial, 159
Oxford Internet Institute, 47, 50, 52,
    70, 74
Oxford Scholarship Online, 146

PDA, 55, 128
Pew Internet and American Life
    Project, 44–5, 50–7, 60–1, 68–9,
    82, 87, 119, 129

Planet Edge Project, 73
podcasts, 15, 67, 87, 159, 161
Productivity Enhancers, 61–2
publishers and e-journals, 112–13
PubMed, 110, 112

radio, 1–2, 5, 7–9, 19, 25, 29–32,
    34–5, 38, 44, 57, 59–60, 71,
    161, 169
Random House, 85
reading behaviour, 95, 113–15
    see also book reading; newspaper
    reading; comics
Rogers, Everett, 24
Roving Librarian project, 120
Royal School of Librarianship at
    Copenhagen, 107

scatter of literature, 107–8
scholarly publishing, 161–2
ScienceDirect, 101, 113
searching behavior, 59–63
Second Life, 68, 148, 160–1
Sim City (computer game), 76
Sky News, 161
social construction of technology
    (SCOT), 26–7
social networking, 5, 13–16, 46,
    55–8, 67–70, 81, 86–7, 89,
    92–3, 118, 128–9, 135, 140–1,
    149–53, 156, 158–9, 161, 163,
    165, 167–9
social shaping of technology (SST),
    23, 26, 105
social web, 149–50
    see also social networking
Sofia's Diary, 159
Sony, 149
Sony's Reader, 85
subject differences in use of
    e-resources, 106–9
SuperJournal project, 97, 110

Sweden, 59
Synthetic Worlds Initiative, 163

tablet PC, 128
TAPin project, 119
task uncertainty, 107–8
technological determinism, 26, 71,
    95, 104–5
technology adoption, 4–5
    see also information and
    communication technology
    adoption
telephony, 6, 19, 30, 42, 67
television (TV), 1–2, 5–10, 12,
    19–20, 25, 34–8, 49–50, 57–61,
    65–6, 71, 73, 75, 81, 87, 128,
    135, 137–8, 140, 148–50, 161
    viewing in UK, 29–33, 43–4
    see also Google Generation TV
    viewing
television generation, 65–6
There, 160
Trailing Boomers, 53, 56
TULIP project, 97

University of Chicago, 101, 112
University of Georgia, 114
University of Illinois, Urbana-
    Champaign, 112
University of Malaysia, 104
University of Manchester, 135
University of Minnesota, 110
University of North Carolina, 115
University of Southern California,
    46

University of Strathclyde, 103
University of Tennessee, 116
University of Tennessee at Knoxville,
    113
US National Institute for Literacy,
    136

Vanderbilt University Medical
    Center, 116
VCRs, 35–6
VHS technologies, 22, 122
video games:
    cognitive benefits, 75–8
    use of, 38, 78–80
virtual worlds, 68, 92, 145, 160–1,
    168, 171
Vodafone, 148

Wark, McKenzie, 167
Washington State University, 100
Web 2.0, 13–14, 67–70
    educational use, 14–15
    impact on higher education, 158
Web of Knowledge, 120
Web of Science, 112
WebCT, 120
Webkinz, 86
weblogs – *see* blogging
WiFi Internet, 50
Wikipedia, 87, 118, 149, 152, 157

Yahoo!, 69, 132
Yahooligans, 118
YouTube, 14, 59, 69–70, 149–50,
    158–9, 167

Breinigsville, PA USA
23 November 2009
228074BV00003B/2/P